Instructor's Manual and Test Questions
to accompany
Elliot Aronson's

The Social Animal

Ninth Edition

Charles Petranek
University of Southern Indiana

Ruth Thibodeau
University of California, Santa Cruz

Wendy Dunn
Coe College, Cedar Rapids, Iowa

Daniel A. Lehn
Coe College, Cedar Rapids, Iowa

Elliot Aronson
University of California, Santa Cruz

Worth Publishers

Printed in the United States of America

ISBN 0-7167-0151-0

First printing 2003

Worth Publishers
41 Madison Avenue
New York, NY 10010
www.worthpublishers.com

Contents

Introduction

The purpose of this manual is to provide assistance to instructors of social psychology who are using Elliot Aronson's *The Social Animal* for their courses. It is intended to help make the task of teaching more enjoyable for instructors by enhancing their efforts to convey material in an exciting and accessible manner.

In the first portion of the manual, a separate chapter is devoted to each corresponding chapter of *The Social Animal*. The basic content of the chapter is presented in outline and summary form, and key terms and concepts are listed. The manual also provides ideas for teaching material from *The Social Animal*, as well as suggestions and resources for lectures that complement the chapter's offerings. In addition, ideas for student projects and discussion topics are offered, along with a list of supplementary readings. A new feature in the ninth edition is experiential learning exercises, which can be conducted in the classroom with oral and written debriefing. Books and articles in the readings section may be used as references for students who are interested in more information about a given topic or as additional sources of lecture material. Each chapter ends with a selection of multiple-choice and essay questions.

The second part of the manual provides a bank of multiple-choice questions based on the research articles presented in *Readings About The Social Animal*, edited by Elliot Aronson. In composing their exams, instructors who use the *Readings* volume may wish to include these questions, which tend to probe for more detailed information about experimental findings and procedures. In a few instances, questions from the *Readings* cover material that is also covered in questions based on *The Social Animal*.

Finally, the manual concludes with a list of films relevant to each chapter, along with the addresses of film distributors. Films have been listed separately to assist the instructor in ordering in a timely fashion, and many may be available from local university libraries. Although the films on the list come well recommended, it is a good idea to preview a film before using it in the classroom.

We hope this manual provides useful ideas to enliven theory and research in social psychology for your students and helps to make your life as an instructor a little easier as well. Your comments and suggestions regarding this manual are most welcome and may be addressed to: Danielle Pucci, Media and Supplements Editor, Worth Publishers, 41 Madison Avenue, New York, New York 10010.

Charles Petranek, Ruth Thibodeau, Wendy Dunn,
Daniel A. Lehn, and Elliot Aronson

1

What Is Social Psychology?

Terms & Concepts

social influence
hindsight bias
amateur social psychologists
professional social psychologists
Aronson's first law
dispositional view

Chapter Overview

Chapter 1 offers a working definition of social psychology as the study of the influences that people have upon the beliefs or behavior of others. A general orientation to the field and its methods is provided, including several illustrations of the broad range of questions and real-world phenomena that are of central interest to social psychologists. Key issues and questions include:

How are people influenced by one another? Why do they accept social influence—that is, what's in it for them? What are the variables that increase or decrease the effectiveness of social influence?

How does one person come to like another person? How does a person develop prejudices against an ethnic or racial group? Is prejudice akin to liking—but in reverse—or does it involve an entirely different set of psychological processes?

Most people are "amateur" social psychologists. Because we spend so much of our time interacting with other people, it is not surprising that most of us develop our own intuitive theories about human behavior. However, our everyday understanding of social behavior lacks the rigor and impartiality of careful scientific investigation. Systematic research is important because, in many instances, "common sense" hypotheses about human behavior turn out to be false when carefully investigated.

Aronson's first law is that "People who do crazy things are not necessarily crazy." When situational pressures are strong, people are often led to behave in ways that are unpleasant, destructive, or bizarre. Although some of this behavior may be due to individual psychopathology, social psychologists find it more useful to try to understand the situational variables that move otherwise "normal" people to engage in unappetizing or seemingly "crazy" behavior. This point is illustrated dramatically in a classic study conducted by Zimbardo and his colleagues, in which psychologically healthy young men were randomly assigned to play the roles of guard and prisoner in a "simulated prison" set up at Stanford University. Within a few days, the majority of subjects had taken their roles to heart: "prisoners" became dehumanized and servile, while "guards" took pleasure in their cruel treatment of prisoners.

Lecture Ideas & Teaching Suggestions

Common Sense and Science. One way to help students appreciate the limitations of common sense in explaining social behavior is to present several examples of research findings that either contradict most people's intuitions, or that offer a more complex picture of behavior than common sense would suggest. One method of doing this is to ask the class to respond as "amateur social psychologists" to a series of true-false statements regarding various social-psychological phenomena. After hearing students' responses, you can proceed to discuss some of the research that is relevant to each statement. Here are some examples, taken from later chapters in the book.

1. When it comes to liking other people, we are attracted to people who are similar to us. (True—but not always. See Jones, Bell & Aronson on the conditions under which we tend to prefer dissimilar others, and Winch's research on need complementarity in long-term relationships. Chapter 8.)

2. If you were alone in a big city and hurt yourself, you would be more likely to get help if there were ten people standing nearby, rather than one or two. (False. Research by Latane & Darley and others shows that the greater the number of bystanders, the lower the chances that someone will help. Chapter 2.)

3. Doing a favor for someone will increase the possibility that they will like you. (True—but not always. Jones' research indicates that doing favors may backfire if the recipient feels manipulated or that "strings" are attached to the favor. Also, sometimes getting someone to do *you* a favor will make them like you more, according to work by Jecker & Landy. Chapter 8.)

4. If someone rewards you for performing an interesting activity (e.g., by paying you money), you'll probably like that activity even more. (False. Deci's research on the effects of rewards on intrinsic motivation indicates just the opposite. Chapter 5.)

5. If you're feeling angry, the best thing to do is "blow off a little steam" by venting some of your hostility. This reduces the chances that you will behave in a far more hostile or aggressive manner in

the future. (False. Several studies testing the "catharsis hypothesis" have demonstrated that rather than reducing aggression, violent behavior increases the likelihood of even greater violence in the future. Chapter 6.)

This exercise serves two purposes: It underscores the need to use scientific methods in studying social behavior, and it provides students with a brief introduction to some of the topics and phenomena that will be covered later in the course.

Power of the Situation. A demonstration of the "power of the situation" can be achieved by describing the experimental setting and procedure of one of the classic studies in social psychology—such as Asch's conformity experiment or Milgram's study of obedience, both from Chapter 2. (This exercise should be done before students have read these studies.) After giving a detailed description of the study, ask students to imagine how they think they would have acted in the same situation. Typically, students will greatly underestimate the extent to which they themselves, and other people, would conform under such circumstances. Next, explain the actual results of the study and the reasons why the situational pressures had such a powerful impact on subjects. You may then want to invite students to comment on these findings and to reconsider whether they still think they would have been able to resist the pressure to conform. Finally, this demonstration can be used as a point of entry into a methodological discussion of why simply asking people how they would behave in a given situation is likely to lead to invalid conclusions.

Applying Social Psychology. Discussing some of the applied uses of social-psychological findings is an effective way to introduce students to the importance of the field and its relevance to real-world issues. Research in the areas of law and health offer some interesting examples of applied social psychology. For material, you may wish to draw upon studies presented in later chapters: For example, Haney's research on the "death qualification procedure" is covered in Chapter 2, and Loftus's work on memory distortion in eye-witness testimony is presented in Chapter 4. Health-related research includes Axsom and Cooper's study of obesity and justification of effort (Chapter 5) and McAlister et al.'s use of the "inoculation technique" to prevent teenagers from smoking (Chapter 3). Additional sources of material may be found in: Oskamp, S. (1984), *Applied Social Psychology*, Englewood Cliffs, NJ: Prentice-Hall. Also, you may want to refer to issues of *Applied*

Social Psychology Annual, The Journal of Social Issues, and *The Journal of Applied Social Psychology.*

Projects and Discussion Topics

1. PROJECT: For a few days, carefully observe events and behavior (your own and others') in everyday life that strike you as the kinds of phenomena that would interest a social psychologist. (A good strategy is to pretend you are an anthropologist studying a completely foreign culture, or an alien visiting from another planet.) Keep a journal of these observations, including your own hypotheses, explanations, and questions regarding the behavior and events you have observed. Share your observations and interpretations with your classmates.

2. PROJECT: Examine several copies of newspapers and magazines, looking for examples of behavior and events that would interest a social psychologist. Does the report contain any explicit or implicit explanations of the behavior being described? If so, do these explanations reflect a "situational" or "dispositional" view of the world? What kind of evidence, if any, is presented to support these interpretations? Bring a few examples to class and be prepared to describe your findings.

3. PROJECT: Ask students to say "Hi" to 20 people on campus and 20 people off campus. They are to note any differences in people's reactions. Is the response rate better or worse on campus? Do people smile more on campus or not? Or students can say "Hi" to 20 males and 20 females. Does it make a difference if the student is male or female? There can be comparison of results in the next class. Does it make a difference if the males or females are younger or older? The need to control for the age variable and many other variables is essential to good research. What type of people are the most responsive and who are the most likely to give a response? Can we generalize that the campus or town is friendly or not?

4. DISCUSSION: Consider one or two of the following sets of questions. a) What makes a person prejudiced? How can prejudice be reduced? b) Why are two people attracted to each other? What makes two people dislike each other? c) Why do people engage in violent behavior? Why do people cooperate or help each other?

d) Why do people conform to the behavior and opinions of others? When do they tend to think and act independently? For each set of questions, list as many possible answers as you can think of, based on common sense and your intuitions about social behavior. Share your ideas with other students in your discussion group, noting the similarity and differences in your explanations. On what basis could you decide the relative merits of these different "hypotheses" about human behavior? Is common sense and evidence gained from personal experience a sufficient basis for deciding the relative merits of these different "hypotheses"? Why or why not?

5. DISCUSSION: What does Aronson mean by the statement: "People who do crazy things are not necessarily crazy?" Do you agree or disagree? What are the broader implications of explaining unpleasant or bizarre behavior as primarily the result of individual "craziness" or "badness"? Why, in your opinion, is this kind of interpretation of behavior so common in our society? On the other hand, what issues regarding individual responsibility would be raised if we were to explain all problematic behavior as the result of situational pressures and influences?

Experiential Learning Exercises

Experiential Learning Exercises are offered as a way to have the students in class experience the various social psychological concepts. It is one thing to lecture or read or discuss an idea, but it is another actually to feel the concept. For example, cognitive dissonance theory is an interesting theory that explains a great deal of behavior. Instead of talking about it, one could experience it by playing the experiential exercise, Standing on the Issues. One could stand on the side of the room that is opposed to her true feelings on a topic like capital punishment. When her group is asked to present a short argument, she can present four ideas to support her new position. Later during the oral debriefing she could reveal that she argued against her original position. That night she would write a paper about her new position and hand the paper in. In the majority of cases she will come to believe in her new founded position.

Often times these are power exercises because students become emotionally involved rather than being passive. There are guidelines. It has to be a voluntary exercise. Students can participate or not, but they have to observe. There should be no physical or mental harm. Anyone can quit at any time. There is no physical violence. There should not be great deception and it should always be debriefed. There should be adequate time for oral debriefing. Written debriefing is highly recommended, which allows the participants to sort out their emotions and logically connect the exercise to the concepts in the text. The general guidelines for ethical behavior in experiments on page 345 of the text should be followed. The excitement these experiential exercises bring to the classroom is well worth the effort.

An excellent way to require papers in this class is to have a 3–5 page paper after each classroom experiential exercise. Students should discuss the events, emotions, their analysis, applications to the real world, and an evaluation. The analysis can be evaluated by the quality of social psychology terms that are utilized in the paper tying the exercise to the theories. There have been professors who have lectured on a very limited basis with this text and spent the majority of class time conducting these experiential learning exercises. The students had written debriefing after every exercise and pursued the ideas from the text to understand their behavior and to write better papers.

People can gain more information and ideas for simulations and experiential learning exercises by joining the North American Simulation and Gaming Association: *www.nasaga.org*. Membership is free online.

Experiential Exercise

1. SOLEMON ASCH'S CONFORMITY EXPERIMENT. The professor should replicate the Asch conformity experiment in class. The day before class four sets of cards should be made. The first one has an inch difference in the three lines, the second one has a half inch difference, the third one has an inch difference and the fourth one has ¼ difference with the lines not all in one line. The professor should arrive early to class and ask 9 or 12 students to help out. They are instructed what to say. They will give the correct answers on the first two sets of cards and incorrect answers on the last two sets of cards. During class the professor asks for volunteers to help in this exercise. The professor picks the nine "confederate" students and three "naïve" students (later arriving students). All twelve students step outside and the professor picks three "confederate" students and one "naïve" student. They come into the classroom and the three "confederates" are asked individually which line is most like X. The "naïve" student is asked last. In general

one-third of the time the "naïve" subject will go along with the group and experience social influence. It happens most often with the ¼ difference in the card, which emphasizes searching for social reality when the physical reality is unclear. The oral debriefing is about conformity and the reasons for it.

2. AWARENESS EXERCISE. Often times in a class students do not get to know each other. To remedy this the professor should write a brief interview schedule with three personality questions and three group questions. The students have to collect information and student names. The personality questions can be: name one personality trait that best describes you, do you consider yourself to be optimistic or pessimistic? And Why? A second line should be included so the interviewed students can reveal another fact about themselves. The group questions can be: What is your racial or ethnic background? Are you from an urban or rural or suburban area? Have you visited a foreign country? If yes, which one? The oral debriefing can consist of asking students what interesting information they discovered and share it. Participants can be asked what information they revealed and why. There can be a discussion whether group characteristics or personality traits influence people the most. The written debriefing would consist of these questions and dispositional and group influences.

Additional Readings

Aron, A. & Aron, E.N. (1989). *The heart of social psychology: a backstage view of a passionate science.* Lexington, MA: Lexington Books.

Campbell, D. & Tavris, C. (1975, December). The experimenting society: To find programs that work, government must measure its failures. *Psychology Today,* pp. 46–56. (Advocates using scientific method to assess social programs.)

Festinger, L. (1980). *Retrospections on social psychology.* New York: Oxford University Press.

Kipnis, D. (1994). Accounting for the use of behavioral technologies in social psychology. *American Psychologist, 49,* (3), 165–172.

Loftus, E.F. (1991). Resolving legal questions with psychological data. *American Psychologist, 46,* 1046–1060.

Petranek, C.F., Corey, S. & Black, R. (1992). Three Levels of Learning in Simulations: Participating, Debriefing and Journal Writing. *Simulation & Gaming, 23,* (2), 174–185.

Petranek, C.F. (1994). A Maturation in Experiential Learning: Principles of Simulation and Gaming. *Simulation & Gaming, 25,* (4), 345–356.

Petranek, C.F. (2000). Written Debriefing: The Next Vital Step in Learning with Simulations. *Simulation & Gaming, 31,* (1), 108–118.

Tetlock, P.E. (1994). The psychology of futurology and the future of psychology. *Psychological Science, 5,* (1), 1.

West, S.G. & Wicklund, R.A. (1980). *A primer of social psychological theories.* Monterey, CA: Brooks/Cole.

Wiggins, J.G., Jr. (1994). Would you want your child to be a psychologist? *American Psychologist, 49,* (6), 485–492.

Multiple-Choice Questions

Answer: b
Page: 4

1. Aronson defines social psychology as:
   a. how people learn to behave in accordance with society's rules.
   b. the influences that people have upon the beliefs or the behavior of others.
   c. how societies and social groups work.
   d. the study of roles and social norms.

Answer: c
Page: 4

2. In his first chapter, Aronson defines social psychology as the study of:
   a. human behavior and mental processes.
   b. people and events.
   c. social influence.
   d. actions that appear to be crazy but are not.

Answer: d
Page: 4

3. "The influences that people have upon the beliefs and behavior of others" is the text's definition of:
   a. dispositions.
   b. the self-fulfilling prophecy.
   c. the hindsight effect.
   d. social psychology.

Answer: a
Page: 6

4. Once we know the outcome of an event, we have the sense that we knew all along that things would turn out as they did. The term for this phenomenon is:
   a. the hindsight effect.
   b. common-sense social psychology.
   c. the self-fulfilling prophecy.
   d. the "deja vu" effect.

Answer: b
Page: 7

5. According to Aronson's text, the statement that we are all "amateur" social psychologists means that:
   a. we all give advice to our close friends and relatives.
   b. we all try to figure out why people act as they do, and we develop explanations for their behavior.
   c. we don't have as much training as professional social psychologists.
   d. our theories about human behavior are too complex.

Answer: b
Page: 7

6. According to the "hindsight effect" you would predict which of the following results:
   a. People would be more likely to blame a prisoner than a guard for a prison uprising.
   b. If after a race were over, people were asked how confident they were that a particular horse would win, they would remember being more confident if he did win than if he did not.
   c. We tend to behave the way that people expect us to.
   d. We are more likely to make situational judgments when explaining our future behavior and make dispositional explanations when explaining our past behavior.

Answer: d
Page: 7

7. In his or her attempts to understand human social behavior, the professional social psychologist has the advantage of being able to:
   a. study at the same time all of the factors that influence people in a situation.
   b. know how to control every individual's behavior.
   c. create and study exact duplicates of actual situations and events.
   d. control the influence of irrelevant factors when studying a problem.

Answer: a
Page: 7

8. Which of the following is NOT an advantage that professional social psychologists have over amateur social psychologists?
   a. Professionals use observation of social phenomena in their thinking about social phenomena, whereas amateurs cannot.
   b. Professionals can make things happen.
   c. Professionals can hold everything constant except what they are interested in studying.
   d. Professionals' conclusions are based on more precise data.

Answer: c
Page: 8

9. According to "Aronson's first law," people who do crazy things:
   a. are, by definition, crazy.
   b. may not be crazy, but are different from normal people.
   c. may be crazy, but may also be normal people trying to adjust to extraordinary social influences.
   d. are perceived as crazy by people with rigid standards for behavior.

Answer: d
Page: 8

10. Explaining unpleasant behavior by labeling people "crazy" or "sadistic":
   a. is useful because it allows us to develop tests to help classify people.
   b. is dangerous because it makes these people angry and violent.
   c. is useful because it warns the general public to watch out for certain people.
   d. is dangerous because it gives the general public a false sense of security and invulnerability.

Answer: a
Page: 8

11. Aronson states, "People who do crazy things are not necessarily crazy." By this he means that:
    a. situations can cause most normal people to behave in abnormal ways.
    b. psychosis, at least from a social psychological point of view, does not exist.
    c. people generally think of others in very much the same way they think of themselves.
    d. human behavior can be explained by using the scientific method.

Answer: d
Page: 8

12. Which of the following best reflects a dispositional view of human behavior?
    a. "That test was so difficult no one could do well."
    b. "Mandy is so attractive that the men just flock around her."
    c. "When I don't eat breakfast, I feel rotten all day."
    d. "Bob is so self-centered that he has trouble getting along with other people."

Answer: d
Page: 8

13. Tomoko explains that her teacher is a kind, gentle person and that is why Tomoko does well in school. Tomoko's appraisal of her teacher is best thought of as an example of:
    a. Aronson's first law.
    b. the hindsight effect.
    c. the situational view.
    d. the dispositional view.

Answer: a
Page: 8

14. People tend to explain the causes of other people's behavior as being the result of their personalities. Thus, if Luke gets a bad grade on a test, it must be because he is stupid. This tendency is called:
    a. the dispositional view.
    b. the self-fulfilling prophecy.
    c. Aronson's first law.
    d. the hindsight effect.

Answer: d
Page: 8

15. You and a friend are watching the news and hear a report regarding a murder in New York City, witnessed by dozens of bystanders—none of whom attempted to help the victim or even telephone the police. Your friend expresses utter disgust at this incident, remarking "People who live in big cities have no compassion for others. They lack fundamental decency—all they care about is themselves." Your friend's remark best reflects:
a. astute insight into the effects of living in large cities.
b. the primacy effect.
c. a situational view of the world.
d. a dispositional view of the world.

Answer: d
Page: 8–9

16. In Zimbardo's "prison" study, how were subjects assigned the role of prisoner or guard?
a. Younger men were made prisoners so as to better replicate the actual prison situation.
b. More intelligent subjects were assigned to be guards.
c. Based on the results of a psychological test, those with more stable personalities were assigned to be guards.
d. By flipping a coin, that is, randomly.

Answer: d
Page: 8–9

17. The subjects in Zimbardo's prison study were:
a. prison guards.
b. prisoners.
c. both prison guards and prisoners.
d. normal, stable young men.

Answer: b
Page: 9

18. In Zimbardo's "Stanford Prison Experiment," young, psychologically normal men were randomly assigned to the role of playing a guard or a prisoner. After five days, the "prisoners" grew withdrawn and unsympathetic, while "guards" became sadistic and brutal. In general, the results of this study probably indicate that:
    a. the veneer of civilization is very thin, and the true nature of humans is to be callous and unfeeling.
    b. the situation is often primarily responsible for behavior, not the personalities of subjects.
    c. prisoners are basically antisocial and, thus, are unable to cope with the prison environment.
    d. guards probably choose their profession because they enjoy power and being brutal.

Answer: c
Page: 10–11

19. Why did Zimbardo discontinue his prison experiment?
    a. The public judged it to be unethical.
    b. All of his subjects quit.
    c. The subjects became too involved with their "prisoner" or "guard" role.
    d. The procedure was completed and the data were so clear and impressive that it did not need to be continued.

Essay Questions

1. In your own words, what is Aronson's definition of social psychology? Give an example of behavior that social psychologists would be interested in studying.

2. Is social psychology simply common sense? Why or why not? Why is it important to conduct scientific investigations of hypotheses about social behavior?

3. Describe three advantages that professional social psychologists have over amateurs.

4. "People who do crazy things are not necessarily crazy." Explain the meaning of this statement and how it is relevant to a social-psychological perspective on understanding social behavior. What are some of the drawbacks of explaining unpleasant behavior by labeling it as sadistic or crazy?

5. Define and give an example of a "dispositional" view of the world.

2

Conformity

I. Introduction

"Johnny Rocco" deviance study (Schachter)
"Groupthink" (Janis)

II. What is Conformity?

Asch experiment
Why do people conform: group pressure or to be correct?

III. Variables That Increase or Decrease Conformity

Variations on Asch's basic experiment
The effects of: unanimity, prior commitment, self-esteem, cultural
differences, task ability, composition group

IV. Rewards and Punishments Versus Information

Physical reality versus "social reality"
Social influence and behavior (O'Leary & Aronson,
Cialdini et al.)
Social influence and emotion (Schachter & Singer)
Social influence: Life and death (Haney)

V. Responses to Social Influence

Compliance, identification, internalization
Power, attractiveness, credibility

VI. Obedience as a Form of Compliance

Milgram's studies of obedience
Disobedience in the Milgram experiments

VII.   The "Uninvolved" Bystander as Conformist

"Lady in Distress" experiment (Latané & Rodin)
Epileptic "attack" experiment (Darley & Latané)
"Good Samaritan" study (Darley & Batson)
Costs and benefits of helping (Piliavin, Baron)

VIII.   A Note on the Ethics of Experiments

Terms & Concepts

anticonformity
groupthink
concurrence-seeking
unanimous majority
social reality
compliance
identification
internalization

power
attractiveness
credibility
secondary gain
behavior modification
bystander intervention
empathy

Chapter Overview

Chapter 2 focuses on the topic of conformity, defined as a change in a person's behavior or opinions as a result of real or imagined pressure from a person or group of people. Basic issues covered in the chapter include:

Is conformity good or bad? As a society, Americans are ambivalent about the merits of conformity—nonconformists or individualists are valued, while deviates and oddballs are scorned. On the other hand, conformists and "sheep" are devalued, while the "team player" is lauded. When the chips are down, however, we tend to value conformity over nonconformity—a fact reflected in the findings of Schachter's "Johnny Rocco" study in which the person expressing the "modal" viewpoint was most attractive to other group members. Although conformity is necessary to the smooth running of daily life, an illustration of its negative aspects can be found in the phenomenon of "groupthink," a maladaptive decision-making process that appears to have contributed to the Challenger space-shuttle tragedy.

Why do people conform to group pressure? Variations on Asch's "line judgment" study indicate that a unanimous group opinion, low self-esteem, and lack of expertise are contributing factors. In addition, greater conformity is produced when the group is composed of experts, similar others, and when the acceptance by other group members is important to the individual. Factors that decrease conformity include prior public commitment to an opposing attitude or behavior, as well as the presence of another group member who opposes the group's opinion. People may conform due to group pressure or to be correct. Research shows that the greater the privacy a subject has, the less conformity, suggesting that group pressure is a motivating factor.

When physical reality is uncertain, we tend to rely on "social reality"—the behavior and attitudes of others—as a guide to appropriate action. This form of conformity is motivated by our need for information, rather than our desire to avoid punishment (e.g., social rejection) or gain a reward (e.g., love and acceptance). This tendency is vividly demonstrated in Schachter and Singer's experiment of the effects of others' behavior on an individual's emotional experiences.

Three major forms of response to social influence are compliance, identification, and internalization. The least permanent of the three, compliance is motivated by the desire to avoid punishment or gain reward. Compliance is a response to the power held by the agent of influence. Identification is motivated by a person's desire to be similar to the person or group exercising influence. Thus, identification depends on the attractiveness of the source of influence. Internalization is motivated by the desire to be right, or correct, and represents the most permanent form of social influence. The key component underlying internalization is the credibility of the source of influence.

Acts of compliance, while often temporary, can have consequences that are far from trivial. This point is dramatically demonstrated in Milgram's classic studies of obedience to authority, in which subjects believed they were delivering lethal doses of shock to fellow subjects as part of a "learning" experiment. Variables that decrease obedience to authority include: reducing the perceived "legitimacy" of the authority figure, the subject's closer proximity to the victim, and the physical absence of the authority figure.

Why don't bystanders come to the aid of victims of injury or crime? In the notorious Kitty Genovese case, dozens of neighbors watched passively for 30 minutes as a young woman was stabbed to death outside of her New York City apartment. Not one helped or even picked up a phone to call the police. Experiments by Latane, Darley, and their colleagues indicate that conformity processes underlie the apparent apathy of onlookers at the scene of an emergency. According to their findings, the greater the number of bystanders, the least likely any single one of them is to offer assistance. Nonintervention, in this case, can be viewed as an act of conformity. For each individual bystander, the behavior of other people at the scene provides important cues regarding appropriate behavior. Thus, the failure of others to respond to the emergency serves as a potent model of nonintervention for each individual onlooker. Observers do, though, sometimes respond, especially when they believe they can provide assistance and when they find themselves in a situation in which they cannot escape or ignore the emergency situation.

Lecture Ideas & Teaching Suggestions

Dramatic Examples of Conformity. Students' interest in the topic of conformity can be readily engaged through the presentation of dramatic examples from history or current events. Examples include: the My Lai massacre, the atrocities of the Third Reich, the mass suicide at Jonestown, and the Challenger shuttle disaster. Such illustrations of conformity processes at work tend to make a profound and lasting impression on students, leaving them with an acute awareness of the relevance of social psychology to real-world events and problems. (See "readings" section for background material and analyses of these events.)

Demonstrating Conformity. The ease with which most people obey the commands of authority figures can be vividly demonstrated in the classroom. For example, at the beginning of class, ask all students to perform some sort of odd behavior—such as putting their pen or pencil behind their ear, or standing up and turning around three times. Ask students why they complied with your strange request, and use their responses as a way of introducing the topic of obedience to authority. After concluding this demonstration and discussion, you may also want to illustrate the phenomenon of reactance, which involves the tendency for people to resist conformity pressures when they feel their freedom is being threatened. Thus, after reminding students that people tend to blindly obey the dictates of authority, ask them once again to perform some kind of silly behavior. On this second occasion, the chances are very good that many students will refrain from carrying out your command. You could use their refusal to obey as a springboard for explaining the concept of reactance and our need to see ourselves as autonomous, self-governing individuals. At this point, you may wish to move on to a broader discussion of the high value placed on individual freedom in American society—as illustrated by the reactance phenomenon, as well as our national penchant for idealizing nonconformity and rugged individualism in history, fiction and films. Yet, this value is also at odds with our tendency to reward conformity and punish deviance, to conform to fads and fashions of all kinds, as well as the practical necessity of conformity for the smooth functioning of everyday life. A more detailed discussion of American ambivalence regarding the issue of conformity and individualism can be found in the introductory section of Chapter Two.

The Good Society. One way to make the concepts of compliance, identification, and internalization come alive for students is to introduce them within the context of the conditions necessary for the creation of "the good society." After explaining these three forms of social influence—and their component factors of power, attractiveness, and credibility—ask students to consider which form of social influence they believe stands the best chance of promoting their idea of a "good society." Elaborate on students' responses and help them to articulate their notions of an ideal (or improved) society and the conditions necessary for its realization. You may wish to discuss (or assign for student reading) B.F. Skinner's *Walden Two* as an example of a utopian society built on principles of compliance, generated by the systematic use of principles of operant conditioning.

Projects and Discussion Topics

1. PROJECT: For one week, carry a pocket-sized notebook with you and record examples of conformity as it occurs in everyday life. In keeping this diary, draw upon your own experiences of conformity, as well as your observations of others' responses to social influence. (Some possibilities: interactions with dorm members or housemates; behavior in public places such as bus stops, supermarkets or movie theaters.) Choose three examples from your diary and analyze them from a social-psychological perspective, drawing upon insights gleaned from readings and lectures on conformity.

2. PROJECT: Recall and describe any incidents in your life in which you witnessed an emergency or similar situation in which help was needed. What were your feelings and behavior in these situations? Did you offer assistance? Why or why not? Ask two friends to tell you about their experiences with emergency situations. What factors seemed to play a role in whether they either helped or did not help?

3.   PROJECT: Make a list of several groups to which you belong—
     both informal as well as formally organized ones. (Examples might
     include: your immediate family; your college dormitory; your
     church or temple; your social psychology class; a group of casual ac-
     quaintances; a close circle of friends; political, volunteer, or campus
     organizations, etc.) Next, think of situations in which you might
     feel some pressure (however subtle) to conform to the opinion or
     behavior of the majority of the members of each group. In which of
     these groups would you be more likely to conform? Conversely, in
     which groups would you be likely to feel greater amounts of free-
     dom to resist conformity pressures? Based on your knowledge of
     group conformity, explain the social-psychological factors and pro-
     cesses that could account for the different levels of conformity you
     might display within each of these groups.

4.   PROJECT: Either alone or with a friend or classmate, engage in a
     mild form of non-conformist behavior in a public setting. Record
     the reactions of onlookers, as well as your own feelings while per-
     forming this behavior. Discuss your "experiment" in class. (If this
     exercise is done in pairs, one person can be the non-conformist,
     while the other carefully observes and takes notes on the verbal and
     non-verbal responses of unsuspecting others. Partners can then
     switch roles.) Some possibilities: 1) stand backwards while waiting
     in line at the grocery store or cafeteria; 2) arrive early for class, sit
     behind or next to a classmate, and proceed to hum loudly or sing
     for a minute or two; 3) when riding an elevator, face the back wall
     instead of the doors, or make somewhat sustained eye contact with
     a fellow passenger; 4) stand overly close to someone while having a
     conversation with him or her.

5.   DISCUSSION: Research on conformity, such as Milgram's studies
     of obedience and Zimbardo's prison simulation, indicates that un-
     der certain conditions people who are otherwise moral and decent
     are capable of engaging in acts of considerable cruelty toward oth-
     ers. What issues do these findings raise regarding the problem of
     holding individuals responsible for their actions? Given our under-
     standing of the power of situations in influencing behavior, can you
     think of ways to use this knowledge to reduce the likelihood of
     conformity-based acts of inhumanity?

6. DISCUSSION: What are the ethical problems raised by Milgram's obedience study? What justifications could be made for conducting this study? Do you think the study should have been performed? Why or why not?

7. DISCUSSION: Think of a time when you found yourself in the midst of a situation in which you behaved or reacted "out of character"—that is, in a manner very different from your accustomed mode of behavior. Describe the nature of this situation and your feelings regarding your own behavior. Try to make sense of your experience in light of your knowledge of conformity and the power of situational pressures. Share your experiences and insights with other members of your discussion group.

8. DISCUSSION: Ask class members to think of emergency situations they may have observed or been involved in, for example, a car accident, near-drowning, and so forth. Ask them to describe how they and others reacted. Try to get them to analyze the similarities and differences between their experiences and the research results of the bystander intervention studies.

Experiential Exercises

1. THE DRINKING GAME. This is a social simulation that emphasizes the social pressure in our society to drink and to be competitive. This is a type of conformity that few people realize happens to them. Participants are assigned profiles of the types of drinks they like to consume. If they match up with people who have similar drinking patterns, they will receive more chips. There is no alcohol in the simulation. As students "consume" more alcohol, their chances of having bad things (going to jail or to the hospital or to the cemetery) increase. In this competitive atmosphere they are frustrated being in the hospital or jail. Often times participants will lie and cheat to get more chips (drinks), so they can win. The social influence is very strong in the game and yet most feel they can resist it. They cannot. The pressure to conform comes from within the individual as well as from the group. There are designated drivers in the game and are often rejected by others because they are different. It can be played in 25 minutes and orally

debriefed with the rest of the class. The written debriefing can consist of many social psychological terms and theories to describe their behavior. They should be encouraged to compare the simulation to their own life and apply the lessons to themselves. Students can analyze their drinking patterns that are very unconscious. The simulation was developed by Charles Petranek and can be purchased from:

> Petranek Consulting Services, Inc.
> 2712 Harmony Way
> Evansville, IN 47720
> Phone: 812-426-1617

2. The Solomon Asch experiment that was described in chapter 1 can obviously be utilized in the classroom for this chapter.

Additional Readings

Allen, V.L. (1975). Social support for non-conformity. In L. Berkowitz (Ed.), *Advances in experimental social psychology* (Vol. 8). New York: Academic Press.

Colman, A.M. (1991). Crowd psychology in South African murder trials. *American Psychologist, 46,* 1071–1079.

Janis, I.L. Groupthink. (1971, November). *Psychology Today,* pp. 24–26. (A "groupthink" analysis of several high-level government decisions.)

Janis, I.L. (1982). *Groupthink: Psychological studies of policy decisions and fiascos.* (2nd ed.). Boston: Houghton Mifflin.

Kelman, H.C. & Hamilton, V.L. (1989). *Crimes of obedience: Toward a social psychology of authority and responsibility.* New Haven, CT: Yale University Press.

Kelman, H.C. & Lawrence, L.H. (1972, June). American response to the trial of Lt. Calley. *Psychology Today,* pp. 41–45, 78–81. (Discusses obedience to authority in light of Milgram's studies and the case of Lt. Calley and the My Lai massacre in Vietnam.)

Kruglanski, A.W. (1984, November). Freeze-think and the Challenger. *Psychology Today,* pp. 43–46. (A social-psychological analysis of the events and faulty decision-making strategies surrounding the space-shuttle Challenger tragedy.)

Latane, B. & Darley, J.M. (1970). *The unresponsive bystander.* New York: Appleton-Century-Crofts.

Milgram, S. (1974). *Obedience to authority.* New York: Harper & Row.

Muson, H. Blind obedience. (1978, January). *Psychology Today,* p. 112. (Panelists John Dean, Stanley Milgram, Thomas Szasz, and Herbert Speigal discuss the problem of conformity to pressure from authority figures.)

Nissani, M. (1990). A cognitive reinterpretation of Stanley Milgram's observations on obedience to authority. *American Psychologist, 45,* 1384–1385.

Osherow, N. (1992). Making sense of the nonsensical: An analysis of Jonestown. In E. Aronson (Ed.), *Readings about The Social Animal* (6th ed.). New York: Freeman.

Pines, M. (1976, January). Unlearning blind obedience in German schools. *Psychology Today,* pp. 59–65. (Describes efforts of German schools to teach students how to resist conformity pressures.)

Saks, M.J. (1992). Obedience versus disobedience to legitimate versus illegitimate authorities issuing good versus evil directives. *Psychological Science, 3,* (4), 221–223.

Skinner, B.F. (1976). *Walden Two.* New York: Macmillan. (Skinner's novel depicting a utopian society based on compliance via the systematic use of operant conditioning.)

Speer, A. (1970). *Inside the Third Reich: Memoirs* (R. Winston & Winston, Trans.). New York: Macmillan.

Multiple-Choice Questions

Answer: d
Page: 12

1. Generally speaking, nonconformity
   a. is usually admired by others in our culture.
   b. is highly adaptive.
   c. is highly maladaptive.
   d. may be either adaptive or maladaptive, depending on the situation.

Answer: d
Page: 12

2. In an experiment by Schachter, subjects engaged in a group discussion of a juvenile delinquent named Johnny Rocco and were asked to suggest treatment for him ranging from "very lenient" to "very hard." When later asked how much they liked other members of their group—some of whom were confederates of the experimenter—subjects gave the highest ratings to:
   a. the "slider" confederate—who first deviated, but later conformed, to the opinions of real subjects on how Johnny should be treated.
   b. the "leader" confederate—who played a major role in influencing the opinions of real subjects on how Johnny should be treated.
   c. the "reluctant" confederate—who refrained from voicing any opinion until all the other subjects had decided on how Johnny should be treated.
   d. the "modal" confederate—who consistently conformed to the opinions of real subjects on how Johnny should be treated.

Answer: a
Page: 12

3. Aronson describes an experiment in which groups of subjects discuss the punishment appropriate for "Johnny Rocco," a juvenile delinquent. In this experiment, subjects best liked a confederate when he played the role of a:
    a. person who agreed with the group (conformist).
    b. person who disagreed with the group (deviate).
    c. person who originally agreed and then came to disagree with the group (lost soul).
    d. person who disagreed and then came to agree with the group (slider).

Answer: a
Page: 12

4. Because Joe's parents can't stand his wild friend Larry, Joe spends even more time hanging out with Larry. Joe's behavior is best thought of as an example of:
    a. anticonformist.
    b. nonconformist.
    c. individualistic behavior.
    d. antisocial behavior.

Answer: d
Page: 14–15

5. According to Aronson's analysis of the Challenger disaster, which of the following most likely did *not* contribute to the disaster?
    a. NASA had already conducted two dozen successful launches.
    b. A schoolteacher who was on board, which created more publicity than normal.
    c. At NASA a lift-off was a more desirable decision than a delay.
    d. NASA engineers assured management that all safety measures had been taken.

Answer: c
Page: 15

6. According to Janis, groupthink most often leads a group to make:
    a. mostly good quality decisions.
    b. mostly average quality decisions.
    c. mostly poor quality decisions.
    d. some very good and some very bad decisions.

Answer: b
Page: 15

7. Disastrous decisions made by members of the Third Reich, Nixon's "palace guard," and NASA officials involved in the launch of the ill-fated Challenger space shuttle were a consequence of a maladaptive decision-making strategy Irving Janis calls:
    a. mind-guarding.
    b. groupthink.
    c. high-risk conformity.
    d. collective momentum.

Answer: b
Page: 15

8. According to Irving Janis, the maladaptive phenomenon of "groupthink" is more likely to occur when:
    a. groups are composed of diverse members who seek agreement in order to overcome their different points of view.
    b. concurrence-seeking processes override realistic considerations of alternative courses of action.
    c. differences among group members prevent the group from reaching a well-considered, realistic decision.
    d. the desire of each group member to be well-liked by other group members overrides concurrence-seeking processes.

Answer: c
Page: 15

9. Which of the following is *not* a characteristic of groupthink?
    a. the perception of invulnerability
    b. the seeking of unanimity
    c. the illusion of too many good alternatives
    d. a strong leader who does not challenge the group to express doubts

Answer: a
Page: 15

10. Which of the following would *not* be a productive strategy to prevent groupthink from occurring?
    a. moving quickly to consensus before too many opposing views are expressed
    b. seeking all the information you can get
    c. having a nondirective, less powerful leader
    d. trying to reduce the cohesiveness of the group

Answer: d
Page: 17

11. Which of the following statements about Asch's conformity experiments is *true?*
    a. Subjects were rewarded with money when they answered correctly.
    b. Subjects were rewarded with money when they went along with the group.
    c. The judging task was very difficult.
    d. Only one group member was a naïve subject.

Answer: b
Page: 17

12. In Solomon Asch's experiment on conformity what were some of the findings:
    a. Roughly half of the responses of the naïve subjects went along with the group.
    b. Around one-third of the responses of naïve subjects went along with the group.
    c. Roughly half of the naïve subjects conformed once.
    d. Around 90% of the naïve subjects conformed once.

Answer: a
Page: 18

13. In Asch's conformity experiments, the discomfort felt by subjects who expressed agreement with the incorrect judgments of the majority could result from the conflict between two important goals. It was suggested that the goals in conflict are:
   a. the goal of being correct and the goal of staying in the good graces of others by living up to their expectations.
   b. the fear of being wrong and the fear of being right.
   c. the goal of being correct and the goal of making others appear to be conforming and wishy-washy.
   d. the goal of being admired and the goal of expressing one's individuality.

Answer: a
Page: 18

14. According to Aronson, most people believe that they are motivated by a desire to _____ whereas others are motivated by a desire to

   _____.
   a. be correct; be respected by others
   b. be respected by others; be correct
   c. get rewards; avoid punishments
   d. avoid punishments; get rewards

Answer: b
Page: 18

15. Research indicates that when people observe a conformity experiment like Asch's (in which subjects conformed to the erroneous judgments of others regarding the length of lines) they typically predict that:
   a. the subjects will exhibit *less* conformity than they actually do.
   b. that they, *personally*, would exhibit less conformity than the subjects they are observing.
   c. that they, *personally*, would exhibit about the same amount of conformity as the subjects they are observing.
   d. that they, *personally*, would exhibit more conformity than the subjects they are observing.

Answer: b
Page: 19

16. In studying the relationship between conformity when making judgments in public versus private, the general finding is that when subjects are given more privacy:
    a. they conform more.
    b. they conform less.
    c. they make better decisions.
    d. they make poorer decisions.

Answer: a
Page: 20

17. If a person makes a prior commitment to a view that differs from the group opinion, he or she will tend to be:
    a. less susceptible to group pressure to conform.
    b. more open to group pressure to conform.
    c. less confident of his or her own view.
    d. more open to conform to the group's opinion on a different issue.

Answer: d
Page: 21

18. In which of the conditions is there likely to be more conformity?
    a. The subject is good at the task.
    b. There are no experts in the group.
    c. The other members of the group are not important to the naïve subject.
    d. The naïve subject is from a collectivist society like Japan.

Answer: a
Page: 21–23

19. In which situation is there likely to be more conformity?
    a. when women are in an experiment with a male researcher.
    b. when the membership in the group does not matter.
    c. when the group has one dissenter.
    d. when people "in the know" decide not to speak.

Answer: c
Page: 22

20. Imagine you are walking down the street and passed by a driver who needed money for the parking meter. According to research on compliance, under which of the following conditions would you be most likely to give the driver some spare change?
    a. when the request for change came from a fashionably dressed person
    b. when the request for change came from a poorly dressed person
    c. when the request for change came from a uniformed parking officer
    d. when the request for change came from the driver's young child

Answer: b
Page: 23

21. According to Aronson, when physical reality _____, people's reliance on social reality _____.
    a. increases; increases
    b. decreases; increases
    c. increases; becomes unpredictable
    d. decreases; decreases

Answer: a
Page: 23

22. According to Festinger, conformity is more likely to occur when physical reality is _____ and social reality is _____.
    a. low; high
    b. low; low
    c. high; low
    d. high; high

Answer: c
Page: 23

23. A good rule of thumb to use in predicting conformity in an ambiguous situation is that there will be a greater dependence on _____ when physical reality is lacking as a basis for judgment.
    a. objective reality
    b. personal intuition
    c. social reality
    d. groupthink

Answer: a
Page: 24

24. Studies on conformity and jaywalking indicate that:
    a. pedestrians are less likely to jaywalk when they observe a high-status, well-dressed person who refrains from jaywalking.
    b. pedestrians are less likely to jaywalk when they observe a low-status, shabbily dressed person jaywalking.
    c. pedestrians are more likely to jaywalk in large cities than in small towns.
    d. pedestrians are more likely to jaywalk in small towns than in large cities.

Answer: d
Page: 24

25. Aronson and O'Leary conducted a study designed to encourage water conservation among male students showering at the university field house. They found that students were more likely to conserve water (by turning off the shower while soaping up) after:
    a. a colorful, vivid sign urging water conservation was placed in the shower room.
    b. a water-conserving "model" told them that they, too, should turn off the shower while soaping up.
    c. listening to a high-status university official explain the importance of conserving water.
    d. observing the behavior of a "model" who turned off the shower while soaping up.

Answer: b
Page: 24

26. Aronson describes a study in which male students were observed showering to determine if they complied with a request to conserve water. Subjects showered alone, with a conserving model, or with two conserving models. The percentages of subjects who conserved water in the alone, one model, two model conditions were:
    a. 6%, 8%, 10%, respectively.
    b. 6%, 49%, 67%, respectively.
    c. 6%, 67%, 49%, respectively.
    d. 67%, 49%, 6%, respectively.

Answer: b
Page: 25

27. When are people least likely to throw a flier on the ground?
    a. When there was litter all around.
    b. When a model picked up a discarded fast-food bag and placed it in the trash can.
    c. When the model kicked the fast-food bag.
    d. When there were fliers all on the cars and none on the ground.

Answer: b
Page: 27–28

28. Schachter and Singer (1962) conducted an experiment in which subjects were injected with either adrenalin or a placebo, and were either informed or misinformed as to the real symptoms produced by an adrenalin injection. Later, they were exposed to the behavior of either an angry or a euphoric cohort. Subjects in which of the following conditions were most likely to imitate the behavior of the cohort?
    a. adrenalin - informed
    b. adrenalin - misinformed
    c. placebo - informed
    d. placebo - misinformed

Answer: c
Page: 27–28

29. Schachter and Singer (1962) (in their study in which subjects were injected with adrenalin, but thought they were getting the vitamin "suproxin") demonstrated that:
    a. internal states of physiological arousal are always interpreted by internal cues.
    b. internal states of physiological arousal are interpreted by external cues only when we have a ready explanation for internal causes of the arousal.
    c. physiological arousal for which we have no ready explanation will often be interpreted in terms of various external cues.
    d. internal states are unrelated to external cues.

Answer: d
Page: 27–28

30. In the experiment by Schachter and Singer, some subjects were given a drug causing physiological arousal and were warned about the side effects of the drug (i.e., hand tremors and heart palpitations). How did subjects who were given the same drug, but who were not warned of the drug's effects, interpret their feelings of arousal?
    a. They thought that they were angry.
    b. They felt happy at first, but later felt angry.
    c. They didn't even feel the drug's effects at all, since they had no idea about what they were supposed to feel.
    d. They thought that they were happy or angry, depending on the behavior of the confederate in the experiment.

Answer: a
Page: 28

31. Haney has conducted research on murder trials that use the *death qualification procedure*, in which potential jury members who are opposed to the death penalty are systematically excluded from jury duty. Compared to subjects who did not witness a film segment showing this procedure, subjects who did observe the procedure were more likely to:
    a. believe that the defendant was guilty and would end up receiving the death penalty.
    b. believe that the defendant was innocent but would end up receiving the death penalty anyway.
    c. believe that the judge thought the defendant was innocent.
    d. believe that the defense attorney thought the defendant was guilty.

Answer: b
Page: 29

32. Six-year-old Lisa finds hitting her little brother is the quickest way to get him to stop bugging her. Her mother, however, finds Lisa's behavior unacceptable, and threatens to take away her favorite toy for a whole week if she hits her brother again. Lisa stops hitting her brother. Lisa's behavior illustrates what form of response to social influence?
   a. identification
   b. compliance
   c. secondary gain
   d. identification

Answer: a
Page: 29

33. Influencing someone by means of insisting that he or she behave in a particular way is called:
   a. compliance.
   b. identification.
   c. modeling.
   d. determinism.

Answer: a
Page: 29

34. Suppose you saw a small child eating lima beans with obvious reluctance. When asked why she was eating them if she wasn't fond of them, she replied, "Because Big Bird eats his vegetables, and I want to be like him!" What type of conformity is she displaying?
   a. identification
   b. internalization
   c. reactance
   d. compliance

Answer: d
Page: 30

35. Even though you believe college tuition should be increased to meet rising expenses, you go along with a group of friends as they organize a protest for lower tuition. This is an example of:
   a. diffusion of responsibility.
   b. reactance.
   c. audience inhibition.
   d. identification.

Answer: a
Page: 30–31

36. Which of the following is *not* characteristic of internalization?
    a. It is based on the admiration or liking of another.
    b. It is the most deeply rooted and permanent response to social influence.
    c. It is based on the desire to be right.
    d. The behavior is internally or intrinsically motivated.

Answer: a
Page: 31–32

37. According to Aronson, power is the essential component in:
    a. compliance.
    b. internalization.
    c. identification.
    d. deindividuation.

Answer: b
Page: 32

38. The essential component of internalization is:
    a. power to reward or punish.
    b. being convinced the new attitude is correct.
    c. admiration of another person.
    d. obedience to authority.

Answer: c
Page: 31–32

39. Three responses to social influence are compliance, identification, and internalization. The major component for each of them, respectively, is:
    a. power, liking, and loving.
    b. status, attractiveness, and reason.
    c. power, attractiveness, and credibility.
    d. power, attractiveness, and liking.

Answer: c
Page: 31

40. Fear of negative consequences would be the major motivation in which of the following?
    a. internalization
    b. identification
    c. compliance
    d. all of the above

Answer: c
Page: 32

41. The type of conformity which is most likely to persist the longest is that which results from:
    a. social reality.
    b. compliance.
    c. internalization.
    d. identification.

Answer: b
Page: 33

42. Gary's parents promised him an interest-free loan for a new car, if only he would quit smoking for 3 months. Gary really wanted the car, so he quit. After not smoking for 3 months, he realized he had more energy, more money, and his food tasted better. Gary decided he would not start smoking again. Gary's experience is an example of:
    a. primary gain.
    b. secondary gain.
    c. primary reward.
    d. secondary reward.

Answer: c
Page: 33

43. Bobby's mother promises that if he will take swimming lessons for two weeks, she will buy him a toy he wants. Even though he doesn't want to swim, he complies and, in the process, learns to like swimming. This is best thought of as an example of:
    a. groupthink.
    b. identification.
    c. secondary gain.
    d. anticonformity.

Answer: b
Page: 34

44. In Milgram's study of obedience, which of the following participants was (were) a confederate of the Experimenter?
    a. the Teacher
    b. the Learner
    c. both the Teacher and the Learner
    d. neither the Learner nor the Teacher

Answer: d
Page: 34–35

45. At what voltage level did the majority of subjects stop "shocks" to the learner in Milgram's classic experiment?
    a. 15 volts, slight shock
    b. 150 volts, learner asks out of experiment
    c. 300 volts, learner is silent
    d. 450 volts, "Danger XXX"

Answer: c
Page: 35

46. One implication discussed from Milgram's classic experiment is:
    a. It is important to follow the rules, so society has norms to guide it.
    b. Obedience is important in training soldiers, so there can be a united force.
    c. Many innocent people had been killed by Nazi soldiers because the soldiers said they were only following orders.
    d. Standing up for freedom and liberty is important in our society.

Answer: d
Page: 35

47. Although a group of psychiatrists who were asked to predict the results of Milgram's experiment on obedience thought that _____ percent of the subjects would use the highest possible shock, in fact _____ percent delivered all the shocks available.
    a. almost 100; less than 1
    b. 33; 65
    c. 90; 100
    d. less than 1; 65

Answer: a
Page: 37

48. In his studies of obedience to authority, Milgram found that:
   a. the closer subjects were to the victim, the less they shocked him.
   b. the more similar the victim was to the subject, the less the subject shocked him.
   c. subjects shocked the confederate less when the experiment was conducted at a prestigious university than in a rundown commercial building.
   d. subjects from Australia and Spain were less obedient to authority than subjects from the United States.

Answer: c
Page: 37

49. Meeus amd Raaijmakers found that subjects were more likely to make negative remarks about a job applicant's performance if
   a. the subjects believed the applicant had already been accepted for the job.
   b. the subjects interviewed the applicant face-to-face.
   c. the subjects believed the applicant would not be receiving the remarks until some later time.
   d. the subjects were unfamiliar with the requirements of the job.

Answer: c
Page: 39

50. Research conducted by Latane, Darley, and their colleagues on bystander intervention has revealed that:
   a. people tend to help more when they're in a hurry.
   b. people in big cities help more than people in small towns.
   c. the more witnesses there are to an emergency, the less likely it is that an individual will decide to help.
   d. the more witnesses there are to an emergency, the more likely it is that an individual will decide to help.

Answer: c
Page: 39–40

51. In the "lady in distress" study, in which subjects waiting for an experiment were led to believe that a female experimenter in the next room had fallen and hurt herself, subjects were more likely to come to her assistance when:
    a. they heard her moan, "Oh, my God, my foot . . . I can't move it."
    b. she was silent, as if unconscious.
    c. they were waiting alone in the next room.
    d. they were waiting with a stranger in the next room.

Answer: c
Page: 42

52. In a series of studies on bystander intervention, conducted on the New York subway system, an accomplice of the experimenters staggered and collapsed on the floor of the train. Overall, these studies found that:
    a. the "victim" was offered help more often when the train had relatively few passengers.
    b. the "victim" was almost never offered help, regardless of how crowded the train was.
    c. the "victim" was almost always offered help when he was made to seem obviously ill.
    d. the "victim" was almost never offered help when he was carrying a liquor bottle and was made to reek of alcohol.

Answer: d
Page: 43

53. According to research on bystander intervention, an individual is more likely to be helped when potential helpers:
    a. feel themselves to be very different from the person in need of help.
    b. are great in number.
    c. have trouble determining if the situation is a real emergency.
    d. assume personal responsibility for intervening.

Answer: b
Page: 43–44

54. Studies involving the "costs and benefits" of helping indicate that:
    a. people help more when the costs of helping are high.
    b. people help less when the costs of helping are high.
    c. costs are unrelated to helping, but people help when benefits are high.
    d. emergencies occur so quickly that bystanders do not have time to estimate costs and benefits.

Essay Questions

1. "When physical reality is unclear, other people become a major source of information." Is this statement supported by research? How might the Schachter-Singer experiment (in which subjects were injected with a stimulant or a placebo) or the Latane-Rodin bystander intervention experiment (in which subjects, alone or in pairs, heard a confederate "fall off a ladder") be used to support or disconfirm this statement?

2. *The Social Animal* describes instances of bystander nonintervention, where people failed to help victims of crimes or accidents. Suppose you were to fall from your bicycle and break your leg. How would you arrange things (theoretically) so that people would be more likely to help you?

3. The chapter on conformity reviews several variables that serve to either increase or decrease the degree to which people will exhibit conformity. Briefly discuss FOUR of these factors and how they affect conformity.

4. Define and give examples of compliance, identification, and internalization. Which of these has the most permanent influence on an individual's behavior? What are the social-psychological processes or components underlying the effects of each of them? Under what circumstances might compliance or identification lead to internalization?

5. Define "groupthink" and the social-psychological processes that underlie it. Imagine you were a member of a group that might be subject to "groupthink" processes. Based on your understanding of group conformity, what steps might you take to minimize the problem?

6. Although conformity processes are often a mundane part of daily life, they may also be implicated in more serious matters—some involving life and death itself. Describe Haney's research on the "death qualification procedure" and explain how it illustrates this point.

3

Mass Communication, Propaganda, and Persuasion

     B.   Increasing Trustworthiness

          Contradicting self-interest (Aronson, Walster, & Abrahams; Eagly)
          "Unintentional" persuasion (Walster & Festinger)

     C.   Attractiveness

          Beauty and likability (Mills & Aronson; Eagly & Chaiken)

VIII.   The Nature of the Communication

     A.   Logical versus emotional appeals (Leventhal)

     B.   Fear and the threat of terrorism

     C.   Consensual statistical evidence versus vivid examples (Nisbett)

     D.   One-sided versus two-sided arguments

     E.   Order of presentation (Miller & Campbell)

     F.   Discrepancy (Zimbardo; Hovland et al.; Aronson, Turner, & Carlsmith)

IX.   Characteristics of the Audience

     A.   Self-esteem

     B.   Prior experience of the audience

          Forewarning (Freedman & Sears)
          Reactance (Bensley & Wu; Heilman)
          Distraction/heckling (Festinger & Maccoby)
          Inoculation effect (McGuire; McAlister)

X.   How Well Do the Principles Work?

     A.   Audience resistance to persuasion (Canon)

     B.   Impact of television (Gerbner)

Terms & Concepts

emotional contagion

copy-cat suicide

education vs. propaganda

central route

peripheral route

credibility

one-sided argument

two-sided argument

discrepancy of communication

primacy effect

recency effect

reactance

inoculation effect

attitude

opinion

Chapter Overview

Chapter 3 covers the specific factors and social-psychological processes underlying effective persuasion, as well as the broader implications of living in an age of mass communication. Highlights of the chapter include:

Media influence is pervasive, affecting our opinions, attitudes, and behavior, regardless of whether direct attempts to persuade are involved. For example, executives in charge of news programming can exert a subtle influence on our opinions simply by determining which events are given exposure. Because these decisions are typically based on the entertainment value of events, news coverage does not present a balanced picture of what is happening in the world. Instead, it puts a heavy emphasis on catastrophic events, violence, crime, and other social ills, leaving viewers with an impression of the world as a more dangerous and troubled place than it really is. Similarly, television dramas, sitcoms, crime shows and other forms of entertainment also tend to contribute to this unrealistic view of the world.

Selective emphasis also places the media in the position of determining subsequent events—not simply reporting them. This is well documented in Phillips' research on the role of the media in the phenomenon of "copycat suicides."

Despite widespread skepticism regarding the truthfulness of media advertising, such blatant attempts of mass persuasion tend to be highly effective. In the case of many products, the public will tend to buy a specific brand for no other reason than that it was heavily advertised. Research suggests that mere familiarity tends to increase attractiveness.

There are two major routes to persuasion, the central route that relies on relevant facts that people carefully consider and the peripheral route that uses cues to stimulate acceptance of a message without deep consideration of the issues. Both can be effectively used in advertising.

What characteristics of the communicator contribute to effective persuasion? A crucial factor is credibility, which depends on the communicator being both an expert and trustworthy source of information. One way a communicator can appear more trustworthy is to argue against his or her self-interest. Persuasion is also enhanced when the audience believes the communicator is not trying to influence them. The attractiveness and likability of the communicator also tends to increase the persuasive appeal of a given message, but only when relatively trivial issues are concerned (e.g., such as what shaving cream to buy).

What characteristics of the message serve to increase its persuasive appeal? Fear-arousing messages are likely to facilitate attitude change, but behavior change (e.g., quitting smoking) is likely to occur only when specific, preventive instructions are provided. One-sided arguments tend to be more effective with poorly informed audiences, or audiences that already agree with the communicator's point of view. Conversely, two-sided arguments are more apt to persuade audiences that are well-informed or are initially opposed to the communicator's argument. Finally, the credibility of the communicator is important in determining how discrepant a message should ideally be from the audience's initial position. When a communicator has high credibility, the greater discrepancy between his or her view and that of the audience, the more the audience will be persuaded; but, when the communicator's credibility is doubtful or slim, he or she will produce maximum opinion change at moderate discrepancies.

What characteristics of the audience are important in persuasion? As we have seen, the audience's initial position, and whether it is well-informed or poorly informed about an issue, are significant factors. In addition, individual self-esteem plays a central role: people with low self-esteem tend to be more easily persuaded than people with high self-esteem. The prior experience of an audience is also an important consideration in determining the impact of a persuasive appeal. For example, people who are forewarned of an influence attempt tend to be more resistant to persuasion. Similarly, individuals who are "inoculated" against a future attempt at persuasion—by learning to defend their beliefs against a mild attack—display greater resistance to persuasion. Resistance is also increased by the phenomenon of reactance, which occurs when the individual perceives a persuasive appeal as a threat to his or her freedom of choice. Finally, when an audience is distracted during the presentation of a message, resistance to persuasion is reduced, presumably because the distraction prevents people from coming up with counter-arguments to refute the message.

Lecture Ideas & Teaching Suggestions

Who Says What to Whom? An effective strategy for helping students assimilate and remember the many factors that influence persuasion is to organize the material under the categories of: WHO says WHAT to WHOM? You might want to put this question on the board, listing briefly each set of findings under the appropriate heading as you discuss them. This is also a useful method for presenting a review of material from the chapter prior to exams. Students should also find it helpful to make their own charts of persuasion findings according to these categories.

Persuasion in Daily Life. In our daily lives, we are all subject to a tremendous number of attempts to influence our attitudes and behavior. As a result, the various persuasion tactics used by advertisers and sales personnel is an area that tends to be intrinsically fascinating for most students. Engaging material on sales pitches and other influence strategies, and the social-psychological processes underlying them, can be found in several of the books and articles listed in the suggested readings for this chapter. Of special interest are Pratkanis and Aronson's (1991) *The Age of Propaganda,* and Cialdini's (1988) *Influence: Science and Practice,* both of which explore the methods employed by those who are highly skilled in the art of persuasion. (Note: Some of these strategies are also examined in Chapter 4; thus, a lecture covering this material might provide an effective transition into theory and research on social cognition.)

Routes to Persuasion. Petty and Cacioppo offer an information-processing theory of attitude change. In their view, people process a persuasive message in one of two basic ways: 1) via a central processing route, in which they carefully and systematically evaluate the issues and arguments presented in the message; and 2) via a peripheral route, in which little thought is devoted to the content of the message itself. In the latter case, changes in attitudes result from relatively superficial characteristics associated with the message—such as the attractiveness of the communicator. When people are highly involved in an issue, they are more likely to engage in central processing modes, whereas an issue with low personal relevance will probably evoke peripheral processing. Research and further details are presented in Petty and Cacioppo (1986a, 1986b), which are referenced in the "additional readings" for this chapter.

Projects and Discussion Topics

1. PROJECT: Collect advertisements or public service messages from various magazines or newspapers—paying special attention to those that seem very persuasive or very unpersuasive. Drawing on your knowledge of persuasion tactics, identify the features of these ads that you believe would either maximize or detract from their persuasive impact. (For example, look at such factors as source credibility and attractiveness, the use of vivid information, one- vs. two-sided arguments, the use of fear, and other variables discussed in Chapter 3.) What kinds of people are the different ads directed toward? Can you find examples of ads that might succeed with one kind of audience, but could totally backfire with another kind of audience? Why do you think advertisers might risk alienating some audience members, rather than presenting a message with universal (or near-universal) appeal? Bring some examples to class and share your analyses with your classmates.

2. PROJECT: Go to the children's room of your local public library and locate books and magazines that are designed to be educational. Can you find examples of subtle—or even blatant—forms of propaganda within these books? You might want to pay particular attention to how certain groups in society—the elderly, women, racial minorities—are portrayed or NOT portrayed. In your search, make a comparison of books published in the last 5–10 years and those published earlier. Do there appear to be any changes in the amounts or kinds of "propaganda" presented in children's books over the years?

3. PROJECT: Suppose you were hired to develop a program to persuade high school students to refrain from drinking and driving. Assume that, from the outset, these students tend to believe that drinking and driving is nothing to worry about and that they have been (or will soon be) exposed to peer pressure to do so. What kind

of program would you design? What factors involving the audience, the source of communication, and the message itself would you need to consider in order to enhance the effectiveness of your program? Can you think of any ways to get around the potential problem of students simply "turning off" to your direct efforts to persuade them? Be imaginative! And, for the sake of convenience, assume that you have ample funds to carry out your program. (This project may be done in small groups or individually.)

4. PROJECT: Over the course of one day, keep a diary of all the various attempts to influence your behavior and beliefs and whether or not they were successful. In recording these attempts at social influence, look for messages coming from a broad variety of sources, including television, radio, print media, billboards, product packaging, etc. In addition, be sure to make note of persuasive appeals that come from "live" interaction with friends, family, teachers, sales clerks, strangers, and others you encounter during the day. Finally, make a special effort to look for "hidden" attempts to influence your beliefs and behavior—that is, those that do not constitute direct or obvious efforts to persuade.

5. DISCUSSION: How, and to what extent, does the mass media influence the public's attitudes and behaviors? Do television shows and newscasts, for example, simply reflect what is happening in the world or do they carry the potential to actually cause real-life events? Apart from advertising, do you believe the members of the media engage in deliberate attempts to persuade people to adopt certain opinions and attitudes?

6. DISCUSSION: To the best of your knowledge, how easily are you influenced by attempts to change your attitudes or behavior? Under what conditions are you more or less likely to be persuaded? Do you think your knowledge about strategies of persuasion, propaganda, and communication can help you to resist unwelcome attempts at persuasion? Since we live in an age of mass communication—in which we are subject to a daily onslaught of influence attempts—should children receive some kind of formal training or education about persuasion? Why or why not?

Experiential Exercises

1. This experiential exercise focuses on the central and peripheral appeal models of persuasion. The professor should decide on some topic like capital punishment or physician assisted suicide or sex education in the middle schools or legal gay marriages or national health insurance for everyone or some other controversial topic. The professor should ask two students to present a 3–5 minute talk for the issue in a central appeals manner with many facts, numbers, and straightforward. Second, another 2 students should present a 3–5 minute drama presentation against the issue in a peripheral manner with pictures, music, jiggles, yelling, costumes, and histrionics. An oral debriefing with the students would follow about the effectiveness of each and reasons for the effectiveness. Information in the text would be brought into the analysis discussion. If time would allow, there could even be two more presentations. One presentation would be against the topic in a peripheral manner and the other would be for the issue with a central appeal. There could be a written debriefing paper tying the ideas of the text to the presentations.

Additional Readings

Ball-Rokeach, S.J., Rokeach, M. & Grube, J.W. (1984, November). The great American values test. *Psychology Today*, pp. 34–41. (An experimental TV show assesses the extent to which television can influence basic values and beliefs.)

Cialdini, R.B. (1988). *Influence: Science and practice.* Glenview, IL: Scott, Foresman.

Diamond, E. & Bates, S. (1984, November). The political pitch. *Psychology Today*, pp. 23–32. (Explores the uses of persuasion within the context of political advertising campaigns.)

Entman, R.M. (1993). Framing: Toward clarification of a fractured paradigm. *Journal of Communication, 43*, 51–58. (Special issue: The future of the field: Between fragmentation and cohesion.)

Kipnis, D. & Schmidt, S. (1985, April). The language of persuasion. *Psychology Today*, pp. 40–46. (Covers the conditions under which "soft" and "hard" persuasion tactics work best.)

McGuire, W.J. (1970, February). A vaccine for brainwash. *Psychology Today*, pp. 63–64. (Explores the uses of the "inoculation technique" as a strategy for resisting persuasion.)

Petty, R.E. & Cacioppo, J.T. (1981). *Attraction and persuasion: Classic and contemporary approaches.* Dubuque, Iowa: W.C. Brown.

Petty, R.E. & Cacioppo, J.T. (1986a). *Communication and persuasion: Central and peripheral routes to attitude change.* New York: Springer-Verlag.

Petty, R.E. & Cacioppo, J.T. (1986b). The elaboration likelihood model of persuasion. In L. Berkowitz (Ed.), *Advances in experimental social psychology,* (Vol. 19), (pp. 874–884). New York: Academic Press.

Poindexter, J. (1983, May). Shaping the consumer. *Psychology Today*, pp. 64–68. (A look at how big business monitors consumer habits, and then uses this information to its advantage in creating commercial messages.)

Pratkanis, A.R. & Aronson, E. (1991). *The age of propaganda.* New York: Freeman.

Roskos-Ewoldson, D.R. & Fazio, R.H. (1992). The accessibility of source likability as a determinant of persuasion. *Personality and Social Psychology Bulletin, 18,* 19–25.

Schwartz, L.L. (1991). The historical dimension of cultic techniques of persuasion and control. *Cultic Studies Journal, 8,* 37–45.

Tykocinski, O., Higgins, E.T. & Chaiken, S. (1994). Message framing, self-discrepancies, and yielding to persuasive messages: The motivational significance of psychological situations. *Personality and Social Psychology Bulletin, (20),* 107–115.

Multiple-Choice Questions

Answer: d
Page: 48

1. According to research on the television film, *The Day After*, which graphically depicted the aftermath of a nuclear attack on the United States:
    a. viewers thought that surviving a nuclear war was very unlikely, while nonviewers thought surviving a nuclear war was very likely.
    b. viewers were more preoccupied than usual with thoughts of nuclear war, while nonviewers were less preoccupied than usual with thoughts of nuclear war.
    c. viewers went into "denial" and believed that the movie presented a highly exaggerated depiction of the horrors of nuclear war.
    d. both viewers and nonviewers said they intended to work toward preventing nuclear war by supporting a nuclear-weapons freeze and other antinuclear activities.

Answer: d
Page: 50

2. After a media overexposure of an event like September 11, 2001, citizens are most likely
    a. to engage in rational public debate on national policy.
    b. to allow a variety of ways to show dissent.
    c. to encourage different viewpoints to seek the truth.
    d. to react emotionally and to see basically one perspective.

Answer: c
Page: 51

3. The news media's sensationalizing of events such as suicides and the Tylenol poisonings sometimes incites copycat suicides and copycat poisonings. This phenomenon is known as:
    a. media proliferation.
    b. reactive imitation.
    c. emotional contagion.
    d. forensic journalism.

Answer: b
Page: 51–52

4. In his study of the effects of media coverage of teenage suicides, David Phillips found that:
   a. coverage of the confusion and grief surrounding the suicides produced a decrease in teen suicides following the coverage.
   b. there was an increase in teen suicides following the coverage.
   c. the suicide rate following the coverage remained surprisingly unchanged—pointing to the limited effects of media coverage of news events.
   d. the suicide rate increased moderately at first, followed by a sharp decrease as mental health workers responded to the crisis.

Answer: b
Page: 52

5. Phillips's research on the impact of media coverage of car-crash suicides revealed that following a publicized suicide:
   a. there was a decrease in single-car, one-passenger "suicide" accidents.
   b. victims of "suicide" accidents tended to be of similar age as the victim of the publicized suicide.
   c. there was an increase in multiple-car accidents.
   d. there was an increase in pedestrian fatalities involving hit-and-run drivers.

Answer: d
Page: 54

6. The impact of television commercials on very young children is reflected in the fact that:
   a. most children express a desire to imitate the behavior of TV characters.
   b. fewer than 20 percent of preschool-aged children asked for toys or food they saw advertised on TV.
   c. very young children tend to be quite cynical about advertising claims.
   d. according to their mothers, a majority of preschoolers were able to sing commercial jingles learned from television.

Answer: a
Page: 54

7. According to the text, what percent of tenth-grade students believed that TV commercials were truthful most of the time?
   a. 4 percent
   b. 33 percent
   c. 60 percent
   d. 80 percent

Answer: c
Page: 55–56

8. During the 1988 Presidential campaign Willie Horton was candidate George Bush's (the elder) most valuable player because
   a. he contributed $2 million to his campaign even though it was illegally done.
   b. he was Bush's top political campaign advisor.
   c. Bush used peripheral advertising to discuss this felon's release from prison.
   d. Bush asked him to design central arguments against Dukakis's economic policy.

Answer: b
Page: 57

9. According to Zimbardo, Ebbesen, and Maslach, who analyzed the content of elementary-school arithmetic texts, examples of math problems from most textbooks:
   a. are intentional forms of propaganda designed to brainwash students.
   b. subtly endorse and legitimize the capitalist economic system that is dominant in our society—presenting it as "natural and normal."
   c. are value-free ways of teaching children the basics of mathematics.
   d. reflect alternative systems of economics that threaten our society's established economic practices.

Answer: a
Page: 57

10. Bobby, a second-grader, is working on a problem in his arithmetic book. The problem reads: "Mary and her sister are baking three cakes for the school bake sale. To bake one cake, they will need 2 cups of flour and 1 egg. How many cups of flour and how many eggs will they need to bake 3 cakes?" According to Aronson, Bobby's math problem might be considered by some people to be a subtle form of:
    a. propaganda.
    b. persuasion.
    c. the inoculation effect.
    d. a one-sided argument.

Answer: a
Page: 58

11. Petty and Cacioppo say there are two routes to persuasion:
    a. the central and the peripheral.
    b. the primacy and the recency.
    c. the expert and the trustworthy.
    d. the fluency and the probability.

Answer: d
Page: 58

12. Suppose you watch a TV ad for a deodorant that tells you almost nothing about the product, but presents it being used by beautiful, popular, successful people. The persuasion appeal is:
    a. the primacy effect.
    b. the inoculation effect.
    c. the central route.
    d. the peripheral route.

Answer: a
Page: 58

13. Suppose you see an ad for a deodorant that focuses on how effective it is in comparison tests, how it compares in cost to other products, and that it is all-natural. The persuasion appeal is:
    a. the central route.
    b. the peripheral route.
    c. the logical route.
    d. the inoculation effect.

Answer: d
Page: 59

14. When lawyers and politicians want to persuade, they often use:
    a. strictly central route arguments.
    b. strictly peripheral route arguments.
    c. neither but only logical arguments.
    d. both central and peripheral.

Answer: b
Page: 60–61

15. In a study by Hovland and Weiss, subjects heard arguments regarding the feasibility of atomic submarines. Subjects were more persuaded by physicist J. Robert Oppenheimer, rather than the Soviet newspaper *Pravda*, because:
    a. Oppenheimer was an attractive source and, thus, subjects wished to identify with him.
    b. Oppenheimer was perceived as an expert and trustworthy source of information, unlike *Pravda*.
    c. Oppenheimer's arguments contained vivid examples, whereas *Pravda* presented the information in the form of statistics.
    d. Subjects knew that *Pravda* was arguing against its own self-interest and, thus, could not be trusted.

Answer: a
Page: 61

16. Research in attitude change suggests that in order to be a credible source, a communicator should be both:
    a. expert and trustworthy.
    b. respected and feared.
    c. attractive and intelligent.
    d. trustworthy and intelligent.

Answer: d
Page: 61–62

17. A study by Aronson and Golden revealed that sixth-graders were more persuaded of the importance of arithmetic after listening to the pro-math arguments of a prizewinning engineer, as compared to a dishwasher. However, when the engineer giving the speech was a black man:
    a. all students found his arguments less persuasive than those of the white engineer.
    b. all students found his arguments more persuasive than those of the white engineer.
    c. most students devalued engineering as a profession.
    d. only students who were highly prejudiced against blacks found his arguments less persuasive than those of the white engineer.

Answer: c
Page: 63–64

18. Suppose you are going to organize a program for high school students advocating stricter enforcement of the drug laws. All other things being equal, your most persuasive speaker would be a:
    a. police officer.
    b. concerned and well-liked parent.
    c. person serving a jail sentence for drug possession.
    d. student who has always supported this view.

Answer: b
Page: 65

19. Walster and Festinger conducted an experiment in which subjects "overheard" a conversation between two graduate students, one of whom expressed an opinion on a certain issue. Subjects' opinions were influenced by the graduate student's opinion when:
    a. the graduate student had previously performed a favor for the subject.
    b. the subject believed the graduate students were unaware of his or her presence.
    c. the graduate student was an expert on the particular issue in question.
    d. the graduate student presented a two-sided argument regarding the issue in question.

Answer: d
Page: 66

20. Attractive or likable communicators tend to be more persuasive when they are obviously trying to persuade us. This statement is:
    a. true, but only when the communicator is delivering a message that the audience already agrees with.
    b. false, except when the communicator is an expert source of information regarding the issue.
    c. true, but only when the audience is composed of men.
    d. true, but only in the case of trivial issues.

Answer: d
Page: 68

21. All other things being equal, the overwhelming weight of experimental evidence on fear and persuasion suggests that, *in general,* the more frightened a person is by a communication:
    a. the more likely he or she is to come up with counterarguments that oppose the fear-arousing communication.
    b. the more likely he or she is to refuse to take positive, preventive action.
    c. the more likely he or she is to "go into denial" and refuse to listen to future communications on the same issue.
    d. the more likely he or she is to take positive, preventive action.

Answer: b
Page: 68–69

22. The more frightened a person is by the communication, the more likely he or she is to take immediate preventive action. This statement:
    a. is true for most people.
    b. describes the way a person with high self-esteem might react to the message.
    c. describes the way a person with low self-esteem might react to the message.
    d. is false for most people.

Answer: c
Page: 68

23. According to research presented in the text, people with high self-esteem are most likely to be persuaded by campaigns using:
    a. low fear.
    b. moderate fear.
    c. high fear.
    d. all of the above are equally effective.

Answer: c
Page: 68–70

24. Elizabeth, a high-school student who smokes cigarettes, saw a film in her health class that depicted horrible scenes of people dying from lung cancer. After class, a friend asked her whether the film had convinced her to quit smoking. Elizabeth said no. However, a few days later, she realized she did want to quit and decided to sign up for a program to help her stop smoking. Based on research on persuasion, what might you conclude?
    a. High-fear messages are based on the primacy effect.
    b. Elizabeth was distracted while watching the film.
    c. Elizabeth has low self-esteem.
    d. Elizabeth was experiencing the self-fulfilling prophecy.

Answer: c
Page: 69

25. In the case of people with low self-esteem, communications that arouse a great deal of fear tend to:
    a. be ineffective under all circumstances.
    b. be effective when accompanied by instructions regarding appropriate action.
    c. inhibit immediate action, but are effective after a delay.
    d. persuade the person to take immediate action.

Answer: b
Page: 69–70

26. In a study by Leventhal, some students were exposed to a high-fear message regarding the importance of taking tetanus shots. Later, half of them were given specific instructions about where and when the shots were available, while the other half was not. Compared to the group that received instructions, students who did *not* receive them:
    a. displayed less favorable attitudes toward taking the shots.
    b. displayed equally favorable attitudes toward the shots, but were less likely to actually take the shots.
    c. displayed less favorable attitudes toward the shots, and were less likely to actually take the shots.
    d. were equally likely to take the shots, but only after a 2-day delay.

Answer: d
Page: 70–71

27. According to Aronson's chapter on persuasion, emotional appeals tend to influence _____ and specific instructions tend to influence _____.
    a. actual behavior; attitudes
    b. attitudes; intentions
    c. intentions; attitudes
    d. attitudes; actual behavior

Answer: a
Page: 70

28. Generally, high-fear appeals are more effective than low-fear appeals in producing behavior change when:
    a. specific instructions are provided on how to avoid painful consequences.
    b. the issue is unimportant to the audience.
    c. the issue is moderately important to the audience.
    d. the audience is challenged to come up with their own plan for avoiding painful consequences.

Answer: a
Page: 70

29. Fear appeals seem to function best when:
    a. followed by clear recommendations for reducing arousal.
    b. the fear is extremely high.
    c. the fear cannot be reduced.
    d. recommendations offered produce an increase in arousal.

Answer: b
Page: 70–71

30. According to the text, perhaps the best way to encourage young people to use condoms when having intercourse is to:
    a. print a warning about AIDS on each condom label.
    b. encourage people to think of condoms as part of erotic foreplay.
    c. present the startling statistics about how high the risk of AIDS is for young American heterosexuals.
    d. show explicit film footage of people dying from AIDS.

Answer: c
Page: 71–72

31. With the threat of terrorism since September 11, the government has issued many warnings. The research indicates that:
    a. these warnings are effective because people become more alert.
    b. the warnings are effective because people see the government as trustworthy.
    c. the warnings are ineffective because no one thinks it would happen again, especially after the war.
    d. the warnings are ineffective because the research says one cannot have heightened anxiety without appropriate action.

Answer: c
Page: 73

32. You are in the market for a new car and think you would like to own a Saab. According to research reported by Richard Nisbett and his associates, which of the following would be most likely to influence your decision?
    a. television commercials for Saab that are both informative and emotionally appealing
    b. print ads for Saab that are primarily informative
    c. hearing about the huge repair bills a neighbor's sister had on her Saab
    d. a high ranking made by *Consumer Reports* based on a sample of 75,000 miles of testing

Answer: c
Page: 73–74

33. Energy auditors were more successful in persuading homeowners to make improvements that would increase the energy-efficiency of their homes when:
    a. the auditors were expert and trustworthy.
    b. the auditors showed homeowners' reports of how much money they would save if they made the improvements.
    c. the auditors used highly vivid language and examples when making their recommendations to homeowners.
    d. the auditors used a two-sided argument when making their recommendations.

Answer: a
Page: 74

34. A one-sided argument for why nuclear power should be discontinued would be more persuasive than a two-sided argument with which of the following groups:
    a. a local anti-nuke group
    b. a college physics class
    c. a group of soldiers who had been drafted into the Army
    d. the U.S. Department of Energy staff

Answer: b
Page: 74

35. Which of the following conditions tends to make a one-sided argument *more* effective in persuading an audience than a two-sided argument?
    a. an intelligent and sophisticated audience
    b. a relatively unintelligent and uninformed audience
    c. a very rational and unemotional audience
    d. an audience which is initially opposed to the speaker's argument

Answer: c
Page: 74–75

36. When is a two-sided message likely to be more effective than a one-sided message?
    a. when the position advocated falls within the audience's latitude of acceptance
    b. when the audience is poorly informed and in general agreement with the source
    c. when the audience is well-informed and in general opposition to the position of the source
    d. when the position advocated falls in the audience's latitude of rejection

Answer: a
Page: 74–75

37. Under certain conditions, a two-sided argument may be more persuasive than a one-sided argument because:
    a. a well-informed audience is aware of both sides of the issue and, thus, would tend to perceive a one-sided argument as unfair or biased.
    b. all audiences appreciate hearing both sides of a controversial issue.
    c. an uninformed audience needs to hear both sides of the issue before forming an opinion.
    d. a one-sided argument would probably be confusing to an uninformed audience.

Answer: c
Page: 75–76

38. Suppose you are trying to persuade an educated audience that they should vote for you. Both you and your opponent will speak at a meeting the same day and the election will be held in two weeks. You should choose to speak _____ and give a _____ presentation.
   a. first; one-sided
   b. second; one-sided
   c. first; two-sided
   d. second; two-sided

Answer: a
Page: 76

39. According to Aronson, if you were to give one of two persuasive speeches, you would choose to speak second if the time interval between the first and second speech were _____ and the time interval between the second speech and the audience's action were _____.
   a. long; short
   b. short; long
   c. long; long
   d. short; short

Answer: b
Page: 76

40. Suppose you were running for office and were going to debate your opponent. If you both will present your arguments one right after the other and the election is still several days away, you should probably try to speak _____, in order to make use of the _____ effect.
   a. second; recency
   b. first; primacy
   c. second; primacy
   d. first; recency

Answer: d
Page: 75–76

41. If you wanted to be sure that you had the opportunity to present your point of view first and hope that listeners stopped paying attention to the speakers who followed you, you would be trying to use to your advantage the influence of the:
   a. recency effect.
   b. inoculation effect.
   c. foreplay effect.
   d. primacy effect.

Answer: b
Page: 76

42. In thinking about the relative importance of the primacy and recency effects, the most crucial variable is:
   a. expertise.
   b. time.
   c. trustworthiness.
   d. vividness.

Answer: b
Page: 77–78

43. There appears to be a positive linear relationship between one's attitude change and the credibility of the source of the communication as long as:
   a. the person has high self-esteem.
   b. the message is within one's latitude of acceptance.
   c. a primacy effect is operating.
   d. the argument presents both sides of the issues.

Answer: a
Page: 78

44. Hovland, Harvey, and Sherif conducted an experiment on latitude of acceptance of ideas about the state being "wet" or "dry" on the sale of alcohol beverages. They found that
   a. the greatest change happened when a moderate discrepancy took place between the actual message and the individual's original opinion.
   b. the greatest change happened when an extreme discrepancy took place between the actual message and the individual's original opinion.
   c. it was very difficult to change the elders of the community because they wanted the state "dry."
   d. the greatest change happened for only people who moved from their "dry" position to a "wet" position because they could see the economic benefits.

Answer: a
Page: 79–80

45. According to Aronson, under which of the following conditions of persuasive communication would people's attitudes typically change the most?
   a. when an expert argues an extreme position
   b. when a nonexpert argues an extreme position
   c. when an expert argues a moderate position
   d. when a nonexpert argues a moderate position

Answer: d
Page: 80

46. To change a person's attitude the most, a communicator should present a position that is highly distant or discrepant from the person's initial position.
   a. The statement is true.
   b. The statement is false.
   c. The statement is true only for low-credibility communicators.
   d. The statement is true only for high-credibility communicators.

Answer: b
Page: 80–81

47. Assume a speaker has low credibility with the audience. For maximum attitude change, how discrepant from the audience's initial position should the communication be?
    a. not at all discrepant
    b. moderately discrepant
    c. highly discrepant
    d. Discrepancy is not a significant factor if the speaker has low credibility.

Answer: b
Page: 81–82

48. One way of *decreasing* the persuasibility of members of an audience is:
    a. to feed them desirable food while someone is trying to persuade them.
    b. to forewarn them that someone is going to try to persuade them.
    c. to remind them that even though the speaker might be credible, he or she may not be trustworthy.
    d. to hide from them the fact that someone is going to try to persuade them.

Answer: c
Page: 82

49. "Persuasive communications, if blatant or coercive, can be perceived as intruding upon one's freedom of choice, thereby activating a person's defenses to resist the messages." This statement reflects the central idea of which of the following theories or concepts?
    a. reinforcement theory
    b. the inoculation effect
    c. reactance theory
    d. the primacy effect

Answer: d
Page: 82

50. Martha's mother tells her that she is absolutely never to dye her hair a "funny color." Martha proceeds to dye her hair purple. Martha's behavior is best thought of as an example of:
    a. the primacy effect.
    b. the recency effect.
    c. the inoculation effect.
    d. reactance.

Answer: b
Page: 83–84

51. When a person is exposed to a watered-down attack upon his or her beliefs, this produces resistance to later persuasion because:
    a. the person becomes bored with the topic.
    b. the person gains some practice in defending his or her beliefs.
    c. the person feels that he or she is not conforming to another's wishes.
    d. None of the above is true, since prior exposure *decreases* resistance to later persuasion.

Answer: b
Page: 84

52. McAlister's field experiment was successful in helping seventh-graders resist peer pressure to smoke cigarettes. His strategy involved teaching students:
    a. how to be assertive and just say "no."
    b. a series of counterarguments they could use against peer pressure, such as, "I'd be a real chicken if I smoked just to impress you."
    c. how to educate their peers about the tremendous health risks involved in smoking.
    d. how to maintain high self-esteem, so they would be more resistant to peer pressure.

Answer: a
Page: 87–88

53. According to research by Gerbner and his associates, heavy viewers of television are more likely than light viewers to:
    a. hold exaggerated views about the prevalence of violence in society.
    b. perceive women as having more interests than men.
    c. hold less prejudiced attitudes toward women and racial minorities.
    d. be more easily persuaded by attractive communicators.

Answer: b
Page: 88

54. According to several studies of television crime dramas:
   a. television accurately portrays criminals as committing crimes because of psychopathology or insatiable greed, as happens in the real world.
   b. television tends to ignore situational pressures which lead to criminal activity.
   c. television police officers are portrayed as being about as effective as their real-world counterparts.
   d. heavy viewers of such crime shows tend to be more lenient and to believe in the presumption of innocence for the defendant.

Answer: a
Page: 90

55. The main way in which an attitude differs from an opinion is that an attitude:
   a. includes an emotional component.
   b. is held for a briefer period of time.
   c. pertains to people, not just facts.
   d. is more resistant to change through persuasion.

Essay Questions

1. "The mass media exerts a powerful and pervasive impact on our attitudes and behavior—even if direct attempts at persuasion are not involved." Explain the meaning of this statement, and describe two pieces of research that support it.

2. In your own words, define and discuss the difference between education and propaganda. Why is it often true that, in real life, these two phenomena are difficult to distinguish? Provide an example of how information designed to educate might also serve as a subtle form of propaganda.

3. Give an example of an advertisement using a central route strategy and one using a peripheral route strategy. What is the major feature that distinguishes between these two approaches?

4. What characteristics associated with the audience play a significant role in determining the impact of a persuasive communication?

Why are they important? Support your reasoning by discussing the results of research involving audience characteristics.

5. Suppose you belonged to an antinuclear group that wanted to persuade an audience that the development of nuclear power plants should be curtailed. The audience is composed of relatively uninformed adults who are already somewhat in favor of nuclear power. Based on your readings on persuasion, what kind of message would you want to deliver? Would you give the speech yourself or, if not, what kind of speaker would you want to hire? Provide examples of relevant research to support your arguments.

6. Pretend you are a candidate for public office and you are planning to engage in a debate with your opponent. Given the choice, under what circumstances would you wish to speak first? Under what circumstances would you choose to speak last? Explain the reasoning behind your choices.

7. Compared to logical or rational appeals, how effective are persuasive communications that arouse a high level of fear? Under what conditions are fear-arousing messages most effective in influencing behavior? Under what conditions might they be less effective? Be sure to support your answer with examples of relevant research.

8. In general, how successful are obvious attempts to persuade? Under what special conditions are direct efforts to persuade more likely to succeed? Discuss one piece of research that supports the notion that direct efforts to persuade are effective, and one that indicates that such efforts are relatively ineffective.

4

Social Cognition

IV.   Categorization and Social Stereotypes

    A.   Stereotypic knowledge and expectations (Darley & Gross)

    B.   Illusory correlation (Hamilton)

    C.   In-group/out-group effects (Park & Rothbart; Tajfel)

V.   Re-constructive Memory

    Eye-witness testimony (Loftus)

VI.   Autobiographical Memory

    Rewriting personal histories (Ross, McFarland & Fletcher; Loftus)
    Recovered memories (Loftus)

VII.   How Conservative Is Human Cognition?

    Confirmation bias (Snyder & Swann)
    Hindsight bias (Fischhoff)
    Pros and cons of cognitive conservatism

VIII.   How Do Attitudes and Beliefs Guide Behavior?

    A.   The attitude-behavior relationship in our heads

      LaPiere's innkeepers
      Correspondent inferences (Jones; Jones & Harris)

    B.   When do attitudes predict behavior?

      Attitude accessibility (Fazio; Fazio & Williams)

    C.   Acting on perceptions (Herr)

IX.   Three possible biases in social explanation

    A.   Fundamental attribution error (Bierbrauer; Ross, Amabile & Steinmetz)

    B.   Actor-observer bias (Storms)

C. The self-biases

> Egocentric thought (Jervis; Langer; Petty & Brock)
> Self-serving bias (Weary; Alloy & Abramson)

D. Value of self-biases (Grove, et al.; Taylor; Seligman)

Terms & Concepts

felicific calculus
naïve scientist
consistency
consensus
distinctiveness
cognitive misers
contrast effects
priming
construct accessibility
attitude heuristic
halo effect
false consensus effect
categorization
illusory correlation
in-group/outgroup effects
minimum group paradigm
reconstructive memory
autobiographical memory
self-schema
recovered memory phenomenon
confirmation bias

decision framing
primacy effect
recency effect
attention decrement
interpretive set
dilution effect
heuristics
representative heuristic
availability heuristic
hindsight bias
cognitive conservatism
attitude accessibility
fundamental attribution error
actor-observer bias
dispositional factors
situational factors
self-serving bias
illusion of control
Barnum statement
depressive realism

Chapter Overview

Social cognition refers to a broad class of processes and influences that affect how people make sense out of the social world. Under the right conditions, we are capable of behaving like scientists in our everyday thinking—seeking out and evaluating information in a systematic and rational manner. More commonly, however, our perceptions and judgments are subject to a variety of biases and other distorting influences. It is important to identify and understand these influences because, to a very large extent, our perceptions of the social world play a central role in determining our behavior. Key issues covered in the chapter are summarized below.

The "social context"—how things are presented and described—has a major impact on our perceptions and judgments of people and events. Kelley, for example, argues that people function as "naïve scientists," evaluating information according to its consistency, consensus, and distinctiveness. Also, an object can strike us as better or worse, depending on the characteristics of the objects against which it is compared. This phenomenon, known as the contrast effect, is demonstrated in research showing that men were less attracted to a potential blind date after viewing a television program (*Charlie's Angels*) that featured three glamorous actresses.

One way that people cope with the enormous amount of information they encounter in everyday life is through the use of heuristics, which provide a short-cut method for processing information. Requiring very little thought, heuristics are simple—but often only approximate—strategies for solving problems. For instance, people often use the similarity of objects or the availability of specific examples to make quick judgments. One commonly used heuristic is the halo effect, in which a favorable or unfavorable impression of a person colors our future expectations and inferences about that person. Another heuristic is the false consensus effect, which involves the tendency to overestimate the percentage of people who agree with us on a given issue.

Our perceptions, judgments, and behavior are strongly influenced by the categories we use to define and interpret events and people. Categorization has particularly important consequences when it involves the use of stereotypes. Once we have categorized a person according to a stereotype, our perceptions of that person's behavior, as well as our expectations regarding future interactions, will tend to be consistent with the stereotype. As a result, we are unlikely to process information that contradicts our stereotypes—a tendency which reinforces prejudiced beliefs and behavior.

Human memory is primarily reconstructive in nature. Our recollections do not reflect a literal translation of past events; rather, we recreate many of our memories from bits and pieces of what we can recall, as well as our beliefs and expectations about what should have been. Research on eye-witness testimony offers a compelling demonstration of the real-world implications of reconstructive memory. For example, the use of "leading questions" by interrogators can seriously distort a witness's memory of the facts regarding a crime, leading to erroneous conclusions on the part of those who must weigh the evidence in a given case.

Autobiographical memories are the coherent, integrated memories of individual histories. Recent research has been conducted into the Recovered Memory Phenomenon. The scientists who have done systematic research on the nature of memory have found that repeated instances of traumatic events occurring over a long stretch of time are not usually forgotten. Their research indicates that, while this kind of thing might happen on rare occasions, it simply is not the way memory works. Rather, memories of abuse could be unintentionally planted by the therapists themselves—not with any malevolent motive, but in a sincere attempt to help the client.

Human cognition tends to be highly conservative. That is, people have a strong tendency to preserve their pre-existing knowledge, beliefs, attitudes, and hypotheses. One important benefit of this tendency is that it allows us to perceive the social world as a coherent and stable place. However, as many of the findings presented in the chapter demonstrate, cognitive conservatism can often cause a person to distort events or miss important information. One strategy for avoiding these negative consequences is to try to think of persons and important events as unique, rather than automatically assigning them to a salient category. Another is to remain vigilant regarding our vulnerability to cognitive biases, realizing that, in any particular situation, we may be mistaken in our perceptions and judgments of a person or event.

What is the relationship between beliefs and behavior? Research indicates that a person's attitudes often are not a good predictor of his or her behavior, even though our intuitions suggest otherwise. In part, the common perception that attitudes do correspond with behavior stems from the fundamental attribution error—the tendency to attribute the cause of an individual's behavior to his or her stable personality traits, rather than to situational influences. Certain conditions do, however, increase the probability of attitude-behavior consistency. One of these is attitude accessibility, or the relative ease with which a relevant attitude comes to mind when we encounter an opportunity to act on it.

Cognitive biases involving the self play a major role in allowing us to fulfill an important psychological goal: maintaining and enhancing our view of ourselves. These self-biases include egocentric thought, which involves perceiving the self as more central to events than it actually is. Another is the self-serving bias, which refers to our tendency to make dispositional attributions for our successes, while attributing our failures to situational factors. Although such biases reflect a distorted view of the self, they can play a vital role in psychological health and functioning. For example, the tendency to take responsibility for successes, but not failures, may protect a person from becoming discouraged while pursuing a goal requiring great effort and persistence. Conversely, research has revealed that depressed individuals are not subject to the self-serving bias; rather, their more accurate way of seeing the world leaves them "sadder but wiser."

Lecture Ideas & Teaching Suggestions

How Decisions are Framed. The importance of context in determining how information about the social world is perceived and interpreted is a major issue addressed in Chapter 4. The impact of seemingly minor changes in the way information is presented can be demonstrated in the classroom by using the decision framing example from the Kahneman and Tversky experiment (discussed on pages 129–130 in *The Social Animal*). In this procedure, subjects are asked to choose between two programs for combating an epidemic illness which could kill 600 people unless measures are taken to curb its impact. The programs are presented in two different ways: one that emphasizes the potential for the LOSS of lives, and one in which the information is framed in terms of a given program's potential to SAVE lives. Although, regardless of wording, the respective impact of each program is identical, the majority of subjects tend to reject the program that appears to entail greater loss of life.

To replicate this effect with your students, you will need to give half the class the opportunity to choose between Program A and B as they are presented in Version 1, with the remaining students choosing between the two programs presented in Version 2 (see paragraphs below). A convenient way to do this is to copy both versions on a single sheet of paper, placing one on the top half and the other on the bottom half. The sheets can then be cut in half and randomly distributed to the class, such that each student receives only one version.

VERSION 1 If Program A is adopted, two hundred people will be saved. If Program B is adopted, there is a one-third probability that six hundred people will be saved and a two-thirds probability that no people will be saved.

VERSION 2 If Program A is adopted, four hundred people will die. If Program B is adopted, there is a one-third probability that nobody will die and a two-thirds probability that six hundred people will die.

As with Kahneman and Tversky's subjects, most of the students who received Version 1 should choose Program A; while those who received Version 2 should show a strong preference for Program B. According to Kahneman and Tversky, the power of decision framing in this example stems from the fact that people are more threatened by the idea of losing something than they are by the possibility of gain. In explaining this effect to your students, you may also wish to point out its practical implications, which are demonstrated in the energy conservation study by Gonzales, Aronson, and Costanzo (discussed on pages 130–131). (NOTE: This demonstration should be conducted before students have read Chapter 4. For maximum impact, you may wish to collect students' responses a week or so prior to assigning the chapter, saving the results until you are ready to cover this topic in lecture.)

Attributions for Success and Failure. If you would like to explore the topic of attribution theory in greater depth, you may wish to discuss Weiner's work on attributions regarding success and failure. According to his model, people focus on two major dimensions in attempting to explain the reasons for another person's success or failure at a given task. The first consists of an internal/external dimension, which is similar to the distinction between dispositional and situational attributions for a behavior. The second dimension consists of the distinction between stable and temporary causes of behavior. These two independent dimensions, when combined in various ways, lead to different conclusions about a person's performance as well as different predictions regarding future behavior. For example, confronted with the fact that Ellen received an A on her social psychology exam, we might variously attribute her performance to: 1) stable/internal causes—she is highly intelligent; 2) stable/external causes—the exam was very easy; 3) temporary/internal causes—she put a great deal of effort in studying for the exam; or 4) temporary/external causes—she was very lucky. The kinds of attributions we make will have important consequences for our predictions about Ellen's future performance. Thus, if we believe Ellen succeeded because she is highly intelligent, we are likely to expect her to do well on future exams. On the other hand, if we believe Ellen succeeded primarily because she studied hard (a less stable cause), our predictions would be less certain, since other factors could prevent her from being equally diligent when preparing for exams in the future. In addition to affecting our predictions, our attributions will influence the kind of treatment we believe a person deserves as a result of his or her performance. For example, if Ellen had failed the exam because she was sick, her instructor would probably be more willing to let her take a make-up exam than if she had failed simply because she hadn't studied hard enough. Similarly, we tend to believe that people deserve greater rewards when their success is due to internal factors, such as effort and ability, rather than to luck or other external factors.

More information about Weiner's model, as well as its implications for achievement motivation, can be found in: Weiner, B., Frieze, I., Kukla, A., Reed, L., Rest, S. & Rosenbaum, R.M. (1972). Perceiving the causes of success and failure. In E.E. Jones, D.E. Kanouse, H.H. Kelley, R.E. Nisbett, S. Valins, and B. Weiner (Eds.), *Attribution: Perceiving the causes of behavior.* Morristown, NJ: General Learning Press; and Weiner, B. (1974). *Achievement motivation and attribution theory.* Morristown, NJ: General Learning Press.

Social Cognition and Depression. The interface between social cognition and the fields of clinical and health psychology offers a number of interesting possibilities for lecture material. For example, the application of findings from social-cognition research has improved understanding and treatment of the problem of depression. Work in this area indicates that depressed individuals are typically caught in a vicious cycle of negative thinking, which leads to self-defeating behavior, which leads to negative experiences, which increase negative thinking, and so forth. Cognitive therapies for breaking this cycle involve various strategies for modifying negative thought patterns. One such method is called "attributional style therapy," which involves teaching depressed persons to make attributions that are more typical of nondepressed persons—such as taking credit for success experiences, and focussing on situational factors that contribute to failure. A useful source information on this form of therapy, as well as other cognitive approaches to clinical issues, may be found in Abramson, L.Y. (1988). *Social cognition and clinical psychology: A synthesis.* New York: Guilford. In addition, Taylor (1989) discusses the value of self-biases and other "positive illusions" in maintaining psychological and physical well-being (see additional readings for this chapter).

Projects and Discussion Topics

1. PROJECT: The "contrast effect" involves the tendency for evaluations of an object to reflect the context within which the object is presented. Using friends and acquaintances as subjects, you can try to demonstrate this effect by conducting a modified replication of Kenrick and Gutierres' experiment (in which a "blind date" was

seen as less attractive when young men evaluated her after, as opposed to before, viewing a TV show featuring three glamorous actresses—see page 99.

First, you will need to find photos of THREE very attractive men, and photos of THREE unattractive men. Then, find a photo of ONE moderately attractive man to serve as the "target" photo.

[HINT: Use photos of men whom your "subjects" are unlikely to know, and try to keep extraneous factors—such as age and style of dress—relatively constant for all photos. Good sources for photos are high school or college yearbooks (you can make photocopies), and magazine or newspaper articles that are accompanied by a "mug shot" of the person featured in the article. Also, it's a good idea to use only female subjects for your study.]

The procedure involves having the subject look at only one of the two series of photos: Group A, which contains the three unattractive photos plus the "target" photo; and Group B, which contains the "target" photo and the three highly attractive photos. In each group of photos, put the target photo last, and assign the other three photos to the first, second and third positions in the series. (Keep the order of the photos constant for all subjects.) After assigning the subject to group A or B, ask her to examine the photos from that group. Next, for each of the four photos, ask her: "How physically attractive is this person?" For each photo, have the subject indicate her rating on a 1–7 scale (1 = very unattractive, 7 = very attractive). Use this procedure on at least 10 subjects, working things out so that roughly half of your subjects view Group A, with the other half viewing Group B.

To determine your results, figure out the average rating of the "target" photo from subjects in Group A and compare it to the average rating of the "target" photo from subjects in Group B. Is there at least a 1-point difference in the ratings? If so, is it in the predicted direction—that is, did subjects in Group A, on average, rate the "target" photo as more attractive, compared to subjects in Group B? If so, you have demonstrated the contrast effect, showing that the same photo was rated as less attractive when seen in the context of photos of more highly attractive men. Whatever your results, bring a report of your findings to class and be prepared to discuss them.

2. PROJECT: Search through newspapers and magazines for "advice" columns in which people ask for help with personal problems or discuss their experiences and insights about life. Collect several examples and conduct an analysis of the kinds of attributions people make when discussing their own behavior and the behavior of others. Also, examine the attributions contained in the columnist's responses. In performing your analysis, draw upon your knowledge of attributional biases discussed in Chapter 4. For example, be on the look out for illustrations of the fundamental attribution error, attributions based on stereotypes, the actor-observer bias, the self-serving bias, etc. Bring your examples to class and give a report of your investigation.

3. PROJECT: With a little help from your friends, you can do an informal demonstration of Asch's "primacy effect on impression formation." Tell your friend you are going to describe a person and that, following the description, you want him or her to tell you how much they think they would like this person—based on a 1 (not at all) to 10 (very much) scale. For half of your "subjects," use description A: "Steve is intelligent, industrious, impulsive, critical, stubborn, and envious." For the other half, use description B: "Steve is envious, stubborn, critical, impulsive, industrious, and intelligent." (Note: Be sure not to read the adjectives too rapidly.) Compare the average ratings from Description A and Description B. Did you find a tendency for people to prefer Steve as portrayed in Description A? Share your findings with your classmates.

4. DISCUSSION: Social psychologists have noted that people tend to behave in accordance with their social roles—acting differently in different situations, depending on which "role" the situation demands. Thus, one reason we often perceive other people's behavior as stemming from their stable personality traits is that we usually see them in only one role—say, as a friend or teacher.

Looking at your own behavior, are you the "same" person with all the different people in your life? Make a list of several of the social roles you occupy—for example, friend, son/daughter, brother/sister, wife/husband, student, worker, romantic partner, etc. Next, list some of the persons who typically "see" you in one of these different roles, but not all of the others. If these people all got together to discuss what kind of person you are and how you usually act, would they completely agree in their assessments of you? If not, how might their perceptions of you differ? To what extent are you aware of behaving differently in different situations?

Finally, try to recall an occasion or two when someone you knew fairly well seemed to be acting "out of character"—that is, in a manner that was at odds with your customary notion of his or her personality. How did you react to this "inconsistent" behavior? Did it surprise you? Looking back, can you think of possible situational factors or role requirements that might account for this person's behavior? Compare your observations and experiences with others in your discussion group.

Experiential Exercises

1. BARGNA: A Cross-Cultural Simulation. This simulation was developed by Sivasailam Thiagarajan in cooperation with Barbara Steinwachs for the debriefing and Pierre Corbeil for the French translation. The purpose is to sensitize people to other cultures with their differences and similarities. It can be played in 25 minutes and debriefed for the remaining part of the class. It is most appropriate for this chapter because participants make many first impressions that are based on false assumptions and lead to negative opinions. Participants are in groups and learn a new card game. The game is played in silence for 5–7 minutes. After that the winners move up to a new table and the losers move down. The surprise in the simulation is that each table received slightly different rules, which leads to major confusion and false accusations from primacy. The oral debriefing is essential to understand how cultures might be the same and yet different. The simulation can be purchased from:

    Intercultural Press
    P.O. box 700
    Yarmouth, ME 04096
    Phone: 207-846-5181

2. BAFA BAFA: Cross-cultural simulation. This is a classical social simulation depicting two different cultures. One is competitive and the other is traditional. Participants learn their cultural norms and then travel to the other culture to experience another perspective. It

takes about 2 hours, but it is well worth the time. The debriefing can be along the lines of judgments we make when interacting with different human beings with different customs. Since half the class would be in one culture and half in the other, these "different" people would be friends. This can be purchased from:

Simulation Training Systems
Del Mar, CA
Phone: 1-800-942-2900

3. Attractiveness Rating. The professor can conduct Project 1 in class by obtaining three photos of good-looking men, three photos of unattractive men and one photo of an average person (target individual). These photos can be on PowerPoint or on slides. Group A with the attractive males is shown to half of the class and the others close their eyes. Then Group B with the unattractive males is shown to the second half of the students. Each student rates the individual photo on a 1–7 attraction scale. Both males and females can rate the photos. The results are tabulated on the blackboard with four columns: Group A Females, Group A Males, Group B Females, and Group B Males. The averages should be calculated. The oral debriefing should revolve around Kenrick and Gutierres' experiment page 99. This exercise can also be done with photos of attractive and unattractive females. Comparisons of the results from the males can be compared to the females. The students can write papers tying the classroom experience to the research and they should discuss whether attractiveness plays a part in their dating experience or not.

4. Character Rating. In connection with this first exercise or separate the professor can conduct Project 3 in class as well. The photo of the average person (target individual) can be shown again in class. The professor should ask half of the class to step in the hall for a minute. Then the professor should read slowly the description: "Steve is intelligent, industrious, impulsive, critical, stubborn, and envious." The students rate how well they like this person from 1 (not at all) to 10 (very much). Then ask the other students to return and read the statement slowly, "Steve is envious, stubborn, critical, impulsive, industrious, and intelligent." The students rate how well they like him. The data are collected into four groups, Group A Females, Group A Males, Group B Females, and Group B Males. This can be done for the female target as well. The oral debriefing

can center around primacy effects and making a good first impression. Students speculate about the implications of this experiential exercise.

5.   Seek and Search Rating. The professor can continue rating a target individual. From the research by Paul Herr on page 130 the professor can create two seek a word puzzles. One would have evil names like Charles Manson, Adolf Hitler, Saddam Hussein, and others. Another seek a word puzzle would have positive names like Peter Pan, Pope John Paul, Shirley Temple and others. Half of the class gets one puzzle and the other half receives the second puzzle. Then a non-descript statement is read about a person named Donald. A picture of an average person can even appear on the screen. Then all the students can rate how likeable is Donald on a scale 1–7. This exercise can also be done with names of females who are evil and then rate a non-descript Susan. (It might be difficult to think of a list of evil women who have not been romanticized.)

Additional Readings

Fiske, S. & Taylor, S.E. (1984). *Social cognition.* Reading, MA: Addison-Wesley.

Fowler, R.D. (Ed.). (1994). *American Psychologist, 49,* 439–445. (Six commentaries on Loftus' 1993 article.)

Harvey, J.H. & Weary, G. (1985). *Attribution: Basic issues and applications.* New York: Academic Press.

Lindsay, D.S. (1993). Eyewitness suggestibility. *Current Directions in Psychological Science, 2,* (3), 86–89.

Loftus, E. (1993). The reality of repressed memories. *American Psychologist, 48,* 518–537.

Loftus, E.F. (1979, May–June). The malleability of human memory. *American Scientist,* pp. 312–320. (How subsequent information can distort memory for an event and the implications of this phenomenon for theory and research on memory processes.)

Loftus, E.L. (1992). When a lie becomes memory's truth: Memory distortion after exposure to misinformation. *Current Directions in Psychological Science, 1,* (4), 121–123.

Messick, D.M. & Asuncion, A.G. (1993). The Will Rogers illusion in judgments about social groups. *Psychological Science, 4,* (1), 46–48.

Offir, C.W. (1975, April). Floundering in fallacy: Seven ways to kid yourself. *Psychology Today,* pp. 66–68. (Covers common errors in human thinking.)

Perlmutter, L.C. & Monty, R.A. (1977). The importance of perceived control: Fact or fantasy? *American Scientist, 65,* pp. 759–765. (A review of experimental evidence regarding the benefits of the "illusion of control" for performance and well-being.)

Rubin, D.C. (1975, September). The subtle deceiver: Recalling your past. *Psychology Today,* pp. 38–46. (Current beliefs have a distorting impact on how we remember the details of our personal past.)

Slovic, P., Fischhoff, B. & Lichtenstein, S. (1980, June). Risky assumptions. *Psychology Today,* pp. 44–48. (Offers several examples of problems posed by errors in human thinking and judgment.)

Snyder, C.R. (1985, September). Excuses, excuses. *Psychology Today,* pp. 50–55. (Discusses self-protective attributions and other strategies people use to sustain a positive self-image.)

Taylor, S.E. (1989). *Positive illusions: Creative self-deception and the healthy mind.* New York: Basic Books.

Multiple-Choice Questions

Answer: a
Page: 95

1. Jane is trying to decide whether she should marry Jim. She sits down with a piece of paper and makes a list of all the positive aspects about marrying Jim, and then a list of all the negative aspects. After looking at both lists, she can see that the good things outweigh the bad. So, she calls Jim up and says, "OK, let's set a date for the wedding!" Jane's way of making up her mind is an example of:
   a. felicific calculus.
   b. using "distinctiveness" information in making a decision.
   c. decisional framing.
   d. the contrast effect.

Answer: b
Page: 95

2. Judy decides to withdraw from her psychology class because she believes she must drop one of the classes she is taking, and the psychology class is the most boring and meets at 8:00 a.m., a time of day during which she would rather sleep. Judy's behavior is best thought of as an example of:
   a. the halo effect.
   b. felicific calculus.
   c. the actor-observer bias.
   d. the fundamental attribution error.

Answer: d
Page: 95

3. Harold Kelley's view of social cognition is that people attempt to function as:
   a. cost accountants.
   b. cost-benefit analysts.
   c. amateur social psychologists.
   d. naïve scientists.

Answer: c
Page: 95–96

4. According to Kelley, people look for which of the following kinds of information in explaining behavior?
   a. continuity, consensus, and distinctiveness.
   b. contiguity, consensus, and distinctiveness.
   c. consistency, consensus, and distinctiveness.
   d. consistency, covariation, and distinctiveness.

Answer: c
Page: 96

5. Suppose you notice that Fred becomes very embarrassed when the subject of knives comes up. In fact, he is the only person you have ever seen react in this way when you talk about knives, and he has never before expressed any concern about knives. According to Kelley, Fred's behavior is very high in:
   a. consistency.
   b. consensus.
   c. distinctiveness.
   d. reactance.

Answer: c
Page: 97

6. The term "cognitive miser" refers to our tendency:
   a. to meticulously count up all the pros and cons of a particular decision.
   b. to expect others to do our thinking for us.
   c. to take shortcuts in processing complex information.
   d. to put self-interest over the interests of others when processing information.

Answer: d
Page: 98

7. Jill is in the market to buy a used car. She visits a car lot and tells the salesperson she is looking for something under $4,000. The salesperson first shows her a car that has very high mileage, a dented fender, and needs a new clutch. The asking price is $3,700. Shocked, Jill wonders, "Who on earth would pay that much for this piece of junk?" The salesperson then shows her a much nicer car—in fact, one that she thinks would suit her needs perfectly. Jill really needs to get a car as soon as possible, so she decides to buy it right then and there—even though it costs $4,800. Jill's decision has been influenced by:
   a. the representativeness heuristic.
   b. the availability heuristic.
   c. the context effect.
   d. the contrast effect.

Answer: c
Page: 98

8. Suppose you are ready to buy your textbooks for your first semester in college. You are unsure as to how much these books will cost, and when your bill is rung up at the register, the total is $200. According to the context effect, you will more likely think that the books are a bargain if the person ahead of you in line:
   a. pays $150 for her books.
   b. pays $200 for her books.
   c. pays $400 for her books.
   d. finds a mistake in her bill.

Answer: b
Page: 99

9. In an experiment by Kenrick and Gutierres, male college students were asked to evaluate a potential blind date before or after watching the television show *Charlie's Angels* (which features three glamorous actresses). Compared to subjects who rated the blind date before watching the show, those who gave their ratings *after* the show:
   a. found her more attractive, due to the halo effect.
   b. found her less attractive, due to the contrast effect.
   c. found her equally attractive, due to the consensus effect.
   d. found her less attractive, but only if they themselves were highly attractive—due to the availability heuristic.

Answer: d
Page: 99

10. If you were a young woman and were about to go out with a male blind date, you should hope that he has just been watching a movie that starred:
    a. attractive men.
    b. unattractive men.
    c. attractive women.
    d. unattractive women.

Answer: d
Page: 101

11. Aronson argues that recently activated or frequently activated concepts are more likely to readily come to mind and thus be used in interpreting social events. This phenomenon is called:
    a. context effects.
    b. reactance.
    c. heuristics.
    d. priming.

Answer: b
Page: 101–102

12. Heath and her colleagues asked a group of physicians to imagine themselves being exposed to the AIDS virus while working. A similar group of physicians received no such instruction. Heath's major result was that, compared to physicians who had not imagined exposure to AIDS, those who had imagined being exposed were more likely to:
    a. actually get AIDS.
    b. believe they were at a higher risk for getting AIDS.
    c. be extra careful with procedures that posed an AIDS risk.
    d. refuse to treat AIDS patients and those infected with HIV.

Answer: a
Page: 102

13. Iyengar and colleagues conducted a study in which subjects watched specially edited news programs for a week. Generalizing from their results, if you wanted to have college students focus on the issue that tuition is too expensive, you would:
    a. run articles in each issue of the college newspaper, thereby keeping the issue in front of the students.
    b. present the tuition issue in a high-fear campaign.
    c. present the issue only in one or two early issues, thereby depending on the primacy effect.
    d. link tuition-setting to corruption in the President's office, thereby using the halo effect.

Answer: c
Page: 102–103

14. The effects of category priming on social judgment are illustrated by the tendency:
    a. for "gain" information to be more influential than "loss" information.
    b. for "loss" information to be more influential than "gain" information.
    c. for the public to see as most important those social and political issues that receive the most media coverage.
    d. for people to base their first impressions of another person on inaccurate information.

Answer: c
Page: 103

15. John, a car salesman, is trying to persuade a customer to trade in his gas-guzzling, 8-cylinder car for a new 6-cylinder model. So he says to his customer, "Think of all the extra money you'll have if you buy this fuel-efficient model!" According to Kahneman and Tversky, John's sales pitch would be much improved if he had said:
    a. "Not only is this model fuel efficient—it has a great safety record, too!"
    b. "Look at this article by *Consumer Report*. No other model in its class gets this kind of mileage on the freeway!"
    c. "Think of all the money you're losing on that gas-guzzler—dollar bills are flying right out of the exhaust pipe every time you drive!"
    d. "Buying this fuel-efficient model is a good way to show your concern for the environment!"

Answer: b
Page: 104

16. Aronson reports the results of an experiment in which people who were asked to insulate their homes were given information either about how much money they would save, if they insulated, or lose, if they didn't insulate. Based on results of this study, if you were trying to sell insulation, you would be wise to:
   a. emphasize how much is saved by insulating.
   b. emphasize how much is lost by not insulating.
   c. emphasize both savings and losses, based on the halo effect.
   d. emphasize neither savings or losses, since money is not something people are reluctant to discuss.

Answer: d
Page: 105

17. Asch's study on the primacy effect on impression formation indicates that:
   a. positive information is more influential than negative information in determining overall impressions of another person.
   b. negative information is more influential than positive information in determining overall impressions of another person.
   c. first impressions are usually more accurate than impressions based on later information.
   d. information received first is more influential than later information in determining overall impressions of another person.

Answer: a
Page: 105

18. Suppose you are planning to take a class from a professor about whom you know nothing. Just before class starts, a friend of yours describes the professor as inflexible, wordy, an easy grader, and kind to students. If the primacy effect is operating, you are most likely to think of the professor as:
   a. inflexible.
   b. wordy.
   c. an easy grader.
   d. kind to students.

Answer: a
Page: 106

19. You are a college professor grading the exams of students in your class. Student A and Student B both got 25 correct out of a total of 40 multiple-choice questions. However, Student A got the first 15 items correct, but missed 10 out of the last 25 items. Student B, on the other hand, got the first 15 items wrong, but had correct answers for the last 25 questions. According to research by Jones and his colleagues, what kind of impression would you be likely to have of these students?
    a. Student A is smarter than Student B.
    b. Student B is smarter than Student A.
    c. Student A and Student B are equally intelligent.
    d. Student A became overconfident while taking the exam, while Student B started off insecure but gained confidence over time.

Answer: b
Page: 106

20. Which of the following explanations have been offered to account for research findings on the *primacy* effect in impression formation?
    a. the latter items on a list receive more attention and, thus, have more impact on judgment.
    b. the first items on a list create an initial impression that is then used to interpret subsequent information.
    c. the first items on a list have a "priming effect" on subsequent items.
    d. the latter items on the list are more easily remembered than the first items.

Answer: a
Page: 106

21. The attention decrement explanation attempts to explain the basis for which of the following?
    a. the primacy effect
    b. the illusory correlation
    c. the hindsight bias
    d. the contrast effect

Answer: b
Page: 106

22. The tendency for neutral or irrelevant information to weaken a judgment or impression is referred to as:
    a. the priming effect.
    b. the dilution effect.
    c. the primacy effect.
    d. the halo effect.

Answer: b
Page: 107

23. A politician running for re-election is suspected of having misused campaign funds during the last election. Based on the "dilution effect," he or she can reduce the impact of this negative public image by:
    a. appearing in ads designed to defend his or her good character.
    b. appearing in ads that include irrelevant information—such as a story about his or her childhood.
    c. appearing in ads that cast doubt on the honesty of his or her opponent.
    d. appearing in ads with film or TV celebrities who believe in his or her innocence and will say so on camera.

Answer: a
Page: 107

24. One way that we make sense out of the vast and dizzying array of information that comes our way is through the use of heuristics, which are
    a. simple, but often only approximate, rules for solving problems.
    b. simple, but highly accurate, rules for solving problems.
    c. complex, but often only approximate, rules for solving problems.
    d. complex, but highly accurate, rules for solving problems.

Answer: b
Page: 108

25. You and a friend are visiting a new city and would like to splurge and go out for a fine meal. You look at the restaurant listings in the newspaper and find one that is very expensive. Your friend says, "Let's go for it. With prices like that, we're bound to have an incredible dining experience." In making her decision, your friend most likely was guided by:
    a. the "priming" effect.
    b. the representative heuristic.
    c. the contrast effect.
    d. the primacy effect.

Answer: d
Page: 108

26. John is described as being introverted, shy, logical, hard-working, not much fun, very intelligent, and having a weird sense of humor. These characteristics match your stereotype of accountants. If you are asked whether John is more likely to be an accountant or a salesman, you are very sure he must be an accountant. This result is predicted from:
    a. the contrast effect.
    b. the primacy effect.
    c. the attitude heuristic.
    d. the representative heuristic.

Answer: d
Page: 108–109

27. The representative heuristic helps to explain why, in some instances, we tend to base our judgments of other people on:
    a. a careful consideration of their individual characteristics.
    b. their actual behavior, even when it conflicts with their personalities.
    c. how well they have treated us, or others, in the past.
    d. stereotypes regarding their gender, race, appearance, etc.

Answer: b
Page: 110

28. After watching a news report of a plane crash, people are more likely to overestimate the frequency of plane crashes in general. This error in judgment is due to:
   a. the representative heuristic.
   b. the availability heuristic.
   c. the false consensus effect.
   d. confirmation bias.

Answer: d
Page: 111

29. Elizabeth, a literature major, believes that the author James Joyce was the most brilliant writer since Shakespeare. A friend asks her if Joyce had positive attitudes about women, or whether he was very sexist. Elizabeth has no knowledge whatsoever about Joyce's private life. Based on the attitude heuristic, which of the following responses would Elizabeth be likely to give?
   a. "He was probably a real sexist—most men of his time were."
   b. "I'm not sure. When I read his biography, I'll let you know."
   c. "If he was sexist, he was probably only conforming to the norms of his time."
   d. "No—he couldn't have been a sexist. I'm sure of it."

Answer: b
Page: 111

30. Suppose Pat believes that President Clinton is a wonderful President and Mike believes he has gross deficiencies. Both are asked to assess the truth of these two statements: A. President Clinton has had many lurid affairs with a wide variety of women, including several members of his staff; and B. President Clinton, although admitting to an extramarital affair early in his life, has since that time remained a faithful husband. Based on the attitude heuristic, we would predict that Pat would believe _____ to be true and Mike would believe _____ to be true.
   a. statement A; statement B
   b. statement B; statement A
   c. neither A nor B; neither A nor B
   d. none of the above since the attitude heuristic does not apply to this example

Answer: c
Page: 112

31. The halo effect occurs when:
   a. we like a person whose attitudes are similar to our own.
   b. we gain a favorable impression of a person who reminds us of someone we already know and like.
   c. a favorable or unfavorable impression of someone biases our future expectations and inferences about that person.
   d. we like a person whose actions make us look good.

Answer: c
Page: 112

32. Suppose you see Mary do very poorly on a classroom test. From this you conclude that Mary is not only stupid, but also has few friends, a poor personality, a difficult family life, and a hard time in everything she does. You have committed an error called:
   a. the primacy effect.
   b. the context effect.
   c. the halo effect.
   d. the attitude heuristic.

Answer: a
Page: 112

33. The false consensus effect implies that we:
    a. overestimate the number of people who agree with us.
    b. underestimate the number of people who agree with us.
    c. rely too heavily on the primacy effect.
    d. don't rely heavily enough on the primacy effect.

Answer: d
Page: 112

34. The tendency to overestimate the percentage of other people who agree with us on a given issue is referred to as:
    a. the conformity bias.
    b. the representativeness heuristic.
    c. the hindsight bias.
    d. the false consensus effect.

Answer: d
Page: 112–113

35. Under which of the following conditions are we least likely to use heuristics in making decisions about social events?
    a. when we are overloaded with information
    b. when the decisions are not very important
    c. when we have little information to use in making the decision
    d. when we have plenty of time to make the decision

Answer: a
Page: 113

36. Which of the following words comes closest in meaning to "category?"
    a. stereotype
    b. heuristic
    c. halo effect
    d. illusory correlation

Answer: b
Page: 114

37. In a study by Darley and Gross, in which subjects were exposed to different stories about a fourth-grader named "Hannah," the effects of stereotypes on social judgment were apparent when:
   a. Hannah was depicted as coming from a poor background.
   b. Hannah's performance on an achievement test was ambiguous, *and* she was also depicted as coming from a poor background.
   c. Hannah's performance on an achievement test indicated low ability.
   d. Hannah was depicted as not trying hard to achieve.

Answer: d
Page: 115

38. Which of the following is a good example of self-fulfilling prophecy?
   a. This student loves to be around attractive people because he feels good.
   b. This student has a broken arm and cannot write well.
   c. This student has no health insurance because his parents are part of the working poor.
   d. This student comes from a poor neighborhood. The teacher assumes he is not smart and consequently the child does poorly.

Answer: b
Page: 116

39. In informal surveys, people consistently overestimate the extent to which lesbians are likely to contract the AIDS virus—when, in fact, lesbians have the lowest rate of HIV infection, compared to male homosexuals and heterosexual men and women. This example illustrates:
   a. the false consensus effect.
   b. illusory correlation.
   c. in-group favoritism.
   d. the attitude heuristic.

Answer: a
Page: 116

40. One of the most common ways of categorizing people is to divide the world up into two groups—the in-group (one's own group) and the out-group. This tendency leads to:
   a. the perception that one's own group is "better" and more deserving than the out-group.
   b. the perception that greater similarity exists among members of the out-group, than among members of one's own group.
   c. a primacy effect when dealing with in-group members and a recency effect when dealing with out-group members.
   d. a primacy effect when dealing with out-group members and a recency effect when dealing with in-group members.

Answer: a
Page: 116–117

41. In Tajfel's research (in which subjects are randomly assigned to Group X or Group W) subjects who are total strangers, but who share the same meaningless label, tend to:
   a. express greater liking for, and allocate more rewards to, others in their own group.
   b. compete against members of their own group—as a form of "sibling rivalry."
   c. perceive greater similarity among members of their own group than among members of the other group.
   d. fabricate elaborate reasons to explain why they feel a sense of "belonging" to their own group.

Answer: b
Page: 118

42. Loftus conducted a study in which subjects saw a film clip of a car accident. Some subjects were asked about how the cars "hit" each other and others were asked about how they "smashed into" each other. The main result of this study was that subjects who were asked about how the cars "hit" were more likely to:
   a. refuse to answer.
   b. estimate a lower rate of speed for the cars.
   c. rely extensively on stereotypes.
   d. experience cognitive dissonance.

Answer: b
Page: 118–119

43. Research on social cognition indicates that human memory:
   a. is a literal translation of past events.
   b. is reconstructed from bits of information that we recall, as well as our expectations about what should have been.
   c. functions according to the "cognitive miser" principle.
   d. operates very much like a computer program.

Answer: a
Page: 118–119

44. Research by Loftus on eye-witness testimony has revealed that:
   a. "leading" questions can distort both a witness's memory and his or her judgments of the facts in a given case.
   b. conformity pressures created in the courtroom lead witnesses to say whatever they think is expected of them.
   c. "leading questions" are confusing to witnesses, which makes them change their testimony.
   d. the courtroom atmosphere makes witnesses nervous, which leads to memory deficits and distorted testimonies.

Answer: d
Page: 119–120

45. Self-schema refers to:
   a. the tendency to develop goal-directed plans that guide behavior.
   b. the tendency to see others as we see ourselves.
   c. the tendency to create false memories.
   d. the tendency to organize our personal history into an integrated whole.

Answer: a
Page: 120

46. The main point of the Ross, McFarland and Fletcher article that studied attitudes about bathing and teeth brushing was that:
   a. attitudes we hold can influence how we remember our own behavior.
   b. we generally see ourselves as having better attitudes but worse behaviors than our friends.
   c. we generally see ourselves as having worse attitudes but better behaviors than our friends.
   d. people can be persuaded to bathe and brush their teeth if they can be convinced that bathing and teeth brushing are beneficial to them.

Answer: d
Page: 120–122

47. According to most cognitive psychologists:
   a. it would be wrong to accuse a family member of sexual abuse based solely on recovered memories.
   b. repeated instances of longterm, childhood traumatic events are usually not forgotten.
   c. there is no scientific evidence of a specific link between child sexual abuse and family characteristics listed in self-help books.
   d. all of the above.

Answer: b
Page: 124

48. The confirmation bias refers to the human tendency:
    a. to believe that other people share our views.
    b. to verify our pre-existing knowledge, hypotheses, and beliefs.
    c. to perceive persons or events that are similar on one dimension as being similar in all other dimensions.
    d. to find "loss" information more compelling than "gain" information.

Answer: a
Page: 125

49. Although Alex had no idea who would win a particular football game, after the game was over he claimed to have been "99% certain" that the winning team would be victorious. Alex's behavior is best thought of as an example of:
    a. the hindsight bias.
    b. priming.
    c. the representativeness heuristic.
    d. a context effect.

Answer: c
Page: 125

50. According to Greenwald, a positive feature of cognitive conservatism is that:
    a. it keeps inaccurate information from influencing our realistic and well-established categories for understanding the world.
    b. it helps us to make decisions in a rational and efficient manner.
    c. it allows us to perceive the social world as a stable, coherent place.
    d. it helps us to remain open to new information that will enhance our functioning in the world.

Answer: b
Page: 126–127

51. LaPiere conducted a study in the 1930s in which he wrote to restaurants and hotels to ask if they would allow Chinese people to eat or sleep there. He later visited these same establishments with Chinese friends and observed whether or not the friends were served. His results showed that about _____ percent of the places said they would not serve Chinese and that in reality about _____ percent of them actually did serve the Chinese.
   a. 90; less than 1
   b. less than 1; 90
   c. 50; 50
   d. 60; 40

Answer: b
Page: 127

52. Tom explains his wife's success in her job as being the result of her intelligence and determination, thus explaining her behavior in terms of her traits that are like the behavior. The text would consider Tom's explanation to be an example of:
   a. hindsight bias.
   b. correspondent inference.
   c. priming.
   d. a contrast effect.

Answer: c
Page: 128

53. One condition under which attitudes are a fairly good predictor of behavior is when:
   a. we hold positive attitudes toward the particular behavior.
   b. we want to look good in the eyes of others.
   c. the attitude relevant to a given behavior is highly accessible.
   d. we are under strong pressure to conform to the behavior of others.

Answer: b
Page: 130

54. What did Paul Herr discover in his research on accessibility of hostility?
   a. If subjects worked a seek and search puzzle with gentle people's names, they rated the target person later as hostile because the picture they saw was of an ugly person.
   b. If subjects worked a seek and search puzzle with hostile names, they later played very competitively in a game.
   c. If the subjects worked a seek and search puzzle with gentle names, they lost interest and got bored with the game.
   d. If the subjects worked a seek and search puzzle with hostile names, they were silent in a group activity because they had too much hostile energy to speak.

Answer: c
Page: 131–132

55. The general human tendency to overestimate the importance of personality or dispositional factors when explaining the causes of social behavior is called:
   a. the halo effect.
   b. the hindsight bias.
   c. the fundamental attribution error.
   d. the actor-observer bias.

Answer: d
Page: 131–132

56. Julie sees a stranger do poorly on a test. She automatically assumes that the stranger is stupid. She has committed an error best thought of as:
   a. a context effect.
   b. an attitude heuristic.
   c. a representative heuristic.
   d. the fundamental attribution error.

Answer: d
Page: 133

57. In the "quiz show" study conducted by Ross, Amabile and Steinmetz, subjects were randomly assigned to serve as "questioners" or "contestants." Observers who watched the simulated quiz show tended to perceive the "questioners" as more knowledgeable than the "contestants." The observers committed the error of:
   a. assigning favorable characteristics to high-status persons as compared to low-status persons.
   b. equating intelligence with verbal skills.
   c. making situational attributions for behavior, rather than dispositional ones.
   d. underestimating the impact of social roles in explaining behavior.

Answer: a
Page: 134

58. The actor-observer bias involves the tendency for actors to attribute their own actions to _____ and to attribute the actions of other people to those peoples' _____.
   a. situational factors; personal dispositions
   b. personal dispositions; situational factors
   c. positive heuristics; negative heuristics
   d. negative heuristics; positive heuristics

Answer: a
Page: 136

59. Although Susan was only peripherally involved in getting her friend elected as the president of the senior class, she felt her friend could never have won without Susan's support. Susan's feeling is best thought of as an example of:
   a. egocentric thought.
   b. the fundamental attribution error.
   c. the hindsight bias.
   d. the actor-observer bias.

Answer: b
Page: 138

60. Jim is concerned about his future, so he visits a "psychic" who tells him: "You are a person who can succeed in life. You have many talents that could be developed—ones that could bring you great prosperity. Sometimes you're afraid of taking risks, but you can spot a good opportunity when you see one." Jim leaves the psychic's office convinced that he has what it takes to be a success in life. The psychic's message

    a. is an example of decision-framing on the part of the psychic.
    b. is an example of a "Barnum statement."
    c. has made Jim fall prey to the effects of illusory correlation.
    d. probably indicates nothing true about Jim.

Answer: d
Page: 139

61. Rifka takes two tests for which she studies equally hard. She gets an A on one and a D on the other. She explains that she got the A because she is "smart" in that subject and got the D because the test was unfair and too difficult. Rifka's explanation is best thought of as an example of:

    a. the contrast effect.
    b. the actor-observer bias.
    c. the fundamental attribution error.
    d. the self-serving bias.

Essay Questions

1. Some theorists have proposed that people are rational thinkers and decision-makers, while others believe social cognition is often subject to biases and other distorting influences. Compare and contrast some of the central ideas that characterize these two perspectives, indicating which you find more convincing. What conditions are necessary for human cognition to operate on a thoroughly rational basis? How common are these conditions in everyday life?

2. In general, how does the "social context"—the way things are presented and described—influence our social judgment and cognition? Discuss the significance of TWO of the following contextual factors: a) contrast effects, b) priming, c) decision-framing, d) the order in which information is presented. Describe how these factors influence social judgments in everyday life and provide research evidence to support your answer.

3. What is the "primacy effect" and how does it influence the impressions we form of other people? Describe one piece of research that demonstrates this phenomenon. What two explanations have social psychologists offered in an effort to account for the existence of this effect?

4. What are heuristics? Under what circumstances are we likely to rely on them when making social judgments? Select two heuristics and discuss how they influence our thinking in daily life. Support your answer with examples of relevant research.

5. "Human memory is primarily reconstructive in nature." What does this statement mean? What are its implications for social cognition? How does research on eyewitness testimony demonstrate this point?

6. It's New Year's Eve, and you've been invited to a large party where there will be lots of people you've never met before. When you arrive, the person hosting the party hands you a blue party hat to wear and you put it on. As you mingle through the crowd, you notice that some people are wearing blue hats like yours, and other people are wearing green party hats. By the end of the evening, you realize you have spent most of your time with people wearing blue hats. Somehow, they just seemed to be nicer people—they even

dance better than those other people wearing green hats. Moreover, a guy with a green hat bumped into you at one point during the evening and spilled your drink! Given your knowledge of social cognition (and despite the somewhat far-fetched nature of this scenario), how could you explain your perceptions and judgments? If this were a costume party, how might you act if you were in charge of awarding prizes for the best costume? Be sure to support your answer with examples of relevant research.

7. To what extent do cognitive processes operate in a conservative fashion? What are the benefits and drawbacks of this tendency in human cognition? What steps can be taken to reduce the negative consequences of cognitive conservatism?

8. How do cognitive biases involving the self contribute to the goal of maintaining and enhancing our view of ourselves? Of what value are such biases, and what are the potential consequences of not having them? Describe two self-biases, providing research evidence that demonstrates their effects.

5

Self-Justification

I. Introduction

Self-justification and rumors (Prasad; Sinha)
Cognitive dissonance theory (Festinger)
Smoking (Gibbons)
Perceptual distortion (Hastorf & Cantril)

II. Dissonance Reduction and Rational Behavior

Biased information-processing (Jones & Kohler; Lord, Ross, & Lepper)

III. Dissonance as a Consequence of Making a Decision

Postdecision dissonance (Ehrlich; Brehm; Johnson & Rusbult; Simpson et al.)
Historical examples
Foot-in-the-door technique (Freedom & Fraser; Pliner)

IV. Irrevocability of decisions

Gambling (Knox & Inkster)
Low-balling (Cialdini)
Immoral behavior (Mills)

V. The Psychology of Inadequate Justification

A. Inadequate rewards

Internal and external justification
Saying is believing (Festinger & Carlsmith; Cohen)
Race relations (Leippe & Eisenstadt)

B. What constitutes external justification

Eating grasshoppers (Zimbardo)

C. What is inadequate justification?

Cheating (Mills)

111

B. Alternative explanations of dissonance effects

Bem's "self-reference" analysis
Well-defined prior beliefs (Jones; Piliavin)

C. Dissonance as a state of arousal

Task interference (Pallak & Pittman)
Misattribution of arousal (Zanna & Cooper; Bond)

XII. Practical Applications of Dissonance Theory

Three Mile Island
Weight loss (Axsom & Cooper)
AIDS prevention
Water conservation
The Waco, Jonestown, and Heaven's Gate tragedies
Osama bin Laden

XIII. Dissonance Reduction and Culture—Japanese Students

XIV. "Man" Cannot Live by Consonance Alone

Terms & Concepts

cognitive dissonance
rational vs. rationalizing
foot-in-the-door technique
low-balling
inadequate rewards
turning play into work
justification of effort

irrevocable decisions
internal justification
external justification
inadequate justification
justification of cruelty
self-fulfilling prophecy
psychology of inevitability

Chapter Overview

The social-psychological process of self-justification, which involves our tendency to justify our actions, behaviors, and feelings, is the topic of Chapter 5. The main tenets of cognitive dissonance theory are presented briefly and provide a framework for understanding the cognitive and motivational components that underlie self-justification processes. Throughout the chapter, the broad implications of the theory are discussed, as well as its application to a multitude of real-world situations and social phenomena. Highlights of the chapter are covered below.

In formal terms, cognitive dissonance (Festinger, 1957) is defined as a state of tension that occurs whenever an individual simultaneously holds two cognitions (attitudes, beliefs, etc.) that are psychologically inconsistent or contradictory. Because dissonance is unpleasant, people are motivated to reduce it—much as they are motivated to reduce hunger or thirst. Dissonance may be reduced by changing one or both cognitions in such a way as to render them more compatible (or consonant) with each other, or by adding more cognitions that help to reconcile, or bridge the gap between, the original cognitions.

In simpler terms, dissonance or self-justification processes generally occur when we find ourselves acting in a manner that contradicts our beliefs and attitudes—in particular, our conceptions of ourselves as good, decent, wise, and intelligent individuals. In order to justify our contradictory actions, we tend to change our attitudes or behaviors to make them more consistent with our previous behavior. For example, confronted with the health hazards associated with smoking, an inveterate smoker who can't or won't quit may reduce dissonance in a variety of ways—by discounting research on cancer as inconclusive or by stressing the benefits of smoking ("I may lead a shorter life, but it will be a more enjoyable one."). Thus, cognitive dissonance theory does not picture people as entirely rational beings; instead, it pictures them as rationalizing beings. We humans are motivated not so much to BE right; rather, we are motivated to believe we are right (and wise, good, intelligent, etc.).

Dissonance often occurs following a difficult or important decision. Once people have committed themselves to a particular choice, they typically justify their decisions by viewing the chosen alternative more positively, and the rejected more negatively, as compared to before the decision was made.

When people have inadequate external justification for a particular dissonance-arousing behavior, they tend to look for internal justification for the behavior in order to reduce dissonance. The search for internal justification often leads to changes in relevant attitudes and behaviors. This principle is illustrated in the classic Festinger and Carlsmith experiment, in which subjects lied to a "fellow student" by telling him that a boring task was interesting. Subjects who were paid only $1 for telling the lie rated the task as more interesting than subjects who were paid $20 for lying. Unlike the $1 subjects, the $20 subjects had sufficient external justification for lying and, thus, had no need to reduce dissonance by changing their perceptions of the task.

The phenomena of justification of effort is also associated with a lack of adequate external justification for one's behaviors. Thus, the Aronson and Mills experiment on mild versus severe "initiation" demonstrates that when we suffer or work hard for a goal, we come to place a high value on that goal—in order to justify the expenditure of effort and the sacrifices we have endured. Similarly, justification of cruelty occurs when we have acted in a cruel or unkind manner toward someone who does not deserve such treatment. Lacking sufficient justification, we tend to devalue the innocent victim of our unkind actions.

Refinements of Festinger's original formulation of dissonance theory have highlighted the role of the self-concept, pointing out that dissonance is greatest when individuals act in a manner inconsistent with their customary notions of themselves as good and competent. As a result, relatively higher levels of dissonance are likely to occur when we have done something "stupid" or immoral. In addition, freedom of choice plays a central role in dissonance arousal. When people perceive their actions as constrained by some external source, little dissonance is aroused.

Bem's "self-reference" analysis of dissonance effects offers an alternative interpretation of dissonance theory. Bem's notion is that the results of dissonance experiments reflect nothing more than reasonable inferences people make about their attitudes, based upon their perceptions of their own behavior. Where the inconsistency between attitudes and behavior is significant and clear, however, research evidence supports dissonance theory over Bem's self-reference interpretation.

Lecture Ideas & Teaching Suggestions

Self-presentation Strategies. Theory and research on self-justification rests on the notion that people are often motivated to avoid unpleasant information about themselves and will engage in acts of cognitive distortion in order to accomplish this goal. A related area of research you may wish to cover in lectures involves our tendency to represent ourselves to others, as well as ourselves, in the best possible light. The various ways that people attempt to create a desired social image are referred to collectively as self-presentation or impression management strategies. Jones and Pittman have developed a useful taxonomy of such strategies, each of which facilitates the achievement of a different self-presentational goal. These general strategies are:

Ingratiation, in which the main goal is to present the self as likable. Ingratiation tactics include paying compliments or conforming to the opinions of others.

- Intimidation, in which the main goal is to arouse fear in others, thereby allowing the actor to control the outcome of the interaction to his or her advantage. Intimidation may involve the use of threats or the exercise of power within a relationship of unequal authority.

- Self-promotion, in which the actor attempts to impress others with his or her competence, in regard to either a specific skill or general ability (e.g., intelligence). In promoting the self, the individual tends to focus on personal strengths and accomplishments, while downplaying or ignoring weaker areas. The self-promoter is vulnerable, however, to having to "make good" when claims of competence are put to the test.

- Exemplification, in which the main goal is to display an image of integrity by appearing noble or as a long-suffering martyr in the pursuit of a worthy goal. The use of exemplification is frequently designed to make others feel guilty or morally inferior to the actor.

- Supplication, in which the goal is gaining the sympathy of others. Presenting the self as weak or dependent often evokes feelings of protectiveness or obligation from others. As a result, the actor may reap practical or psychological benefits that might not be offered if he or she displayed a competent self-image.

In addition to the above strategies, researchers have explored other tactics for achieving self-presentational goals. For example, self-handicapping (Berglas & Jones, 1978) is employed when a person wishes to maintain the appearance of competence in the face of a likely threat to that competence. In such instances, people prearrange convenient excuses for failure so their later failure can be attributed to external causes. Thus, a tennis player who is unsure of her ability to beat her opponent may announce prior to the match that she only got three hours of sleep the night before. Basking in reflected glory (Cialdini et al., 1976) is another self-presentation tactic, which allows the individual to feel competent as a result of his or her association with successful others. For example, Cialdini and his colleagues (1976) found that students were more likely to wear clothing that announced their campus affiliation the day after their college football team won a game, compared to after a defeat. Further details on these self-presentation strategies may be found in: Jones, E.E. & Pittman, T.S. (1982). Toward a general theory of self-presentation. In J. Suls (Ed.), *Psychological perspectives on the self.* Hillsdale, NJ: Erlbaum; Berglas, S., & Jones, E.E. (1978). Drug choice as an externalization strategy in response to noncontingent success. *Journal of Personality and Social Psychology, 36,* 405–417; Cialdini, R.B., Borden, R.J., Thorne, A., Walker, M.R., & Freeman, S. (1976). Basking in reflective glory. Three (football) field studies. *Journal of Personality and Social Psychology, 34,* 366–375.

The Importance of Theory. In reviewing research on self-justification processes, you may wish to take advantage of the opportunity to discuss the importance of theory to the scientific enterprise. Cognitive dissonance theory provides a useful illustration of the properties of a good theory in its ability to: 1) organize and integrate existing empirical findings within a simple framework; 2) explain a broad range of phenomena; and 3) provide a fertile source of testable hypotheses that otherwise might not have occurred to researchers. An effective way to illustrate the integrative power of dissonance theory is to describe briefly the results of several dissonance studies, each representing a social-psychological phenomenon that—on the surface—bears little resemblance to the others. Experimental findings from different sections of the chapter can be presented, such as: 1) Prasad's rumor study; 2) Brehm's post-decision study; 3) Mill's cheating study; 4) Deci's research on "turning play into work"; 5) Aronson & Mills' justification of effort study; and 6) Glass's study of victim derogation. After presenting the results of each of these studies, the basic principles of cognitive dissonance theory can be set forth. The studies you have previously described can then be reviewed, with the goal of showing how these diverse findings are all predictable from the theory's basic tenets.

Cognitive Dissonance Theory Diagram
Characteristics of Individual

Instance 1		*Instance 2*	
Ideas	Attitudes	Ideas	Attitudes
Beliefs	Behavior	Beliefs	Behavior

If these characteristics are similar from Instance 1 to Instance 2, there is **harmony, consistency, and stability.** Life is no problem.

If there is inconsistency from Instance 1 to Instance 2, there is **dissonance, discord and conflict** within the individual. For example, "I read the research that says smoking is harmful and yet I smoke."

Dissonance → Tension → Tension Reduction → External Justification
Or
Internal Justification

External Justification works   → if one is **forced.**
    →   if one receives a **large reward.**

(Justification is that one was forced or one got paid enough for the action.) Life is back in **Harmony.**

What if one is not forced or there was not large reward, then there is *still tension.* **Inadequate Justification.**

Internal Justification is needed to reduce this tension.
Can't change behavior. → **But can Change attitude to fit behavior**
    → **But can Distort perception to fit behavior**
    → **But can Change view of "evidence" to fit behavior**

For example, "I smoke but the research does not apply to everyone. George Burns smoked and lived to be 100 years old."

For example, "I had a decent wife but she made me mad by her smart remarks, and I had to hit her. She is mean and deserved to be hit but I am still a decent person." (This action is still wrong and punishable by law, but it is an insight.)

For example, one acts in a mindless fashion like getting dressed in the morning. Then one spends the day justifying one's crazy clothes.

Behavior can be explained because someone sets a goal and accomplishes the deed. However, another large part of behavior can be explained by saying we perform an action and then think of reasons for the behavior. We justify our actions five to twenty times a day or more.

Finally, to give students a sense of the historical context of scientific discoveries, you might also wish to discuss the "revolutionary" nature of dissonance theory. In the late 1950s, when dissonance theory appeared on the scene, reinforcement theory was the prevailing framework for understanding behavior. In many instances, however, predictions based on dissonance theory were at direct odds with reinforcement principles. For example, Aronson and Mill's experiment on the effects of mild versus severe initiations demonstrates that people tend to prefer a goal for which they have suffered or expended great effort. Reinforcement theory would have predicted the opposite result: greater hardship or effort should have made the goal less, rather than more, attractive.

Projects and Discussion Topics

1. PROJECT: For about a week, keep a journal of instances in which you find yourself experiencing dissonance and engaging in efforts to reduce it. Refer back to Chapter 5 to gain some insight into the kinds of situations that are likely to arouse dissonance and elicit self-justifying thoughts and behaviors. Some of these are: a) after making a decision; b) after working hard for a goal that might not have been worth the effort; c) after succumbing to the temptation to do something against your beliefs; d) after resisting the temptation to do something against your beliefs; e) after hurting someone's feelings; f) having to "make the best" of an inevitable situation. (Make a special note of times when you felt dissonance under circumstances that were not covered in the chapter, if such situations occur.) For each entry in your journal, describe what provoked the dissonance, how it made you feel, and how you reduced it. Finally, if you did not reduce dissonance in a given situation, do your best to explain why you failed to do so.

2. PROJECT: Imagine that you are the parent of a 5-year-old girl named Lisa. It's the beginning of the summer and you've decided it's time for Lisa to learn how to swim. So, you enroll her in swimming lessons that a couple of her friends will be also attending. Unfortunately, the swimming lessons are rather expensive and the location is a fairly long drive from your home. Still, you figure, the goal of teaching Lisa to swim is well worth the trouble and expense. Lisa, however, is not crazy about the idea. When the morning of the first class arrives, Lisa puts her little foot down

and says she doesn't want to go. This is a real dilemma. On the one hand, you don't want to force her to go to the classes—even though you've already paid for them. However, you also know that Lisa possesses a great deal of natural athletic talent and is sure to be a good swimmer. Moreover, you are convinced that once she gets over her initial hesitation, she will thoroughly enjoy being able to swim and play in the water with her friends. You also suspect she will feel really proud of herself for having learned a new skill.

Based on your knowledge of cognitive dissonance, how would you handle this problem? Write a scenario describing the steps you would take to persuade Lisa to give swimming a try and how you think she would respond. In devising your strategy, pay special attention to the implications of the psychology of inevitability, the "foot-in-the-door" technique, and the effects of rewards on intrinsic motivation. Finally, looking back on your behavior as a parent, do you suspect there might have been times when you were experiencing dissonance and engaging in self-justifying behavior? If so, what was dissonance-arousing and why?

3.   DISCUSSION: How would self-justification processes be engaged during a time of war? Here are a couple of situations to consider.

  A. First, put yourself in the shoes of a hypothetical combat soldier. You think of yourself as a good person—you love your family and friends—and they all love you. Suddenly, you are in the midst of a war zone and are faced with a situation of killing or being killed on a daily basis. You're 19 years old, you're far from home, and you're scared. Now, imagine you are that soldier and you find yourself in the following situations:

  1. Face-to-face with an armed enemy who is about to kill you. You shoot first, killing him instead.
  2. Face-to-face with a civilian who, in your eyes, physically resembles "the enemy." He has something in his hand—you're not sure what it is, but you think it might be a grenade and that he might be about to kill you. He takes a step toward you. Panic grips you, and you shoot him. You look at what he was holding and find it was not a weapon after all. You have killed an innocent civilian.

Under which of these two circumstances are you more likely to experience dissonance? Why? How would you be likely to reduce it?

B. Consider a different scenario. Imagine you are in the Army Reserves. You enlisted during a time when jobs were scarce, you had no money for an education, and your country had not been involved in armed conflict for a number of years. You figure it's your best chance of getting some kind of job skills, and perhaps a college education when your period of enlistment has ended. Considering these very real benefits, you block from your mind the possibility that a war could break out and you would be called upon to serve in it. The thought scares you and, besides, you grew up hearing about Vietnam and feel that it was an immoral war. Then, just six months before your period of enlistment is to end, a war breaks out in the Middle East and you are called up on "active duty." How do you suppose you would feel about this war and your involvement in it? Would you tend to think it was a "just" cause? How would you feel about people who opposed the war? In particular, how do you think you would feel about those who took the position, "I support our troops, but I oppose the war"? What would their view imply about your involvement in the war?

Share your reflections on these scenarios with members of your discussion group. Can you think of any other situations associated with war that would be likely to arouse dissonance? For example, consider the public's reaction to hearing that, contrary to early reports of war casualties, a great number of innocent civilians had been killed by our bombs. How would this information tend to influence public support for the war and the conclusion that our actions were morally correct and necessary? How might this impact differ for people who were consistently opposed to the war from the start, compared to those who, after some doubt and soul-searching, had decided they supported the war?

4. DISCUSSION: Aronson has stated that people "cannot live by consonance alone." Discuss your interpretation of this statement and its implications. What are the limitations of protecting our egos through dissonance reduction? Why might it be important to

admit our mistakes? Why is it that we are usually so reluctant or unable to do so? What steps could we take in order to facilitate the chances of learning from our mistakes? Drawing on your personal experience, try to recall a situation in which it was relatively easy for you to admit a mistake. Discuss and analyze this situation with others in your group to see if you can determine the conditions that facilitate being able to face the truth about your behavior in a fairly non-defensive manner. Are these conditions the same for others?

5. DISCUSSION: Elementary-school teachers often use a reward system (such as offering children small prizes) in order to motivate their students to do well on their schoolwork and to maintain discipline in the classroom. Based on your knowledge of dissonance theory, what are the possible drawbacks of relying on such a system? What steps could teachers take to avoid or counteract these potential negative effects? How might dissonance theory be applied to other practical issues in real life? For example, consider such issues as teen-age pregnancy, substance abuse, water conservation, AIDS prevention, or any other problem that interests you. Can you think of ways that dissonance theory might shed light on such problems—either by deepening our understanding of them, or helping to solve them?

Experiential Exercises

1. STANDING ON THE ISSUES. The professor should write down ten statements about controversial topics. For example, "I am in favor of spanking in the middle school." "I am in favor of gun control." "Welfare mothers should have to be employed to receive benefits." "I am in favor of lowering the drinking age to 18." Then in class the professor should have all the students stand in the front of class and the chairs should be moved to the side. The first statement is read and the students have to stand on the issue by moving to the right if they agree or be in the middle if they are undecided or move to the left if they disagree. As the groups form, friends can see how their friends are voting and it might affect them. Each group then develops four or six arguments that support their viewpoint. The professor points to each group and asks for one or two people to present their arguments in two minutes. There is no debate or rebuttals but that can be a possibility. Then the participants

are asked if they would like to change their position and move to another position. After that another topic is voted on after the professor reads it.

From a Cognitive Dissonance Theory perspective what happens to a student who deliberately chooses one issue that is directly opposed to what he/she believes. Then during the presentation of arguments he/she speaks in behalf of the group. The professor has to tell the students that they personally should try this once if they want. The question from a Cognitive Dissonance perspective is whether this student will come to believe their statements about their new position. Surprisingly, during the written debriefing in their papers a majority of them detail the reasons for their new belief.

Another angle to mention to the students is to encourage them to vote for a new position during the second voting whether they are convinced or not. How do they view themselves and how do others view them after this public act? The oral debriefing is filled with cognitive dissonance ideas. Applications can be made to their lives as well.

Additional Readings

Aronson, E. (1978). The theory of cognitive dissonance: A current perspective. In L. Berkowitz (Ed.), *Cognitive theories in social psychology*. New York: Academic Press.

Aronson, E. (1980). Persuasion via self-justification: Large commitments for small rewards. In L. Festinger (Ed.), *Retrospections on social psychology*. New York: Oxford University Press.

Bem, D.J. (1967, June). When saying is believing. *Psychology Today*, pp. 21–25. (Bem offers an alternative explanation for cognitive dissonance findings.)

Greene, D. & Lepper, M.R. (1974, September). How to turn play into work. *Psychology Today*, pp. 49–54. (A discussion of the use of rewards can undermine intrinsic motivation.)

Saxe, L. (1991). Lying: Thoughts of an applied psychologist. *American Psychologist*, 46, (4), 409–415.

Sinclair, R.C., Hoffman, C., Mark, M.M., Marlin, L.L. & Pickering. T.L. (1994). Construct accessibility and the misattribution of arousal: Schachter and Singer revisited. *Psychological Science, 5,* (1), 15–19.

Wicklund, R.A. & Brehm, J.W. (1976). *Perspectives on cognitive dissonance.* Hillsdale, NJ: Erlbaum.

Multiple-Choice Questions

Answer: c
Page: 145

1. The combined results of rumor research conducted by Prasad and Sinha were that following a natural disaster, people who lived in the towns directly affected by the event were more likely to _____ the possibility of impending disaster, while those living in relatively undamaged, neighboring towns tended to _____ the possibility of impending disaster.
   a. be prepared for; be unprepared for
   b. be anxious about; be unconcerned about
   c. downplay; exaggerate
   d. think about; repress

Answer: c
Page: 145–146

2. Cognitive dissonance is defined as a state of tension:
   a. that occurs whenever a person is motivated to change his or her attitudes.
   b. that occurs when a person thinks and acts irrationally.
   c. that occurs when a person simultaneously holds two cognitions that are psychologically inconsistent.
   d. that occurs when a person is unaware of his or her conflicting cognitions.

Answer: c
Page: 146

3. The main idea behind cognitive consistency theories, such as dissonance theory, is that incompatible attitudes:
    a. are easily extinguished.
    b. are easy to change.
    c. make us feel uncomfortable.
    d. are very rare.

Answer: c
Page: 147–149

4. According to a survey gauging people's reactions to scientific evidence that smoking cigarettes causes cancer:
    a. smokers who were planning to quit believed the report even more than nonsmokers did.
    b. smokers believed the report, but nonsmokers rejected it.
    c. smokers were far less likely to believe the report than nonsmokers were.
    d. smokers were likely to believe the report, but still refused to quit smoking.

Answer: c
Page: 150

5. In 1997 a few members of Heaven's Gate, a religious cult, bought a telescope to view a comet. They returned the telescope a few days later and said that it was faulty because there was no spaceship behind the comet. This action is
    a. not consistent with cognitive dissonance theory.
    b. consistent with cognitive dissonance theory because this is an external justification.
    c. consistent with cognitive dissonance theory because it is an internal justification.
    d. just crazy.

Answer: c
Page: 151

6. The responses of students from both campuses to a film of a roughly played football game between Dartmouth and Princeton indicated that _____ may be one important means of reducing dissonance.
   a. vicarious expression of aggression
   b. revenge-taking strategies
   c. actual perceptual distortion
   d. blaming the victim

Answer: a
Page: 152

7. According to dissonance theory, people are generally more motivated to:
   a. believe they are right, rather than to actually be right.
   b. be right, rather than simply believe they are right.
   c. have others believe they are right, rather than actually being right.
   d. be rational, rather than simply subjective.

Answer: b
Page: 153

8. Lord, Ross, and Lepper showed articles favoring and opposing capital punishment to groups of students who either opposed or were in favor of it. The results of this study showed that reading articles on both sides of the controversial issue:
   a. brought the attitudes in the students closer together in a "middle" position.
   b. actually increased the difference in attitudes between the two groups.
   c. increased the self-esteem of members of both groups.
   d. decreased the self-esteem of members of both groups.

Answer: d
Page: 152–154

9. Which of the following is *not* cited by Aronson as a possible way for people to reduce dissonance?
   a. changing their attitudes
   b. distorting their perceptions
   c. selectively exposing themselves to only certain information
   d. worrying more about the inconsistency that gives rise to the dissonance.

Answer: b
Page: 154–155

10. Suppose you are ready to buy a new car. You have great difficulty choosing between Brand A and Brand B. Finally, you buy Brand A. According to dissonance theory, after you have driven the car for a few weeks, you will be most likely to emphasize:
   a. the poor mileage you are getting in Brand A.
   b. how convenient the Brand A car is to park and drive.
   c. how pretty the Brand B car was.
   d. how you should have taken more time to make this difficult decision.

Answer: a
Page: 155

11. Jim has trouble deciding whether to buy a good-mileage, poor-maintenance MGB or a poor-mileage, easy-care Camaro. Finally, he buys the MGB. According to cognitive dissonance theory, he will probably spend most of his time concentrating on:
   a. the good mileage he gets.
   b. wondering when his car will break down.
   c. the unimportance of good mileage.
   d. the advantages of a low-maintenance car.

Answer: c
Page: 155

12. According to dissonance theory, we tend to experience dissonance after making an important decision because:
   a. we often feel forced into choosing a particular alternative.
   b. the rejected alternative seems more attractive than the chosen alternative.
   c. the chosen alternative is seldom entirely positive, while the rejected alternatives are seldom entirely negative.
   d. we hardly ever have enough time to make a good decision.

Answer: a
Page: 155–156

13. After choosing between two equally attractive appliances, women in Jack Brehm's study rated the appliance they selected:
   a. as more attractive than the one they rejected.
   b. as less attractive than the one they rejected.
   c. as equally attractive as the one they rejected.
   d. as less attractive than a group of similar appliances they were not allowed to choose from.

Answer: a
Page: 156

14. Joe is given the choice between two record albums he has already ranked as numbers 4 and 5 on a 1–10 scale. Joe chooses #4. Two weeks later when Joe is asked to rerank the ten albums, he reranks #4 as #2. This example is best predicted by:
   a. cognitive dissonance theory.
   b. reactance theory.
   c. stereotyping.
   d. the "just-world" hypothesis.

Answer: c
Page: 156

15. Carole has two boyfriends, Tim and Craig, whom she likes very much. Both of them really like her, too. She has decided, however, that dating both of them is making her life too complicated. After careful consideration, she decides to stop seeing Tim and to continue dating Craig. According to dissonance theory, which of the following is most likely to happen as a result of her decision?
    a. She and Tim will continue to be good friends.
    b. Tim will develop an intense dislike for Craig.
    c. Craig will seem more attractive than ever.
    d. Tim will seem more attractive, making her regret her decision.

Answer: a
Page: 156

16. Suppose Bob and Tom are asked to rate the attractiveness of a group of young women about their same age and a group of women about the same age as their mothers. Bob is engaged to be married, whereas Tom is dating many women. Generalizing from an experiment conducted by Simpson and his colleagues, you should expect that, in comparison to Tom, Bob would see the younger women as _____ attractive and the older women as _____ attractive.
    a. less; equally
    b. more; equally
    c. equally; more
    d. equally; less

Answer: b
Page: 155–156

17. Bill and Mary are concerned because they feel their 13-year-old son spends too much time playing video games. One day, they came across a magazine article describing the positive and negative effects of video games on child development. After reading the article, Bill and Mary decided to show it to their son. According to dissonance theory, what would be the most likely impact of reading the article?

a. Bill and Mary would stop worrying, now that they knew that video games had positive effects.

b. Bill and Mary would be more convinced than ever that video games are a bad influence on their son.

c. Their son would be more convinced than ever that video games were a bad influence on him.

d. Bill and Mary, as well as their son, would develop a more balanced view of video games.

Answer: a
Page: 158

18. Freedman and Fraser, in their door-to-door study in which housewives were asked to sign a petition or put an ugly sign in their yard, found that subjects who agreed to a _____ request first were _____ likely to comply with another request.

a. small; more

b. large; less

c. small; less

d. large; more

Answer: c
Page: 158

19. The foot-in-the-door technique:
    a. is a method of encouraging people to do a small favor after they've refused to comply with a larger request.
    b. is a method of encouraging people to do a favor for us after we have granted them a small request.
    c. is a method of encouraging people to do a larger favor after they've agreed to an initially small request.
    d. is a method of using increasingly larger rewards to encourage people to comply with increasingly larger requests.

Answer: b
Page: 159

20. Bettors at a race track who were asked how confident they were about their chances of winning:
    a. were more confident the more money they bet.
    b. were more confident right after having placed their bets.
    c. were less confident right after having placed their bets.
    d. were equally confident both before and after placing their bets.

Answer: d
Page: 159

21. All other things being equal, cognitive dissonance following a decision is *greatest* when:
    a. the decision was not engaged in freely, but was coerced.
    b. the consequences of the decision were not foreseeable.
    c. the decision-maker has low self-esteem.
    d. the decision is irrevocable.

Answer: c
Page: 160

22. A local store advertises a great sale on a certain computer. When you get to the store, the salesperson informs you that they are all out of that particular model, but that they have another model that is "even better" than the sale model for "only" $500 more. This sales technique is known as
   a. foot-in-the-door.
   b. bait-and-hook.
   c. lowballing.
   d. switching.

Answer: b
Page: 161–162

23. According to Mills's study of cheating among sixth-graders, students _____ after having resisted the temptation to cheat on an exam.
   a. developed more tolerant attitudes toward cheating
   b. adopted harsher attitudes toward cheating
   c. were more tempted to cheat in the future
   d. actually performed better on later exams

Answer: b
Page: 163–164

24. According to dissonance theory, as the external justifications for performing an act *decrease*, the need to find internal justifications for performing the act tends to:
   a. decrease.
   b. increase.
   c. remain the same.
   d. decrease rapidly, followed by a gradual increase.

Answer: a
Page: 165–166

25. Festinger and Carlsmith (1959) performed an experiment in which subjects were asked to lie to a "fellow student" for either $1 or $20. For subjects in the $1 condition, dissonance was created by the cognitions "I am an ethical person" and "I have told a lie." Based on the results of this study, which of the following statements best expresses how subjects probably reduced this dissonance?
   a. "I did not really tell a lie—what I said is quite true."
   b. "Though I told that person a lie and I know it, what she doesn't know won't hurt her."
   c. "Lying is a terrible thing."
   d. "I guess I'm not really a very ethical person at all."

Answer: a
Page: 165–166

26. In a study discussed in the text, students were paid either $20 or $1 for telling collaborative subjects that a dull task was actually interesting. Which group showed greater attitude change in actually rating the task as interesting?
   a. the group that told the lie for $1
   b. the group that told the lie for $20
   c. the group that refused to tell the lie for $1
   d. the group that refused to tell the lie for $20

Answer: d
Page: 165–166

27. The amount of dissonance produced when a person engages in an attitude-discrepant act is *greatest* when the rewards are:
   a. much greater than would be needed to induce the act in question.
   b. so small that the act fails to occur.
   c. secondary reinforcers.
   d. just sufficient to induce the act.

Answer: b
Page: 166

28. As part of a psychology experiment, Ed and Todd write essays saying that seat belts are unnecessary and laws requiring them should be abolished. From a questionnaire given several weeks before, it is known that both Ed and Todd are actually in favor of laws requiring seat belts. In the experiment, Ed is given a very small reward for writing an essay, while Todd is given a large reward for writing the essay. If their attitudes are subsequently measured, what is the most likely result?
   a. Todd will favor seat belts more than before; Ed will be more opposed.
   b. Todd's attitude about seat belts will not change; Ed's will become stronger that seat belts are unnecessary.
   c. Todd's attitude about seat belts will not change; Ed's will become stronger that seat belts are necessary.
   d. Todd will favor seat belts more than before; Ed's attitudes will not change.

Answer: b
Page: 165–166

29. Ginny is asked to give a speech in favor of requiring all students to take two years of a foreign language, although her personal position is for no such requirement. Under which of the following circumstances would you expect her attitude to undergo the most change in favor of the requirement?
   a. She agrees and is paid $1,000.
   b. She agrees and is paid $10.
   c. She decides not to give the speech, even though she is offered $1,000.
   d. She decides not to give the speech, even though she is offered $10.

Answer: c
Page: 166–168

30. Suppose you wanted to convince someone who is opposed to marijuana that it should be legalized. According to cognitive dissonance theory, what would be the best way to change that person's attitude?

a. Give him or her a substantial reward to openly endorse the legalization of marijuana.

b. Provide that person with as many convincing arguments and facts as possible in favor of marijuana until he or she changes his or her attitude.

c. Offer the person a small reward to openly endorse legalization, but one just large enough to get him or her to endorse it.

d. Create the illusion that everyone else favors legalization, so that disagreeing will make the individual feel uncomfortable.

Answer: a
Page: 166–168

31. According to cognitive dissonance theory, a disadvantage of the use of large rewards is:

a. the intrinsic value of the rewarded behavior may be reduced.

b. work may be turned into play.

c. people will assume that their behaviors have an internal source.

d. people will eventually grow tired of the rewards and will refuse to perform the behavior.

Answer: c
Page: 166–168

32. Which of the following is *not* an important element in activating dissonance reduction processes?

a. The person's decision cannot be changed—it is irrevocable.

b. The person's action was voluntary—it was not forced.

c. The person was given large rewards.

d. The person's self-concept is threatened by the decision or action.

Answer: d
Page: 168

33. Imagine that someone asked you to do something you found very distasteful—such as eating a handful of sugar-coated beetles. For the sake of argument, let's say that you complied and ate the beetles. According to dissonance theory, under which of the following conditions would you be most likely to find the experience of eating beetles enjoyable?
   a. when your best friend offered you a large reward for eating them
   b. when a person you disliked offered you a large reward for eating them
   c. when your best friend offered you a small reward for eating them
   d. when a person you disliked offered you a small reward for eating them

Answer: b
Page: 169

34. Aronson argues that the key to understanding whether or not dissonance will be aroused is whether or not the subject:
   a. is aware of his original attitude.
   b. feels his behavior violates his self-concept.
   c. has time to think about his actions or must act spontaneously.
   d. hurt another person.

Answer: a
Page: 169–170

35. Dissonance effects are *greatest* when:
   a. people feel personally responsible for their actions and their actions have serious negative consequences.
   b. people feel personally responsible for their actions and they have low self-esteem.
   c. the person's actions have serious negative consequences whether the person feels responsible or not.
   d. the person's actions have serious negative consequences and the person has low self-esteem.

Answer: b
Page: 169–170

36. Aronson argues that typically when dissonance arises it is because the subject:
    a. has a low self-concept.
    b. has done something stupid or immoral.
    c. cannot internally justify his or her actions so must seek external justification.
    d. all of the above

Answer: a
Page: 170

37. Suppose the fund-raising chairperson of a non-profit organization tells you he has heard of a new fund-raising approach in which, when people are asked for contributions, they are also told, "any amount you contribute will be appreciated, even a penny will help." Being a student of social psychology you should respond that, if he uses this technique, he can expect that:
    a. more people will give and the average size of the gifts will not decrease.
    b. more people will give, but the gifts will be smaller.
    c. fewer people will give, but the gifts will be larger.
    d. fewer people will give, and the gifts will be smaller.

Answer: c
Page: 171–172

38. Deci discovered that if you are rewarded for performing a fun and interesting puzzle:
    a. the puzzle becomes easier to solve than if you are not rewarded.
    b. the puzzle becomes harder to solve than if you are not rewarded.
    c. you become less likely to play with it later, when you are not rewarded.
    d. you grow more likely to play with it later, when you are not rewarded.

Answer: c
Page: 172

39. George bought his 6-year-old grandson, Pete, a set of paints for his birthday. Hoping to encourage the little artist, George told him he would give him $1 for every painting he made, which Pete thinks is a lot of money. According to Deci's research on the effects of rewards, which of the following is most likely to happen as a result of George's offer?
   a. Pete will love painting and will want to grow up to become an artist.
   b. George will have to start paying Pete more and more money, to justify his original decision to pay Pete.
   c. Pete will see painting as a way to make money, not as something enjoyable in itself.
   d. Pete will refuse to paint, due to feelings of reactance.

Answer: b
Page: 173

40. According to cognitive dissonance theory, if Abby wanted her roommate Rachel to pick up her clothes instead of leaving them on the floor, Abby would get the most behavioral change if she:
   a. severely punished Rachel when she threw her clothes down.
   b. used a very mild punishment that was enough to get Rachel to pick up her clothes.
   c. used a very mild punishment that was not enough to get Rachel to pick up her clothes.
   d. did not use any punishment whatsoever.

Answer: b
Page: 174–175

41. In Freedman's study, children who were given mild threats of punishment for playing with a robot toy:
   a. were more likely to play with the toy than those who received severe threats.
   b. refused to play with the toy even after Freedman had left and several weeks had passed.
   c. refused to play with the toy while Freedman was present but began playing with it as soon as he left.
   d. played with the toy, but liked it less than the children who received severe threats.

Answer: a
Page: 175

42. Suppose you conduct an experiment in which a child is placed in a room with a highly attractive toy. Generalizing from Freedman's research, you could diminish the child's attraction to the toy by:
    a. using a mild threat of punishment for playing with the toy.
    b. using a severe threat of punishment for playing with the toy.
    c. using no threat of punishment for playing with the toy.
    d. using a mild promise of reward for playing with the toy.

Answer: a
Page: 175–177

43. Suppose you are responsible for planning the initiation of new members to a group to which you belong. Generalizing from Aronson and Mills's study on the effects of initiation on liking of the group, you would do well to make the initiation process:
    a. difficult or unpleasant.
    b. easy and pleasant.
    c. closely resemble the activities of the group.
    d. very different from the regular activities in which the group engages.

Answer: c
Page: 176–177

44. Which of the following conclusions is supported by Aronson and Mills's experiment in which subjects underwent either a severe or a mild initiation in order to join a boring discussion group?
    a. The more you like something, the harder you will work for it.
    b. The less you like something, the harder you will work for it.
    c. The harder you work for something, the more you will like it.
    d. The harder you work for something, the less you will like it.

Answer: c
Page: 177

45. Why is it, according to dissonance theory, that we evaluate favorably those goals we've had to suffer for?
    a. The goals themselves *are* valuable; otherwise we wouldn't go to all that time and trouble.
    b. Deep down, people really like to work hard for what they get.
    c. We are motivated to justify the time and effort we've spent.
    d. Reaching the goal ends our suffering and, thus, is rewarding.

Answer: a
Page: 177

46. In Cooper's study of snake phobia, he found that which of the following groups improved the most:
    a. high effort-high choice
    b. high effort-low choice
    c. low effort-high choice
    d. low effort-low choice

Answer: c
Page: 178–189

47. How does cognitive dissonance explain a husband beating up his wife while he still sees himself as a decent human being?
    a. It cannot explain these evil acts, which are punishable by law.
    b. It explains that the husband learned this violence from his dad.
    c. He convinces himself that his wife deserved the beating from her evil actions.
    d. He knows when stress builds in his life something has to give.

Answer: b
Page: 181

48. In a study by Davis and Jones, subjects volunteered to insult a "fellow student" by telling him he was a shallow, untrustworthy and dull person. How did these subjects justify their hurtful behavior toward the other student, who had done nothing to deserve criticism?
    a. By agreeing to help the other student with a difficult task.
    b. By finding the other student less attractive than before they had insulted him.
    c. By convincing themselves that they had been forced to deliver the insults.
    d. By promising themselves they would never again perform such an unkind act.

Answer: b
Page: 181

49. Dissonance reduction processes can make:
    a. us like a person we hurt, in order to compensate the person for our mistake.
    b. us dislike a person we hurt, in order to justify hurting the person.
    c. us dislike a person we do a favor for, because we come to resent doing the favor.
    d. people with high self-esteem cheat more, because they feel less guilty.

Answer: a
Page: 181

50. In comparison to people with low self-esteem, cognitive dissonance theory suggests that persons of high self-esteem are _____ likely to experience dissonance if they hurt someone and they are _____ likely to derogate a victim whom they have hurt.
    a. more; more
    b. less; less
    c. more; less
    d. less; more

Answer: b
Page: 181

51. Suppose you had volunteered to be in an experiment in which you believe you have just given painful electric shocks to another person. According to cognitive dissonance theory, you would:
   a.   estimate that the shocks were more painful than they actually were.
   b.   have a lower opinion of the victims after the experiment than before.
   c.   have a higher opinion of the subjects after the experiment than before.
   d.   experience a temporary increase in your self-esteem.

Answer: b
Page: 182–183

52. Lucas believes that, because women take longer to learn mechanical skills at his factory, they have less mechanical aptitude, and therefore he is justified in not hiring any women. Lucas's belief system is best thought of as an example of:
   a.   the inoculation effect.
   b.   the self-fulfilling prophecy.
   c.   the initiation effect.
   d.   the "turn about is fair play" effect.

Answer: a
Page: 184

53. Aaron Kay and his colleagues gave different articles before the presidential election to people showing in one set that Gore was most likely to win and in another set that Bush was most likely to win. The subjects rated
   a.   the candidates most desirable if the article depicted his as most likely to be president.
   b.   the candidates the same as before receiving the article information.
   c.   Bush higher if they were Republicans and Gore higher if they were Democrats.
   d.   the race as too close to call and would look to Florida to decide it.

Answer: c
Page: 184–185

54. Darrin Lehman and Shelley Taylor studied college students who lived in Los Angeles, the site of an impending earthquake. In their interviews with students, they found that:
   a. students living in seismically unsafe buildings planned to move to safer structures.
   b. students living in seismically unsafe buildings tended to be less familiar with safety measures than those living in safe buildings.
   c. students living in seismically unsafe buildings tended to underestimate the damage that would result from a major quake.
   d. students living in safer buildings spread more rumors about impending earthquakes.

Answer: c
Page: 186–187

55. In a study by Mettee and Aronson, subjects whose self-esteem had been temporarily lowered were more likely to cheat at a card game than subjects whose self-esteem was temporarily increased. According to Aronson, the results of this study suggest that:
   a. low self-esteem reinforces the belief that cheating is worth the risk of getting caught.
   b. high self-esteem reinforces the belief that cheating is worth the risk of getting caught.
   c. behaving in an immoral fashion is more dissonance-arousing for people with high self-esteem than for those with low self-esteem.
   d. behaving in an immoral fashion is less dissonance-arousing for people with high self-esteem than for those with low self-esteem.

Answer: b
Page: 187

56. How did Aronson and Mettee manipulate self-esteem in their article on self-esteem and dishonest behavior?
    a. They selected subjects who rated themselves as either high or low on a standardized test of self-esteem.
    b. They gave subjects false feedback about their personalities based on results of a personality test they had taken.
    c. They made the cheating task much more tempting for those subjects in the low self-esteem condition.
    d. They told people in the low self-esteem condition that others found them to be physically unattractive.

Answer: d
Page: 189–190

57. Zanna and Cooper conducted an experiment in which subjects received a pill and were told different stories. Some were told that it would arouse them and make them tense. Some were told it would do nothing. And some were told that it would relax them. They all wrote counter-attitudinal essays to create dissonance. Which group changed their attitude the most?
    a. It was a tie between the relaxed and aroused groups.
    b. It was the aroused group.
    c. It was the group who were told the pill would do nothing.
    d. It was the relaxed group.

Answer: c
Page: 190

58. Zimbardo's experiment on the effects of dissonance arousal on pain, in which subjects received a series of intense electric shocks under different conditions, found that:
   a. subjects felt less pain when they were allowed to deliver the shocks to themselves, rather than receiving them from the experimenter.
   b. subjects felt more pain when they were allowed to deliver the shocks to themselves, rather than receiving them from the experimenter.
   c. subjects felt less pain when they volunteered to receive the shocks.
   d. subjects felt less pain when they received a large reward for receiving the shocks.

Answer: d
Page: 191

59. Brehm put hungry subjects in a state of high or low dissonance. According to his results, subjects in the high-dissonance condition said they were _____ hungry and actually ate _____ food than those in the high dissonance condition.
   a. more; less
   b. more; more
   c. less; more
   d. less; less

Answer: a
Page: 191–192

60. According to dissonance theory, the people living nearest to the Three Mile Island nuclear plant during the crisis should:
   a. perceive the Nuclear Regulatory Commission's reassuring statements as more credible because they were committed to staying.
   b. perceive the Nuclear Regulatory Commission's reassuring statements as more credible because they were in favor of nuclear power.
   c. perceive the Nuclear Regulatory Commission's reassuring statements as less credible, because they had the most to lose.
   d. spread around the most frightening rumors, because they had the greatest reason to be scared.

Answer: c
Page: 193

61. According to Axsom and Cooper, what may well be the critical factor in therapy that accomplishes the recovery of the person?
    a. the empathy of the therapist
    b. whether or not the person enters the therapy under a doctor's care
    c. how much effort the person expends in the therapeutic process
    d. the particular type of therapy that is delivered

Answer: d
Page: 193

62. In Axsom and Cooper's study of weight reduction, they found that women in the _____ effort condition reported significant weight loss at

    _____.
    a. low; 4 weeks but not at 12 months
    b. low; 12 months but not at 6 weeks
    c. high; 4 weeks but not at 12 months
    d. high; 12 months but not at 4 weeks

Answer: b
Page: 193–194

63. Aronson and his colleagues found that he was best able to convince students to use condoms regularly when:
    a. they were exposed to a high-fear campaign detailing the awful consequences of getting AIDS.
    b. they were reminded of their own failures to use condoms and they made a speech advocating condom use.
    c. they could obtain condoms for free by simply asking for them.
    d. they were given an embarrassing "lesson" on how to use and remove them.

Answer: a
Page: 195–196

64. In his text, Aronson argues that Jim Jones was able to persuade people to comply with his demands by first making small demands and then increasing them. This analysis is most similar to the research conducted by:
   a. Freedman and Fraser on the "foot-in-the-door" technique.
   b. Freedman on the threat of punishment.
   c. Aronson and Mills on the severity of initiation.
   d. Hastorf and Cantril on the Princeton-Dartmouth football game.

Answer: b
Page: 197–198

65. Haruki Sakai performed Festinger and Carlsmith's experiment about telling a lie for either $1 or $20. In Japan Sakai found that
   a. The results were the opposite.
   b. The experiment was a little different with an observer to the lie and the observer came to believe the lie.
   c. It was nearly impossible to conduct the experiment because the Japanese were too honest to lie.
   d. Sakai had to offer $100 before the Japanese would tell the lie.

Essay Questions

1. According to cognitive dissonance theory, making an important decision is likely to arouse considerable dissonance. Let's say you were in the market to buy a new car. You are torn between buying a compact model—fuel-efficient, inexpensive and reliable—and a foreign sports car, which would be fast, flashy and impressive. Applying the theory of cognitive dissonance, describe what kinds of information you would seek (e.g., what kinds of ads or other information you would attend to) and what your attitudes would be (e.g., about fuel-efficiency, cost, safety, performance, etc.) both: a) before making your decision, and b) after deciding to buy the sports car. Explain the reasoning behind your response, using relevant research examples to support your arguments.

2. What is meant by "the psychology of inevitability"? How can it be explained by cognitive dissonance theory? Illustrate your answer with an example from real life and describe at least one piece of research that demonstrates this phenomenon.

3. Imagine that you are approached by a member of a prominent cult in this country. On his or her invitation, you attend several cult meetings. As a result, you begin to believe that this group has some good ideas, but you still have some doubts about becoming a member. You are asked for a financial contribution, which you give. After several months, you find that you have donated a great deal of time and money to the group. Eventually, without even hearing any new arguments or propaganda, you believe everything the group stands for—they can do no wrong. You have become a devout member of the cult. How would a social psychologist explain this phenomenon? Be sure to cite research to support your answer.

4. Suppose you were a subject in Milgram's experiment on obedience, but for some reason, you were never debriefed. In other words, you were never told that the other person in the experiment was a confederate who didn't really receive the electric shocks you delivered. Suppose that the next day you ran into the other person at the college coffee shop. All other things being equal, how would you feel about that person if: a) you had gone all the way in delivering shocks to him or her? b) you had disobeyed the experimenter and refused to continue after delivering only a few mild shocks? Support your answer with relevant research and theory.

5. Imagine that you volunteered (for no pay) to spend a few hours each day teaching arts and crafts to young children in a day-care center. After several weeks, you discover that you really enjoy working with the children even though they sometimes make a mess and don't follow directions—which occasionally gets a little annoying. Now, suppose a paid position opened up at the center, and you began to receive a fairly good salary for performing the same kinds of work you had previously done for free. How might your attitudes toward your work—and, perhaps, toward the children themselves—change as a result? Explain the reasoning behind your answer, making sure to discuss the distinction between internal and external justification. Support your response with relevant research and theory.

6. Suppose a mother was trying to get her oldest son to stop beating up on his younger brother. Given your knowledge of dissonance theory, what advice would you give this parent on how to proceed? Compare the likely result of your plan with one based solely on compliance (i.e., simple reward and punishment). Discuss research evidence that supports your reasoning.

7. Given what you know about cognitive dissonance, explain why direct efforts to change someone's mind about an important issue are often doomed to failure. Similarly, why would offering someone a reward to change his or her opinion be unlikely to produce real attitude change? Support your answer with relevant research.

8. One of the reasons dissonance theory has attracted great interest is its ability to explain and predict real-world phenomena that are not easily understood in common-sense terms. Describe two "practical applications" of dissonance theory, drawing upon relevant research examples to illustrate your discussion.

6

Human Aggression

I. Aggression Defined

Hostile versus instrumental aggression

II. Is Aggression Instinctive?

Thanatos and the "hydraulic" analogy (Freud)
Animal studies (Kuo; Eibl-Eibesfeldt; Scott; Lorenz; Lore & Schultz)
The effects of learning (Berkowitz)
Regional differences (Nisbett; Cohen & Nisbett)

III. Is Aggression Useful?

A. Survival of the fittest

Evolutionary value (Lorenz; Washburn & Hamburg; Pinker; LeBoeuf)
Value of nonaggressive behavior (Ashley Montagu; Kropotkin)
America as a competitive culture

B. Catharsis

Sports (Patterson)
Direct aggression (Geen; Kahn; Doob & Wood)

IV. Causes of Aggression

A. Neurological and chemical causes

Testosterone (Dabbs; Maccoby & Jacklin)
Gender differences (Eagly & Steffan; Archer & McDaniel)
Alcohol

B. Pain and discomfort (Berkowitz; Carlsmith & Anderson; Griffitt & Veitch)

C. Frustration and aggression (Baker, Dembo, & Lewin)

Nearness of goal (Harris)
Unexpected interruption (Kulik & Brown)
Relative deprivation

D. Social learning and aggression

Attributed intention (Mallick & McCandless)
Aggressive stimuli (Berkowitz)
Anonymity of aggressor (Zimbardo; Mullen)

E. Social learning, violence, and the mass media

TV and movie violence (Liebert & Baron; Josephson; Parke)
Prizefights (Phillips)
Numbing effect of TV violence (Hanratty Thomas)
Why does media violence affect viewers' aggression?
The media, pornography, and violence against women
    (Donnerstein; Malamuth; Linz)
Aggression to attract public attention

V. Toward the Reduction of Violence

A. Pure Reason

B. Punishment

Severe and frustrating forms of punishment (Hamblin)
Harsh prison sentences (*Gideon* v. *Wainwright;* Zimbardo)
Mild punishment (Aronson & Carlsmith; Freedman; Olweus)

C. Punishment of aggressive models

D. Rewarding alternative behaviors

Reinforcing positive behaviors (Brown & Elliot)
Inhibiting the effects of frustration (Davitz)

E. Presence of nonaggressive models

Conformity and nonaggression (Baron & Kepner)

F. Building empathy towards others

Perspective-taking (Feshbach & Feshbach; Hammock &
    Richardson; Obuchi)

Terms & Concepts

aggressive action
hostile aggression
instrumental aggression
Eros
Thanatos
hydraulic theory
sublimate
relative deprivation
social learning
aggressive stimulus
deindividuation
aggressive cues

survival of the fittest
altruistic
catharsis
blaming the victim
amygdala
testosterone
frustration-aggression hypothesis
social learning
scripts
nonaggressive models
empathy

Chapter Overview

Chapter 6 discusses theory and research on aggression, which is defined as a behavior aimed at causing harm or pain. A further distinction is also made between hostile aggression, which serves as an end in itself, and instrumental aggression, an act of aggression that is performed as a means to achieving some other goal besides harm or pain. Important issues and questions covered in the chapter include:

Is human aggression instinctive? The answer to this question is still controversial, and much of the evidence comes from studies of non-human species rather than studies of humans. Although aggression may have an instinctual component in humans, the important point for the social psychologist is that it is modifiable by situational factors.

Is aggression necessary for human survival? It is possible that in the early history of human evolution, highly competitive and aggressive behaviors were adaptive. Given the violent and troubled state of human affairs in recent history, however, the survival value of aggressive behavior is questionable.

Does watching, enacting, or fantasizing about aggression serve a useful function in helping people to "blow off steam," thus preventing future, more extreme acts of violence? The weight of research evidence contradicts Freud's "catharsis" hypothesis, and instead indicates that violence breeds future violence. This is especially the case when aggression is unleashed against an innocent victim, largely due to the kinds of self-justification processes discussed in Chapter 5. Under special circumstances, however, aggressive retaliation can reduce the need for further aggression if something akin to equity has been restored.

Research on the impact of media violence suggests that watching violent programming not only increases aggressive behavior among children but leads to reduced sensitivity to aggressive acts in the real world. Studies using adult subjects—including research on the impact of violent pornography and "slasher" films—demonstrate that these effects are not restricted to children.

The finding that frustration leads to aggression is well-documented. Although frustration is one of the major causes of aggression, other social-psychological factors can intervene either to induce aggression in a person who is experiencing little frustration, or to inhibit aggressive behavior in a person who is frustrated. For example, knowing that the cause of one's frustration was unintentional tends to reduce the likelihood of an aggressive response. Factors that increase the probability of aggression include the presence of aggressive cues in the person's immediate environment. Similarly, the phenomenon of deindividuation, which occurs when a person's actions are cloaked by a sense of anonymity (e.g., as in a large crowd) tends to facilitate aggressive behavior.

Can human aggression be eliminated? Although there are no easy solutions to this problem, various possibilities for reducing violence and aggression have been proposed. These include the use of "pure reason," harsh punishment, punishment of aggressive models, rewarding alternative behavior patterns and building empathy toward others. Of these strategies, developing the capacity for empathy and rewarding nonaggressive behaviors are among the most promising.

Lecture Ideas & Teaching Suggestions

Aversive States and Aggression. In addition to the frustration-aggression relationship that is examined in Chapter 6, you may also wish to discuss the link between aggression and other unpleasant states. Research on human subjects has demonstrated that aggression is heightened in response to several aversive factors, including pain, high temperatures, foul odors, and cigarette smoke. These findings are consistent with the results of a large number of experiments conducted on animals. They also ring true with our everyday experiences. Thus, in introducing a discussion of the effects of aversive states on aggression, you may want to ask your students to think of situations in which they felt more irritable or reacted to others with greater hostility while suffering from an illness or injury. You may also wish to provide an example or two from your own experience.

A thoughtful review and analysis of this body of research may be found in Berkowitz, L. (1983). Aversively stimulated aggression: Some parallels and differences in research with animals and humans. *American Psychologist, 38,* 1135–1144. In this article, Berkowitz also examines the role of cognition in mediating the impact of aversive events on aggression. Moreover, in reconsidering the frustration-aggression hypothesis, he argues that frustrating experiences provoke aggression because they are aversive in nature. In his view, then, the instigation to aggression lies in the aversiveness of the experience, not simply the frustration of having failed to attain a desire goal. Finally, Berkowitz concludes that, while it is clearly impossible to eliminate all aversive events from our daily existence, human beings can learn to refrain from acting on the aggressive impulses stimulated by these events.

The Effects of Alcohol and Drugs. Do alcohol and drugs increase the tendency to engage in aggressive behavior? This question, which may be of interest to your students, has been explored in research conducted by Stuart Taylor and his colleagues. In their experiments, subjects consumed either small or large doses of alcohol and then interacted with a confederate who either did or did not make them angry. Next, they were given an opportunity to aggress against the confederate. The results were that, regardless of the dosage, alcohol did not increase aggression among subjects who had not been provoked by the confederate's behavior. Thus, alcohol, by itself, does not appear to stimulate aggression. For provoked subjects, however, consuming a large dose of alcohol did lead to heightened aggression, while low doses did not have this effect. This same procedure was conducted using small or large doses of marijuana (in the form of THC, the major active ingredient in marijuana). The results of marijuana use were different from the effects of alcohol. Among subjects who had been provoked by the confederate, those who ingested large doses of THC were significantly less aggressive than subjects who received either large alcohol doses or low THC doses. Moreover, subjects with high THC doses even responded less aggressively than subjects who had not consumed any drugs at all. Although based on a fairly small body of research, these findings seem somewhat consistent with the common stereotype of the "violent drunk" and the "mellow" pot-smoker.

Further details on this topic are available in: Taylor, S.P. & Gammon, C.B. (1975). Effects of type and dose of alcohol on human aggression. *Journal of Personality and Social Psychology, 32,* 169–175. Taylor, S.P., Gammon, C.B., & Capasso, D.R. (1976). Aggression as a function of the interaction of alcohol and threat. *Journal of Personality and Social Psychology, 34,* 938–941. Taylor, S.P., Vardaris, R.M., Rawitch, A.B., Gammon, C.B., & Cranston, J.W. (1976). The effects of alcohol and delta-p-tetrahydrocannibol on human physical aggression. *Aggressive Behavior, 2,* 153–162.

Gender Differences in Aggression. Throughout history and across cultures, aggressive activities such as hunting and waging war have been the special, if not sole, province of men. Thus, the issue of gender differences in aggression constitutes an important, and controversial, realm of social-psychological inquiry. In their 1974 review of the findings in this area, Maccoby and Jacklin concluded that males are more aggressive than females, and that these behavioral differences are partly the result of biological factors. More recently, Eagly and Steffen (1986) have noted that gender differences found in social-psychological research tend to be small and are often inconsistent. This is especially true when verbal and other forms of psychological aggression are the focus of study. When it comes to inflicting physical harm, however, these differences tend to be more pronounced, with men displaying higher levels of aggression. For a review and analysis of these findings, see Eagley, A.H., & Steffen, V.J. (1986). Gender and aggressive behavior: A meta-analytic review of the social psychological literature. *Psychological Bulletin, 100,* 309–330.

Projects and Discussion Topics

1. PROJECT: Find a television show that has a reputation for violent themes (detective or police dramas are a good choice). As you watch this program, pretend you are Paxman, an alien from the peaceful planet Pacifica, who has been sent on a mission to learn about life on Earth. Based on what you've seen on this television show—and nothing else—you must transmit a preliminary report back to your planet, describing what you've learned thus far. In your report, describe your observations and conclusions regarding what life is like on Earth, the basic nature of earthlings, and how and why they act as they do. Compare these creatures and their behavior with your own experience of living in a violence-free society.

2. PROJECT: Visit a playground at a time when lots of young children are playing. Look for instances of hostility and aggressive interactions among children, and see if you can determine what provoked them and how they were resolved. Write up your observations and analyses, and share them with your classmates.

3. PROJECT: Collect newspaper or magazine articles describing a violent crime or other incident involving aggression. What factors are described as having provoked the incident? What kinds of attributions concerning the incident are made by the writer, the witnesses, authorities, or other people quoted in the article? Does the article contain any explicit or implicit theories regarding the causes of aggression or its solution? Bring your articles to class and describe your findings.

4. DISCUSSION: Based on research evidence presented in Chapter 6, what are the effects of violent pornography? Given this evidence, do you think steps should be taken to make such pornography illegal? Why or why not? Similarly, research has demonstrated that watching televised violence increases aggressive behavior in children. Should there be policies or laws implemented that restrict the levels of violence contained in children's television shows? Why or why not? Is your opinion the same regarding pornography and children's shows? Why or why not? Share your views on these issues with members of your discussion group.

5. DISCUSSION: You are the parent of a young child whom you would like to see become a peaceful, affectionate, and cooperative adult. To achieve this goal, to what extent would you consider taking the following steps? a) preventing your child from watching violent television shows; b) preventing your child from playing with "violent" toys such as guns, swords, etc.; c) preventing your child from playing with "aggressive" children; d) preventing your child from fighting back, if another child kept bullying him or her. Finally, would you want to eliminate all aggressive behavior in your child? Why or why not? Discuss your decisions, and the reasoning behind them, with your classmates.

Experiential Exercises

1. SEX ON THE BEACH. This simulation emphasizes the sexual diversity and the social pressure in our society to be competitive. Participants are assigned profiles and mingle in the room in a party type atmosphere. There are heterosexuals, bisexuals and homosexuals in the simulation. They can approach and visit with each other. If they both feel comfortable, they approach the sex therapist, who will evaluate their sexual encounter and provide chips. If they match up with people who have similar characteristics, they will receive more chips. A competitive atmosphere develops at the "party". People throw caution to the wind and have more and more partners. There is a secret in the simulation because AIDS is circulating from a couple of people to possibly 75% of the participants. They could stop the spread of the disease if they asked for condoms, but hardly anyone ever does. It can be played in 25 minutes and orally debriefed the rest of the class. During the oral debriefing after they discover many have AIDS, there are many accusations and hostile behavior towards others who might have passed it to them. This simulation demands written debriefing because participants can examine their own behavior. They can write about social influence, sexual diversity, AIDS and social psychological terms to analyze their behavior. The simulation was developed by Charles Petranek and can be purchased from:

    Petranek Consulting Services, Inc.
    2712 Harmony Way
    Evansville, IN 47720
    Phone: 812-426-1617

Additional Readings

Bandura, A. (1973). *Aggression: A social learning analysis.* Englewood Cliffs, NJ: Prentice-Hall.

Berkowitz, L. (1981, June). How guns control us. *Psychology Today,* pp. 11–12. (Review of field and laboratory research on the "weapons effect," offering support for gun-control legislation.)

Donnerstein, E.I., Linz, D. & Penrod, S. (1987). *The question of pornography: Research findings and policy implications.* New York: Free Press.

Feshbach, S. & Malamuth, N. (1978, November). Sex and aggression: proving the link. *Psychology Today,* pp. 110–117. (Explores the link between pornography and aggression.)

Fowler, R.D. (Ed.). (1993). *American Psychologist, 48,* (10), 1054–1087. (Five articles about violence against women.)

Geen, R.G. & Donnerstein, E.I. (1983). *Aggression: Theoretical and empirical reviews.* New York: Academic Press.

Gerbner, G. & Gross, L. (1976, April). The scary world of TV's heavy viewer. *Psychology Today,* pp. 41–45. (Heavy exposure to television leads people to view the world as a more dangerous place.)

Linz, D., Donnerstein, E. & Penrod, S. (1987). The findings and recommendations of the Attorney General's Commission on Pornography: Do the psychological facts fit the political fury? *American Psychologist, 42,* 946–953.

Lore, R.K. & Schultz, L.A. (1993). Control of human aggression: A comparative perspective. *American Psychologist, 48,* (1), 16–25.

Malamuth, N.M. & Donnerstein, E.I. (1984). *Pornography and sexual aggression.* Orlando, FL: Academic Press.

Satterfield, J.M. & Seligman, M.E.P. (1994). Military aggression and risk predicted by explanatory style. *Psychological Science, 5,* (2), 77–82.

Tavris, C. (1982, November). Anger defused. *Psychology Today,* pp. 25–35. (Contrary to catharsis theory, ventilating one's anger tends to increase feelings of hostility.)

Multiple-Choice Questions

Answer: c
Page: 202

1. Which of the following would most likely be considered an act of aggression by Aronson's definition?
   a. a football player tackling a practice dummy
   b. an actor rehearsing a fight scene who accidentally punches a stuntman, breaking his nose
   c. a middle school child angrily, but harmlessly, hits his father
   d. a person whose comment unintentionally hurts a friend's feelings

Answer: c
Page: 202–203

2. Instrumental aggression differs from hostile aggression in that:
   a. instrumental aggression involves the intent to harm another person.
   b. instrumental aggression involves both emotional and physical harm to another person.
   c. instrumental aggression involves harming someone in order to achieve a goal, rather than for its own sake.
   d. instrumental aggression is an end in itself rather than a means to an end.

Answer: a
Page: 202–203

3. Which of the following is an instrumental act of aggression?
   a. dropping a bomb on a ball-bearing factory of the enemy during World War II
   b. the My Lai massacre
   c. a person who hits an enemy in anger
   d. watching a violent boxing match on TV

Answer: a
Page: 203

4. Sigmund Freud would most likely be associated with the idea that aggression:
   a. is instinctive.
   b. is a socially learned response.
   c. needs to be strictly controlled in order to protect a person's mental health.
   d. is a result of societal problems

Answer: c
Page: 203

5. According to Freud, society performs an essential and beneficial function in regulating the instinct of aggression by:
   a. forbidding opportunities for people to express their aggressive feelings.
   b. giving people free reign to express their aggressive feelings at those who provoke their anger.
   c. helping people to sublimate destructive energy into acceptable or useful behavior.
   d. helping people to direct their aggressive energy inward, in the form of self-punishment.

Answer: c
Page: 203

6. Freud believed that aggressive energy could be channelled so that the person's behavior actually worked toward the good of society. He called this process:
   a. catharsis.
   b. vicarious aggression.
   c. sublimation.
   d. Thanatos.

Answer: a
Page: 204

7. Kuo conducted a study in which he raised a kitten in the same cage as a rat. As an adult, the cat refrained from attacking the rat and, in fact, the two became close companions. The cat never chased or attacked any other rats as well. This study indicates that:
   a. aggressive behavior can be inhibited by early experiences.
   b. aggression is not instinctive.
   c. aggression is not instinctive in cats.
   d. the aggressive instinct does not operate when an animal is raised in captivity.

Answer: c
Page: 205

8. According to Berkowitz, who stresses the role of learning in human aggression:
   a. aggressive behavior is almost entirely the result of social influences.
   b. once learned, aggressive behavior is nearly impossible to modify.
   c. aggressive behavior is the result of an interplay between innate propensities and learned responses.
   d. once learned, aggressive feelings must be released through catharsis.

Answer: c
Page: 205–206

9. Overall, research indicates that:
   a. aggression is not instinctive among humans but is instinctive among other animals.
   b. aggression is not an instinct in either humans or nonhumans.
   c. aggression may have an instinctual component in humans, but it is also highly modifiable by situational factors.
   d. over the course of human evolution, aggression has changed from an instinct to a learned behavior.

Answer: c
Page: 205–206

10. The Iroquois Indians lived in peace for hundreds of years as a hunting nation, but in the seventeenth century, trade introduced by Europeans brought the Iroquois into competition with a neighboring tribe. A series of tribal wars developed, and the Iroquois ultimately became ferocious and successful warriors. This series of events suggest that:
    a. warlike behavior is the result of uncontrollable aggressive instincts.
    b. competition inevitably leads to violence.
    c. changing social conditions can lead to changes in aggressive behavior.
    d. aggressive behavior ensures evolutionary survival.

Answer: d
Page: 208

11. Kropotkin's study of chimpanzees documents that when one hungry chimp begs for food from the other, the other chimp reluctantly shares its food. This research is cited to make which of the following points:
    a. like aggression, empathy is learned.
    b. humans and chimps have many behaviors in common; therefore animal studies are useful in understanding human behavior.
    c. aggression has been selected for according to "survival of the fittest."
    d. sharing may be an instinctual behavior.

Answer: a
Page: 209

12. The tension reducing properties of various types of aggressive acts have been called:
    a. catharsis.
    b. repression.
    c. deindividuation.
    d. social facilitation.

Answer: d
Page: 209

13. Catharsis refers to the idea that:
    a. frustration results when a person can't attain his or her goals.
    b. frustration increases the drive, or activity, state of the organism.
    c. modeling increases the probability of aggression.
    d. violence reduces pent-up aggressive energy.

Answer: c
Page: 209–210

14. The catharsis theory of aggression holds that:
    a. aggressive impulses, if kept bottled up, will eventually fade away.
    b. one act of aggression usually leads to further aggression.
    c. one act of aggression reduces the likelihood of further acts of aggression.
    d. frustration leads to aggression.

Answer: a
Page: 210

15. Which of the following perspectives would encourage you to let children watch violent TV programs?
    a. psychoanalytic
    b. frustration-aggression
    c. social learning
    d. instinct

Answer: d
Page: 210

16. John is frustrated by doing poorly on a college chemistry test because he felt he really knew the material. After the test, he thought he would "blow off steam" by going to his favorite bar and playing video games. This example highlights the principle underlying:
    a. reinforcement.
    b. punishment.
    c. instinct.
    d. catharsis.

Answer: a
Page: 210

17. Patterson measured the hostility of high-school football players both one week before and one week after the football season. He found that:
    a. players exhibited an increase in hostility over the course of the season.
    b. players exhibited a decrease in hostility over the course of the season.
    c. players from teams with losing records displayed higher rates of hostility over the course of the season.
    d. players from teams with winning records displayed higher rates of hostility over the course of the season.

Answer: c
Page: 211

18. The analysis of the research on the catharsis theory of aggression suggests that direct acts of aggression:
    a. generally reduce the tendency toward future aggression—Freud was right.
    b. reduce the tendency toward future aggression, because they reduce the effect of social inhibitions.
    c. reduce the tendency toward future aggression if they are done directly, are justified, and restore equity.
    d. reduce the tendency toward future aggression if they are done indirectly, are not justified, and do not restore equity.

Answer: b
Page: 211

19. In a "natural experiment" in the real world, some technicians who were laid off by their company were given a chance to verbalize their hostility against their exbosses, while other technicians did not have this opportunity. Later, when given a chance to talk about their exbosses, workers who had voiced their hostility were _____ than workers who had not voiced their hostility.
    a. less negative in their descriptions of their exbosses
    b. more negative in their descriptions of their exbosses
    c. more likely to feel empathy toward their exbosses
    d. less likely to feel socially inferior to their exbosses

Answer: a
Page: 211

20. Cognitive dissonance theory predicts that once a person has hurt another, he will be _____ likely to hurt the person again in the future. This explanation is _____ the idea of catharsis.
    a. more; contrary to
    b. less; contrary to
    c. more; consistent with
    d. less; consistent with

Answer: c
Page: 212–213

21. In Kahn's experiment, students were allowed to express their hostile feelings towards a medical technician who had made derogatory remarks about them. Compared to students who were not allowed to vent, students who vented:
    a. felt more remorse after expressing their aggression.
    b. expressed the same amount of aggression.
    c. disliked the technician more after expressing their aggression.
    d. were less likely to aggress when given a second opportunity to vent.

Answer: d
Page: 214

22. Which of the following are NOT true about males and females in regards to aggression?
    a. Boys are physically more aggressive than girls.
    b. Women are more often arrested for property crimes than for crimes of violence against people.
    c. Prisoners with higher levels of testosterone in prison violate more rules.
    d. Girls and women engage in more relational aggression than boys and men.

Answer: c
Page: 215

23. Alcohol is involved in _____ percent of violent crimes arrests:
    a. 25.
    b. 50.
    c. 75.
    d. 95.

Answer: a
Page: 216

24. Research on the effect of environmental conditions suggest that higher air temperature:
    a. increases hostility and aggression.
    b. increases physiological arousal, but not aggression.
    c. decreases arousal and thus decreases aggression.
    d. has no effect on arousal or aggression.

Answer: c
Page: 217

25. In the experiment by Barker, Dembo, and Lewin, in which children were delayed or not delayed from playing with attractive toys, the greater aggression of children who were delayed from playing with the toys probably occurred because:
    a. of relative deprivation.
    b. they were angry at the children who weren't delayed from playing with the toys.
    c. they were frustrated at not getting what they had been led to expect.
    d. being delayed caused them to dislike the toys.

Answer: b
Page: 217

26. Barker, Dembo and Lewin's classic study of children who were either delayed or not delayed from entering a room full of attractive toys showed that, with regard to aggression:
   a. children who were delayed from playing with the toys experienced dissonance and were thus less aggressive than children who were not delayed.
   b. children who were delayed from playing with the toys experienced frustration and were thus more aggressive than children who were not delayed.
   c. both groups were equally aggressive, but children who were delayed liked the toys more than children who weren't delayed.
   d. both groups were equally aggressive, but children who weren't delayed liked the toys more than children who were.

Answer: b
Page: 218

27. According to Aronson's analysis, the riots that occurred in Watts and in Detroit *most clearly* exemplified the effects of:
   a. frustration.
   b. relative deprivation.
   c. catharsis.
   d. social learning.

Answer: a
Page: 218

28. In the experiment by Kulik and Brown, subjects attempted to earn money by telephoning potential donors (confederates) for charity pledges. Subjects displayed the most aggression when:
   a. their expectations were high, but their success rate was low.
   b. they were not personally committed to the charity.
   c. the potential donors were rude.
   d. they got a high level of donations but were paid the same as the less successful callers.

Answer: b
Page: 219

29. Aronson explains the high school shootings like Columbine by
   a. pointing to the males who committed the crimes and their high testosterone levels.
   b. examining the relative deprivation in high schools for the youth on the bottom being rejected by the "preppies" on top.
   c. analyzing the macho upbringing these boys have had.
   d. citing all the violence on TV and these boys wanted to make a name for themselves by participating in a major violent act.

Answer: c
Page: 221

30. Martha argues that children should not be exposed to sex and violence on TV because it leads them to behave more aggressively. Martha's view is most consistent with:
   a. psychoanalytic theory.
   b. survival of the fittest.
   c. social learning theory.
   d. the frustration-aggression hypothesis.

Answer: d
Page: 221

31. The social learning theory of aggression does *not* make which of the following assumptions:
   a. children and adults can learn to be aggressive by observing others.
   b. aggression can be maintained when its occurrence results in tangible rewards for the aggressor.
   c. aggression can be maintained by social reward and approval.
   d. human beings are constantly driven toward violence by built-in internal forces or ever-present external stimuli.

Answer: a
Page: 221

32. According to a study by Mallick and McCandless, in which children were kept from achieving a goal by another child's clumsiness, the amount of aggression we express after a frustrating experience is often reduced when:
    a. we learn that the person who has frustrated us actually intended no harm.
    b. we are not allowed to retaliate in an appropriate and moderate manner.
    c. we are threatened with punishment if we retaliate.
    d. we are exposed to an aggressive model just prior to being frustrated.

Answer: b
Page: 222

33. In a study by Berkowitz, subjects were made angry in a room containing either a gun or a badminton racket. Later, when given a chance to administer shocks to a "fellow student," subjects who had been in the room with the gun shocked the other person more than those who had been in the room containing the badminton racket. This study demonstrates:
    a. that anger increases the probability of aggressive behavior.
    b. the power of "aggressive cues" in facilitating aggressive behavior.
    c. that thoughts about playing nonviolent sports—such as badminton—tend to reduce the probability of aggression.
    d. that the theory of "catharsis" is unable to explain aggressive behavior.

Answer: d
Page: 222

34. Generalizing from Berkowitz's research, you would predict that a subject who has just watched a "slasher" movie (in which a beautiful young woman gets brutally raped, beaten, and murdered by a man who was an artist) would be more likely to act aggressively against:
    a. male artists.
    b. female artists.
    c. men who look like the murderer.
    d. beautiful young women.

Answer: a
Page: 222

35. The results of Zimbardo's experiment on deindividuation and aggression, in which some subjects "shocked" a confederate while wearing hoods and loose-fitting robes, suggests that:
    a. anonymity reduces concern over social evaluation, and therefore tends to increase aggression.
    b. individuals are usually more aggressive when alone than in groups because there is no one around to make them feel guilty.
    c. individuals are less aggressive when anonymous because they feel more responsible for their behaviors.
    d. anonymity reduces self-esteem, and therefore increases the likelihood of aggressive behaviors.

Answer: c
Page: 222

36. Zimbardo's research suggests that "deindividuation" contributes to aggression. By this, he means that we are more likely to behave aggressively when we are:
    a. angered.
    b. frustrated.
    c. anonymous.
    d. rewarded for aggressive behavior.

Answer: c
Page: 223

37. Brian Mullen studied lynchings perpetrated from 1899 to 1946, and found that the larger the lynch mobs, the more violent the lynchings. This research suggests that:
    a. catharsis is more likely to occur in large crowds than in smaller groups.
    b. aggressive behavior studied in the laboratory differs greatly from behavior in the "real" world.
    c. being a "faceless" member of a crowd lowers inhibitions against destructive acts.
    d. the process of "groupthink" is less powerful in smaller groups.

Answer: c
Page: 223

38. In Bandura's "Bobo doll" study, children who watched an adult act aggressively toward a plastic, air-filled doll:
    a. admired the adult more than if the adult had not acted aggressively toward the doll.
    b. admired the adult less than if the adult had not acted aggressively toward the doll.
    c. not only imitated the adult's aggressive behavior, but also engaged in new forms of aggressive behavior toward the doll.
    d. wanted the adult to be punished for acting aggressively toward the doll.

Answer: b
Page: 223

39. "Bobo doll" studies found that:
    a. children will perform complex modeled responses for the reinforcement of being able to "beat-up a Bobo doll."
    b. children imitated adults who had been aggressive toward a "Bobo doll," and thus learned new forms of physical and verbal aggression through observation.
    c. children would not aggress against the "Bobo doll," especially after watching an adult do so.
    d. after aggressing against a "Bobo doll," children were less likely to engage in hostile behavior toward their playmates.

Answer: b
Page: 224

40. The results of Josephson's study, in which boys watched violent movies of S.W.A.T. killings or high-action movies and were later exposed to a frustrating situation, indicate that:
   a. exposure to violent stimuli reduces the tendency for frustration to provoke aggression.
   b. exposure to violent stimuli strengthens the tendency for frustration to provoke aggression.
   c. violent stimuli have no effect on the relationship between frustration and aggression.
   d. the effects of violent stimuli on aggression are more powerful than the effects of frustrating situations.

Answer: b
Page: 225–226

41. In his study of the effects of televised prize-fights, sociologist David Phillips found that:
   a. the U.S. homicide rate increased after domestic fights, but *not* after overseas fights.
   b. the more publicity surrounding the fights, the greater the increase in homicides in the following days.
   c. the race of the losers of the fights was related to the race of homicide victims—when blacks lost fights, the rate of white (but not black) homicide victims increased.
   d. the effects of televised fights was more pronounced for older men than younger men.

42. In a study by Thomas and colleague, subjects watched either a violent TV police drama or an exciting volleyball game. When subjects later saw an aggressive interaction between two preschool children, people who had watched the volleyball game:
    a. reacted more emotionally compared to people who had watched the police drama.
    b. reacted the same emotionally compared to people who had watched the police drama.
    c. reacted less emotionally compared to people who had watched the police drama.
    d. reacted with a different emotion compared to people who had watched the police drama.

43. Which of the following is NOT a reason cited by Aronson for why media violence might increase aggression?
    a. it may desensitize us to violence and the suffering of others.
    b. it increases physiological arousal.
    c. it may provide ideas about how to imitate aggressive behaviors.
    d. it may weaken inhibitions against aggression.

44. In Donnerstein's study on the effects of pornography, male subjects delivered more intense shocks to a female confederate:
    a. after viewing an erotic film with the female confederate.
    b. after being asked to describe their sexual fantasies.
    c. after viewing an erotic-aggressive film involving rape.
    d. after expressing their views on the "rape myth."

Answer: b
Page: 228–229

45. In experiments on the effects of violent pornography, Malamuth found that:
    a. men engaged in less violent sexual fantasies after watching a film involving rape.
    b. men were more accepting of violence against women after watching violent pornography.
    c. women were more accepting of violence against women after watching violent pornography.
    d. women were more accepting of the "rape myth" after watching violent pornography.

Answer: d
Page: 229

46. The rape myth is the belief that:
    a. rape occurs much more frequently than we believe.
    b. rape occurs mostly with young girls.
    c. when a woman says "no," she means "no."
    d. women, deep down, want to be taken forcefully.

Answer: c
Page: 229

47. Linz and his colleagues found that, compared to men who watched X-rated, but nonviolent, pornography, men who watched R-rated, violent "slasher" films:
    a. were more likely to believe that women found "slasher" movies sexually arousing.
    b. were less likely to believe that "slasher" movies could have harmful effects.
    c. expressed less empathy for victims of rape.
    d. expressed more empathy for victims of rape.

Answer: b
Page: 229–230

48. The effect of violent pornography is:
    a. similar to the effect of other violent media in that it tends to decrease the level of aggression.
    b. similar to the effect of other violent media in that it tends to increase the level of aggression.
    c. different from the effect of other violent media in that it tends to decrease the level of aggression.
    d. minimal, except among men who have unusually high sex drives.

Answer: c
Page: 230

49. Bushman and Bonacci had an experiment in which people watched violent or sexually explicit or neutral TV shows with advertisements. Under which conditions did men and women recall the advertised products?
    a. under the sexually explicit shows because everything was exciting.
    b. under the violent shows condition because they were impressed with the shock value.
    c. under the neutral conditions because their minds were not cluttered.
    d. women could recall the advertisements under all conditions but the males could only do it under the violent conditions.

Answer: b
Page: 233

50. According to Aronson and Hamblin when punishment is applied to children to stop aggression, what happens?
    a. It does not matter if the punishment is mild or harsh, the aggression will immediately stop and the lesson will last for weeks.
    b. Moderate punishment by an adult who previously was warm and nurturing before will work immediately and for a little while later.
    c. Being firm and harsh in one's punishment sends a strong message to a child for a long time.
    d. When tokens were taken away in one study, the boys stopped aggressing so they could get the tokens to earn enjoyable activities.

Answer: d
Page: 234

51. The text describes a situation in which some convicted criminals were released from prison early due to a technicality, whereas others served out their sentences. In comparing these two groups, the primary finding was:
    a. prisoners who were let out early were found to be much less aggressive.
    b. prisoners who were let out early were found to be much more aggressive.
    c. prisoners who served their full term were less than half as likely to return to prison.
    d. prisoners who served their full term were twice as likely to return to prison.

Answer: a
Page: 238

52. According to Feshbach and Feshbach's correlational study of empathy and aggression in children:
    a. as empathy increases, aggression decreases.
    b. as empathy increases, aggression increases.
    c. empathy eliminates aggressive feelings in children.
    d. there is no significant relationship between empathy and aggression in children.

Answer: c
Page: 239

53. Several methods for reducing aggression were discussed in *The Social Animal*. _____ would seem to be the most effective.
   a. Severe punishment or threats of severe punishment
   b. Punishing aggressive models
   c. Building empathy and rewarding alternative behavior patterns
   d. Pure reason

Answer: d
Page: 232–234

54. Five methods for reducing aggressive behavior are discussed in Aronson's text. These are: (a) pure reason, (b) punishment, (c) punishment of aggressive models, (d) rewarding alternative behavior patterns, and (e) building empathy toward others. Of these, the two methods which presently seem to be the most effective are:
   a. a and d
   b. b and c
   c. c and d
   d. d and e

Essay Questions

1. Is aggression instinctive in non-human animals? Is aggressive behavior instinctive among humans—are we "hard-wired" from birth to behave aggressively toward members of our own species? If not, what other kinds of influences affect the human tendency toward aggression? Be specific and cite research evidence to support your arguments.

2. What arguments have been made to support the idea that aggression is necessary for the evolutionary survival of the human species? What research evidence is consistent with this notion of the "survival of the fittest?" Do you agree with this perspective? Why or why not?

3. There is a popular belief that exposure to, or participation in, aggressive behavior is beneficial because it allows people to release their pent-up aggression. What does research on aggression tell us

about this view? What are the implications of this belief as it affects public policy and the mass media (e.g., pornography, children's television programs, sports, etc.)? Be sure to back up your answer with examples of relevant research.

4. Briefly discuss the relationship between frustration and aggression. What other social-psychological factors influence this relationship? Illustrate your discussion with examples of relevant research.

5. Most everyone would agree that reducing human aggression is a worthwhile goal—one that may be crucial to our survival as a species. Among several possible methods of achieving this goal are punishment of aggressive behavior, rewarding nonaggressive behavior, punishment of aggressive models, and building empathy toward others. Choose two of these methods and discuss their relative merits and limitations. Support your answer with relevant research.

7

Prejudice

I. The Effects of Prejudice

  Self-esteem (Clark & Clark; Goldberg; Swim)

II. Stereotypes and Prejudice

  Stereotypes (Bond; Bodenhausen & Wyer; Steele & Aronson)
  Stereotype Threat (Steele & Aronson)

III. Stereotypes and Attributions

  A. "Ultimate attribution error" (Pettigrew)

  B. Gender stereotypes

    Perception of gender differences (Deaux)
    Cultural stereotypes vs. reality (Eagly, Wood, & Swim;
      Feldman-Summers & Kiesler; Deaux & Emsweiler;
      Swim & Sanna)
    Self-defeating beliefs (Nicholls; Stipek & Gralinski; Jacobs &
      Eccles)
    Effect of self-attributions (Turner & Pratkanis)

III. Blaming the Victim

  Belief in a just world (Lerner)
  Hindsight bias (Fischoff; Janoff-Bulman)

IV. Prejudice and Science

  Biased IQ tests
  Women and persuasibility (Janis & Field; Sistrunk & McDavid)

V. Some Subtle Effects of Prejudice

  Biased interactions (Word)
  Belief creates reality (Snyder & Swann)
  Subtle racism (Frey & Gaertner; Devine)

Hostile sexism, benevolent sexism (Glick & Fiske)
Sexism as a nonconscious ideology (Bem & Bem; Hartley;
   Lipman-Blumen)
The effects of gender stereotypes (Porter & Geis; Baron et al.;
   Bem; Jackson & Cash; Horner)

VI.   Prejudice and the Media

Representation of minority groups (Thibodeau)
Representation of women (Geis)

VII.   Causes of Prejudice

    A.   Economic and political competition

       Competition for limited resources (Dollard)
       Competition and intergroup conflict (Sherif)

    B.   The "scapegoat" theory of prejudice

       Lynchings and cotton prices (Hovland & Sears)
       Burakumin of Japan (Klineberg)
       Frustration and scapegoating (Miller & Bugelski)
       Maintenance of self-image

    C.   The prejudiced personality

       The Authoritarian Personality (Adorno et al.; McFarland)

    D.   Prejudice through conformity

       Conforming to prejudiced norms (Pettigrew; Watson)
       Casual exposure to prejudice (Kirkland)

VIII.   Stateways Can Change Folkways (Reducing Prejudice)

    A.   The effects of equal-status contact

       Integrated vs. segregated housing (Deutsch & Collins)

    B.   The vicarious effects of desegregation

       Psychology of inevitability
       Importance of firm policies (Pettigrew; Clark)

C.   But all other things are not always equal

Desegregation and self-esteem (Stephan)

IX.   Interdependence: A possible solution

Mutual interdependence (Sherif; Deutsch; Keenan & Carnevale)
The cooperative classroom: Jigsaw technique (Aronson et al.;
   Desforges)
Underlying mechanisms (Gaertner)
Cooperation and empathy (Bridgeman)
The challenge of diversity

Terms & Concepts

prejudice	self-attributions
stereotyping	hindsight bias
attributions	self-fulfilling prophecy
stereotype threat	nonconscious ideology
"ultimate attribution error"	androgynous
"scapegoat" theory of prejudice	psychology of inevitability
authoritarian personality	mutual interdependence
equal-status contact	jigsaw technique

Chapter Overview

Prejudice refers to a hostile or negative attitude toward a distinguishable group based on generalizations derived from faulty or incomplete information. Such generalizations are based on stereotypes, which result from the tendency to assign identical characteristics to any person in a group, regardless of the actual variation among members of that group. Chapter 7 examines the social-psychological processes involved in stereotyping and prejudice, as well as other causal factors associated with prejudiced attitudes and behavior. In addition, strategies for reducing prejudice are explored. Important issues covered in the chapter are described below.

Stereotyping is closely linked with the human tendency to make attributions, or causal inferences, about behavior. In ambiguous situations, people are especially likely to commit the "ultimate attribution error," which involves making attributions that are consistent with prejudiced attitudes. In a spiraling fashion, such biased attributions serve to reinforce stereotypes and further intensify a person's prejudice. Research on gender roles offers abundant evidence on the effects of stereotypes on attribution processes. For example, attributions regarding women's achievement typically stress the role of luck and effort, whereas male achievement is associated with high ability.

Prejudice can have a subtle, but potent, impact on the behavior of prejudiced individuals as well as the victims of prejudice. Research revealing major differences in the way white interviewers interact with white and black job applicants illustrates this point (Word et al.). Specifically, interviewers unwittingly engaged in a variety of discriminatory, largely nonverbal, behaviors that produced nervous and less effective behavior on the part of black job applicants. The subtle effects of prejudice are also reflected in the phenomenon of the self-fulfilling prophecy, which refers to our tendency to interact with others on the basis of our erroneous beliefs which, in turn, often causes them to act in ways that validate these mistaken beliefs.

The media play an important institutional role in sustaining prejudice. Although some progress has been made in recent decades, research indicates that underrepresentation and media stereotyping of women and minority group members remains fairly common.

Among the important causes of prejudice are political and economic competition for scarce resources, as well as the tendency for majority group members to "scapegoat" minority groups, particularly during troubled times or in the face of frustrating events.

Conformity processes are a key factor in prejudice. According to this view, when people act in a prejudiced manner, they are often simply conforming to the prevailing norms of their social world. Thus, research reveals that when people move to areas where norms are more prejudicial, their prejudice increases (and vice versa). The conformity hypothesis is also supported by evidence indicating that individuals who characteristically conform to a variety of social norms also show strong prejudice when they live in an environment in which bigotry is the norm.

The events surrounding the Supreme Court's 1954 decision calling for school desegregation provide a context for examining the problem of prejudice reduction. An analysis of these events, as well as evidence from social-psychological research, indicate that prejudice is more likely to be reduced when intergroup contact is based on equal-status relations, is clearly supported by authorities, and involves the interdependent pursuit of common goals. Incorporating these factors, the "jigsaw classroom" offers an effective strategy for reducing prejudice in the classroom. The technique involves the use of interdependent learning groups in which each student's academic performance rests on cooperating, rather than competing, with classmates. Carefully conducted field research has documented the success of the jigsaw technique in increasing self-esteem, academic performance, and facilitating the development of empathy.

Lecture Ideas & Teaching Suggestions

Face-ism. A subtle, but intriguing, manifestation of sexism in our culture is reflected in the phenomenon of "face-ism." Research on this topic by Archer and his colleagues has revealed that visual depictions of men and women differ in the extent to which facial features are given prominence. In several studies they found that, on average, male faces were depicted more prominently than female faces in a variety of visual media, including newspaper and magazine photos, works of art, and pictures drawn by college students. Conversely, in portrayals of women, relatively more space was devoted to the rest of the body. In discussing the implications of their findings, Archer and his colleagues note that they are consistent with gender stereotypes and serve to reinforce sexist notions regarding masculine and feminine domains in life: When it comes to the life of the mind, men are perceived as the natural leaders, whereas physical appearance is of greater importance for women.

To illustrate your discussion of face-ism, you might collect photos from newspapers and magazines that reflect this phenomenon. Before introducing the research findings, you can display these photos in class, asking your students if they detect anything unusual about the way men and women are portrayed. For details on how "face-ism" was measured in these studies, see Archer, D., Iritani, B., Kimes, D.D., & Barrios, M. (1983). Face-ism: Five studies of sex differences in facial prominence. *Journal of Personality and Social Psychology, 45,* 725–735.

The Effects of "Solo Status." Underrepresentation in employment, education, and other areas can cause women and minority group members to occupy a "token" status within an organizational setting. What are the effects of being the only member, or one of the few members, of an underrepresented group in a majority-group setting? Research by Shelley Taylor and her associates indicates that, for example, being the only Afro-American in an otherwise White group, or being the only woman in an otherwise all-male group, has considerable impact on how others perceive the person occupying this "solo status." In general, the minority person is perceived as more prominent and influential, is evaluated more extremely, and is more often categorized in stereotypic terms than a comparable individual within a sexually or racially integrated group. In addition, the minority person is typically perceived as playing a greater causal role in events that occur within the group. People also tend to remember more information about a person who occupies a minority position within a group. Taylor and her colleagues offer an information-processing interpretation of these effects: Because information about the solo individual is more salient, it engulfs one's field of attention. In explaining the effects of "solo status" to your students, you may wish to call their attention to the likely impact of tokenism on the minority person. Given what we know about the self-fulfilling prophecy and the confirmation bias (discussed in Chapter 4), how might the effects of salience influence the behavior of the solo individual? For a discussion of research on the effects of solo status, see Taylor, S.E., Crocker, J., Fiske, S.T., Sprinzen, M., and Winkler, J.D. (1979). The generalizability of salience effects. *Journal of Personality and Social Psychology, 37,* 357–368; and Taylor, S.E., & Fiske, S.T. (1978). Salience, attention, and attribution: Top of the head phenomena. In L. Berkowitz (Ed.), *Advances in experimental social psychology* (Vol. 11). New York: Academic Press.

Prejudice and Stereotypes. It is often difficult for people to acknowledge their stereotypes and prejudices about other people—especially for individuals who place a high value on eliminating prejudice from society. One way to stimulate discussion of personal experiences of prejudice is to ask students to describe the kinds of people who drive different makes of cars—such as Cadillacs, BMWs, Mercedes, Volkswagens, Fords, and Hondas. After eliciting students' stereotypes, you can ask them several questions that pertain to stereotyping processes in general. What is the source of their "knowledge" about the drivers of these cars—advertising? family and friends? direct personal knowledge? How accurate do they think these stereotypes are? Do they believe these stereotypes are useful or destructive? Do they feel prejudiced against drivers of certain cars? For example, are they more likely to get angry if they are cut off in traffic by a Cadillac than a VW? If so, why? Finally, you might also want to illustrate in-group/out-group effects (covered in Chapter 4) by asking students if they feel a special sense of "kinship" or liking for others who drive the same kind of car. Do they perceive same-car drivers, as a group, as more unique and differentiated, whereas drivers of another make of car (e.g., Cadillac) are seen as highly similar to each other? In other words, from the in-group perspective, do out-group drivers "all look alike?"

Projects and Discussion Topics

1. PROJECT: Nearly everyone has been the target of blatant or subtle prejudice at some point in their lives. Whether this has been a frequent or rare occurrence for you, write about some of your experiences as a victim of prejudice. What kinds of stereotypes or labels were applied to you? What do you suppose was the cause of the other person's prejudice? How did being a victim of prejudice affect your self-esteem and behavior? What were your feelings and behavior toward the person who treated you in a prejudiced manner? How did you deal with the situation? Were you in any way able to counteract or defend yourself against their attitudes and behavior toward you? If so, how? Share some of these experiences with your classmates.

2. PROJECT: For one day, make a self-conscious effort to create "self-fulfilling prophesies" in your encounters with others by treating them as if you believed they were friendly, compassionate, competent, etc. (For the sake of ethics, restrict yourself to positive behaviors!) Keep a record of how people responded to your behavior, as well as your own reactions to their behavior. How often did they confirm your expectations, and how did you feel when they did? If and when they didn't, how did that make you feel? In general, what was it like to conduct this "experiment"? Write a report of your findings and observations.

3. DISCUSSION: As you know from your readings, competition is one factor that appears to contribute to the problem of prejudiced beliefs and behaviors. Under what conditions is competition more likely to foster prejudice? Would you advocate eliminating all forms of competition as a strategy for reducing prejudice and aggression? Why or why not? Recall some experiences in your own life in which you felt highly competitive with another person or group of people. How did you feel about your "opponents," and how do you

suppose they felt about you? If the period of competition ended or subsided, did your feelings change about this person or group? In what way? Share your experiences and reflections with others in your discussion group.

4. DISCUSSION: To what extent is prejudice a problem on your campus or in your community? If so, what are some subtle—or even blatant—ways that prejudice is expressed? What are the most common forms of prejudice in your social environment (e.g., racism, sexism, basic intolerance for different points of view, etc.)? Imagine you had the authority and resources to reduce prejudice on your campus or community. What kind of strategies would you implement to achieve this goal?

5. DISCUSSION: Is everyone prejudiced to one degree or another? That is, is it possible to be entirely free of prejudice in our society? Why or why not? How could people become more aware of the subtle ways in which they hold or express prejudiced beliefs and behavior? Describe any experiences you might have had in which you suddenly realized you were acting or feeling prejudiced toward another person or group. Were you surprised to discover this about yourself?

Experiential Exercises

1. THE TAG GAME. This little exercise is simple, but it conveys the ideas of prejudice. The professor is to cut out several different shapes out of wrapping paper and then cut out the same shapes out of different paper. This is repeated until there are enough pieces for the entire class. These pieces are randomly distributed to everyone. All the students stand in the middle of class and are asked to form groups based on their piece of paper. Sometimes people focus on the wrapping paper and others on the design. There is an in-group and an out-group. When the groups have formed people are to look at each other's piece of paper. Then the professor says to find a different group and it is repeated another time. It takes about 10 minutes to play and there could be 20 more minutes of oral debriefing. The purpose is to examine our use of labels to include and to exclude others. What labels in real life do people use to include and exclude others?

2. CHATTER. Participants are given a slip of paper describing the norms for their interaction with the group. Some instructions read:

be two feet away from the person you are talking to, be 6 feet away, only look at your feet when you speak, wait 5 seconds to respond, snap your fingers before speaking and so forth. The professor has the students form groups of four or five. They are to discuss any current topic. The discussion lasts 5 minutes. Prejudicial attitudes quickly develop against the person looking at his shoes, the person six feet away and the person who hesitates before he responds. People learn that prejudices can happen for many reasons. This exercise was developed by Thiagi or Sivasailam Thiagarajan and can be purchased from him:

Workshops by Thiagi, Inc.
4423 East Trailridge Rd.
Bloomington, IN 47408
Phone: 823-332-1478

3. THE PREJUDICIAL INTERVIEWER. On page 255 Carl Word and his associates conducted an experiment that dealt with interviewing people for jobs. He found that white male interviews gave several non-verbal prejudicial clues to minorities and caused the minorities to make more mistakes. In class the professor pairs up white males with minorities and women. If there is not an equal number, any two people will do. The interviewer is to interview the potential employee for a summer job. The interviewer should look disinterested, look at his watch often, look at the floor, almost no eye contact, ask very generic questions and tap his pencil. The roles can be reversed after five minutes. During the oral debriefing the non-verbal clues should be examined and the employee's reaction discussed. This is a great example of a self-fulfilling prophecy. Applications to the real world should be made and students should bring examples from their lives during the debriefing.

Additional Readings

Allport, G.W. (1979). (1954). *The nature of prejudice*. 25th anniversary edition. Reading, MA: Addison-Wesley.

Aronson, E. (1975, February). The jigsaw route to learning and liking. *Psychology Today*, pp. 43–50. (Discusses the prejudice-reducing effects of cooperative learning groups.)

Bem, S. (1975, September). Androgyny vs. the tight little lives of fluffy women and chesty men. *Psychology Today,* pp. 58–62. (Research on androgyny is discussed, as well as the benefits—for both sexes—of having a balance of masculine and feminine traits and qualities.)

Bentancourt, H. & López, S.R. (1993). The study of culture, ethnicity, and race in American psychology. *American Psychologist, 48*(6), 629–637.

Blanchard, F.A., Lilly, T. & Vaugn, L.A. (1991). Reducing the expression of racial prejudice. *Psychological Science, 2*(2), 101–105.

Duckitt, J. (1992). Psychology and prejudice: A historical analysis and integrative framework. *American Psychologist, 47*(10), 1182–1193.

Fiske, S.T. (1993). Controlling other people: The impact of power on stereotyping. *American Psychologist, 48*(6), 621–628.

Jaynes, G.D. & Williams, R.M., Jr. (Eds.) (1989). *A common destiny: Blacks and American society.* Washington, D.C.: National Academy Press.

Kiesler, S., Sproull, L. & Eccles, J. (1983, March). Second-class citizens? *Psychology Today,* pp. 40–48. (Examines how girls are discouraged from using and learning about computers.)

Nelson, L.L. & Kagan, S. (1972, September). Competition: The star-spangled scramble. *Psychology Today,* pp. 53–56. (A discussion of the detrimental impact of competitive individualism on children, and the possibilities for learning how to cooperate.)

Rushton, J.P. (1991). Racial differences: A reply to Zuckerman. *American Psychologist, 46,* 983–986.

Sadker, M. & Sadker, D. (1985, March). Sexism in the schoolroom of the 80s. *Psychology Today,* pp. 54–57. (Research reveals that girls get less feedback and encouragement from teachers, as compared to boys.)

Snyder, M. (1982, July). Self-fulfilling stereotypes. *Psychology Today,* pp. 60–68. (When people act on the basis of their stereotypes, they elicit behavior that confirms and reinforces their prejudiced beliefs.)

Stephan, W.G. & Feagin, J.R. (1980). *School desegregation: Past, present and future.* New York: Plenum.

Sun, K. (1993). Two types of prejudice and their causes. *American Psychologist, 48*(11), 1152–1153. (A response to Duckitt.)

Taylor, D. (1984, January). Toward the promised land. *Psychology Today,* pp. 46–48. (A look at the impact of civil rights legislation in education, employment, and housing.)

Zuckerman, M. (1990). Some dubious premises in research and theory on racial differences: Scientific, social, and ethical issues. *American Psychologist, 45,* 1297–1303.

Multiple-Choice Questions

Answer: d
Page: 241–242

1. Clark and Clark conducted a study that found that even very young children preferred white dolls and thought they were prettier than black dolls. This study was used to make the point that:
   a. the authoritarian personality does exist.
   b. stateways change folkways.
   c. the psychology of inevitability is inescapable.
   d. separate is not equal.

Answer: b
Page: 242

2. In Goldberg's study, in which women read an article supposedly written by either John T. McKay or Joan T. McKay, it was found that:
   a. the women rated the article as better written when they thought a woman wrote it.
   b. the women rated the article as better written when they thought a man wrote it.
   c. the women rated the article as better written when they thought a woman wrote it, but were more persuaded by the message when they thought it was written by a man.
   d. the women thought the "male author" was more intelligent, but rated the "female author" as more likable.

Answer: c
Page: 242

3. In Goldberg's study, in which women read an article supposedly written by either John T. McKay or Joan T. McKay, it was found that:
    a. changing one letter in the author's first name from an "h" to an "a" had no effect on the subjects' rating of the article.
    b. subjects rated the article as better written when the author was a woman than when he was a man.
    c. subjects rated the article as better written when the author was a man than when she was a woman.
    d. the quality of the article was rated equal in both conditions, but the subjects were more persuaded by it when the author was a woman.

Answer: c
Page: 243–244

4. According to Aronson, which of the following is NOT a characteristic of a prejudice?
    a. a hostile or unenthusiastic attitude
    b. a negative attitude toward a particular group which is based on faulty or incomplete information
    c. any positive or negative attitude that predisposes the person
    d. an attitude that could lead to hostile action towards a particular group

Answer: a
Page: 244

5. Julia states, "all football players are just a bunch of thick-headed, beer-guzzling oafs." Her statement is best thought of as capturing the essence of:
    a. stereotyping.
    b. the self-fulfilling prophecy.
    c. the psychology of inevitability.
    d. scapegoating.

Answer: c
Page: 244–246,
249

6. Which of the following is NOT a characteristic of a stereotype?
   a. Stereotyping provides a way of justifying our own biases.
   b. Stereotyping leads people to make attributions that are consistent with their prejudiced beliefs.
   c. Stereotypes are relatively flexible and change if individuals are provided with new information that is inconsistent with their beliefs.
   d. Stereotypes tend to generate self-fulfilling prophecies.

Answer: a
Page: 245

7. Bond and his colleagues investigated a psychiatric hospital that had a racially mixed population of patients but was run by an all-white staff. The results of this study revealed that:
   a. harsher methods of handling violent behavior were used against black patients than against white patients.
   b. black patients committed more violent acts while in the hospital than did white patients.
   c. black patients committed fewer violent acts while in the hospital than did white patients.
   d. the staff's prejudiced treatment toward blacks increased over time.

Answer: b
Page: 246

8. Suppose you are a subject in an experiment and are asked to make a parole decision about two criminals, a Latino, José Ortega, and an upper middle class white man, Matthew Smith. Both men were convicted of embezzling funds from the bank in which they worked. Generalizing from a similar study conducted by Bodenhausen and Wyer, you would most likely recommend parole for:
   a. José but not Matthew.
   b. Matthew but not José.
   c. both José and Matthew.
   d. neither José nor Matthew.

Answer: d
Page: 247–248

9. Steele and Aronson administered the verbal portion of the GRE to black and white students, telling them either that the test was measuring their intellectual ability or that it had nothing to do with their intellectual ability. The results of this study revealed that:
   a. in general, students performed better when they thought the test was important, regardless of race.
   b. in general, students performed better when they thought the test was not important, regardless of race.
   c. black students did better than white, when they thought the test was important, but worse when they thought it was not important.
   d. white students did better than black when they thought the test was important, but not when they thought it was not important.

Answer: d
Page: 247

10. What did Steele and Aronson mean by their term, stereotype threat?
   a. The stereotype of a group would be accepted by all people in society.
   b. The minority group would act out more on the stereotypes about violence and display more violence in society, which would threaten many people.
   c. Society would devote more police resources to stop any minority threat to society.
   d. The individuals who are a minority come to believe the cultural stereotypes and they do not perform as well in society.

Answer: a
Page: 248

11. Attribution theory is most concerned with explaining the:
    a. tendency people have to infer the causes of behavior.
    b. tendency people have to make stereotypic statements about minority group members.
    c. tendency people have to derogate themselves.
    d. tendency people have to look for situational explanations for the behavior of others.

Answer: a
Page: 249

12. According to the ultimate attribution error, if subjects thought a harm-doer was black, they would be more likely to attribute his action to _____. When they thought he was white, they would be more willing to attribute his action to

    _____.
    a. his personality; the situation
    b. the situation; his personality
    c. the minority; the majority
    d. the majority; the minority

Answer: c
Page: 249

13. Frank has started working in an office recently where Mary has worked for several years. Mary is prejudiced against Jewish people, and Frank just happens to be Jewish. While eating her lunch at work one day, Mary noticed that Frank had saved his lunch bag after eating—rather than throwing it in the trash. "How cheap can you get?" Mary thinks. "Those Jews won't spend a nickel if they don't have to!" What Mary doesn't know is that Frank is an avid environmentalist who tries to recycle as many resources as he can. Mary's comment is an example of:
    a. scapegoating.
    b. the psychology of inevitability.
    c. the ultimate attribution error.
    d. the self-fulfilling prophecy.

Answer: b
Page: 249

14. The "ultimate attribution error" has been defined by Pettigrew as:
    a. the tendency to attribute one's own failures to the situation.
    b. the tendency for people to make attributions that are consistent with their beliefs or prejudices about others.
    c. the tendency to make situational attributions about another's behavior.
    d. the tendency to attribute another's behavior to both situational and dispositional factors.

Answer: c
Page: 252

15. Mary believes that she got her job as a lawyer because she has the potential to be a great lawyer. Her sister, Patty, believes she got her lawyer's job because her firm "needed to hire a woman." Suppose both women come up against a very difficult case. Which result would you be more likely to expect, based on research conducted by Turner and Pratkanis?
    a. Mary would work more hours, but be more likely to lose.
    b. Patty would work more hours, but be more likely to lose.
    c. Patty would be more likely to give up.
    d. Mary would be more likely to give up.

Answer: b
Page: 252–253

16. In the Lerner experiment, in which subjects observed the experimenter flipping a coin to decide which of two people would be rewarded for his work, it was later found that:
    a. the nonrewarded person was seen as having engaged in the task for its own sake (dissonance effect).
    b. the nonrewarded person was seen as having worked less on the task (blaming the victim).
    c. the nonrewarded person was liked better than the rewarded one (compensation effect).
    d. the rewarded person came to believe that he had worked harder on the task (self-fulfilling prophecy).

Answer: a
Page: 252–253

17. Which of the following is a good example of blaming the victim?
    a. People blaming a lower class person for being poor because they feel he is lazy, stupid. And does not want to work.
    b. People realizing that sometimes lower class people are poor because society has not provided opportunities for good paying jobs.
    c. After a person breaks his leg in a fall down the steps, people might say that the steps were too steep.
    d. A person is robbed at gunpoint, and people feel that this person is a victim of society, which needs more gun control laws.

Answer: c
Page: 252

18. Believing that the world is a "just place" tends to:
  a. create a more just world by inducing the person to treat others as responsible for their own outcomes.
  b. create a more just world by reducing prejudiced beliefs and attitudes.
  c. create a less just world by leading the person to derogate those who have received bad outcomes through no fault of their own.
  d. create a more just world by committing the person to the belief that it is.

Answer: b
Page: 253

19. Jorge states, "I always knew that that white guy Johnson was a sneak. I'm not at all surprised that they finally caught him stealing money out of the cash drawer." Jorge's statement is best thought of as an example of:
  a. an authoritarian personality.
  b. hindsight bias.
  c. the psychology of inevitability.
  d. mutual interdependence.

Answer: a
Page: 254

20. Suppose Fred and Margaret are both being persuaded about the best way to repair lawnmowers and the best way to choose paint colors to decorate a kitchen. Based on the recent work by Sistrunk and David, you would expect:
  a. Fred to be more persuaded about mower repair and Margaret about decorating.
  b. Margaret to be more persuaded about mower repair and Fred about decorating.
  c. Fred to be more persuaded about mower repair and decorating.
  d. Margaret to be more persuaded about mower repair and decorating.

Answer: c
Page: 255

21. What conclusion did Carl Word and his associates arrive at after conducting experiments on whites interviewing minorities for a job?
    a. White male interviewers spent more time with blacks in the interviewing because they did not want to be labeled as prejudicial.
    b. White male interviewers spent more time with women in the interviews because they were aware of affirmative action.
    c. White male interviewers spent less time with blacks and sat further away which caused the interviewee to become more nervous.
    d. White male interviewers spent less time with women but more time with blacks because all the blacks were males and the interviewers identified more with the males than females.

Answer: c
Page: 256

22. Research on the self-fulfilling prophecy conducted by Mark Snyder and his colleagues has revealed that:
    a. women are more likely than men to be influenced by others' beliefs about them.
    b. introverts are less likely than extroverts to test their hypotheses about other people.
    c. even when we're "open-minded" enough to test our beliefs about others, we can inadvertently produce the very behaviors we expect.
    d. when people are offered large rewards for being correct, they are less likely to use a biased strategy in testing their hypotheses about others.

Answer: b
Page: 256–257

23. Frey and Gaertner, in a study involving prejudice and helping, found that:
    a. whites, wishing to look "open-minded," were actually more willing to help a black than a white person.
    b. whites discriminated against a black person only when such discrimination could be easily rationalized.
    c. whites and blacks discriminate against each other equally.
    d. whites discriminated against blacks when their self-esteem was threatened.

Answer: d
Page: 258

24. What conclusion did Glick and Fiske come to with regards to hostile and benevolent sexism?
    a. In some situations hostile sexism can be beneficial for women because they will fight harder against the stereotype.
    b. In general benevolent sexism is good for women because people have positive feelings towards women.
    c. Both hostile and benevolent sexism are limiting to women because they justify relegating women to traditional roles.
    d. In society there are equal amounts of hostile and benevolent sexism.

Answer: a
Page: 260

25. What is Aronson's conclusion about stereotyping and prejudice?
    a. As people accept a minority's out-of-role behavior to break stereotypes, the more the minority person grows and the majority grows too becoming better human beings.
    b. Minority people have to have more pro-active behavior and out-of-role behavior to force society to change.
    c. The majority in society have to learn to accept minorities more so we can become a better society.
    d. Not much can be done to change prejudicial attitudes and stereotypes because these ideas have been around for years and will continue into the future. All we can do is adjust.

Answer: b
Page: 261

26. According to research by Thibodeau, from the 1940s to the 1960s, the number of blacks depicted in stereotypic roles in *New Yorker* cartoons _____.
    a. increased because of more prejudice in society
    b. decreased but still there was only one main black cartoon figure
    c. increased and there were 12 main black figures
    d. decreased and there were 17 main black figures

Answer: d
Page: 263

27. A study by Florence Geis and her colleagues on the effects of television commercials on women's aspirations found that:
   a. women exposed to sex-stereotyped commercials expressed "fear of failure."
   b. women exposed to sex-stereotyped commercials expressed "fear of success."
   c. women who saw commercials in which men were subservient expressed the desire to have careers and never get married.
   d. women exposed to sex-stereotyped commercials displayed lower levels of achievement aspiration than women who saw commercials in which male-female roles were reversed.

Answer: d
Page: 263–264

28. Which of the following is probably NOT a major cause of prejudice as discussed by Aronson?
   a. personality needs, such as authoritarianism
   b. economic or political competition
   c. scapegoating—the displacement of aggression
   d. one's racial background

Answer: b
Page: 265

29. How did America see the Chinese during the 19th century?
   a. The Chinese were defined mostly in negative stereotypes and only in positive terms when it came to their food in restaurants.
   b. The Chinese were defined in negative stereotypes during economic hard times and in very positive terms when their labor was needed for building the railroad.
   c. When the Chinese first arrived in this country they worked very hard and other people recognized their excellent work habits. By the late 19th century it led to greater advances in industry and trade and became known as the model minority.
   d. During the gold rush days there was little prejudice against the Chinese because it was each man for himself.

Answer: b
Page: 266

30. The subject in Sherif's study of two groups, the "Eagles" and the "Rattlers" were:
    a. college students who volunteered to participate for extra credit.
    b. normal 11–12 year old boys.
    c. male college students.
    d. men age 24–27 from various occupations who volunteered to participate for money.

Answer: a
Page: 266

31. After Muzafer Sherif and his associates had arbitrarily divided boys in a summer camp into two groups, they found that intergroup hostility could be created by providing _____ and reduced by providing _____.
    a. competitive activities; cooperative activities
    b. more intergroup contact; less intergroup contact
    c. negative stereotypes; positive stereotypes
    d. oversufficient rewards; insufficient rewards

Answer: c
Page: 267

32. Hovland and Sears found that, from 1882 to 1930, you could predict an increase in lynchings when the price of cotton declined. This information is best thought of as evidence for:
    a. the authoritarian personality.
    b. the ultimate attribution error.
    c. scapegoating.
    d. the self-fulfilling prophecy.

Answer: b
Page: 267

33. Where did the word scapegoat come from?
    a. It came from the Medieval times when Jews were placed in ghettos and would escape from their neighborhood.
    b. Ancient Hebrews had a custom during atonement where the priest placed his hands on the goat and recited the sins of the people. Then they allowed the goat to escape.
    c. The term developed in the south during the slavery days when blacks would escape from a plantation and yet still carry the burden of slavery with them.
    d. The term developed in the 1960s as child abuse research discovered that parents labeled one child and would abuse that child, who was the scapegoat for all the family's problems.

Answer: a
Page: 268

34. Suppose you asked students to write stories about black and white characters. Some students were prejudiced against blacks; others were not. Some students were frustrated just before they wrote the stories and others were not. Generalizing from a similar experiment, you would guess that the group that would write most negatively about blacks in their stories were:
    a. prejudiced, frustrated students.
    b. non-prejudiced, frustrated students.
    c. prejudiced, non-frustrated students.
    d. non-prejudiced, non-frustrated students.

Answer: b
Page: 270

35. Which of the following is NOT a characteristic typical of an "authoritarian personality"?
    a. conventional, generally conservative values
    b. low respect for authority
    c. intolerant of weaknesses
    d. rigidity of beliefs

Answer: d
Page: 270–271

36. Which of the following is NOT characteristic of people to whom Adorno and his colleagues refer as the "authoritarian personality"?
    a. They tend to be rigid and set in their beliefs.
    b. In general, they tend to be intolerant of weakness.
    c. They tend to possess conventional values and standards.
    d. They tend to be authority figures.

Answer: d
Page: 270–271

37. An "authoritarian personality" is closely linked to which of the following dimensions?
    a. mutual interdependence
    b. the matching hypothesis
    c. the self-fulfilling prophecy
    d. prejudice

Answer: d
Page: 271–272

38. Joe was brought up in a household in which both of his parents worked outside the home, and both they and the children shared responsibilities for housework. When Joe left home and went to college, he joined a fraternity and became friends with some members who held rather sexist attitudes towards women's roles. When Joe came home for the summer, his parents were surprised to find that Joe expected his mother to do his laundry and pick up after him. Joe's new attitudes were most likely a function of:
    a. scapegoating.
    b. his authoritarian personality.
    c. the psychology of inevitability.
    d. conformity processes.

Answer: a
Page: 273

39. Studies on conformity and prejudice have shown that:
   a. individuals who move into areas in which the norm is more prejudiced show dramatic increases in their levels of prejudice.
   b. individuals who are least likely to conform to a wide variety of social norms usually show a higher degree of prejudice in environments that are highly prejudiced.
   c. individuals with nonconformist personalities tend to become less prejudiced when they move into areas that are high in prejudice.
   d. conformity to general norms and specific prejudices such as racism are not related.

Answer: d
Page: 274

40. Aronson's argument that "stateways change folkways" is based primarily on:
   a. reactance theory.
   b. the "just world" hypothesis.
   c. conformity pressures.
   d. the theory of cognitive dissonance.

Answer: b
Page: 275

41. According to *The Social Animal,* when important issues are involved, information campaigns:
   a. have been successful in changing prejudiced attitudes when given adequate media coverage.
   b. generally fail because people are unlikely to listen to information that is incompatible with their prejudiced beliefs.
   c. are effective in eliminating distortions and deep-seated prejudiced attitudes when individuals are forced to listen to the information.
   d. are ineffective in changing prejudiced attitudes unless both sides of the issue are presented.

Answer: a
Page: 275–276

42. When it comes to changing deeply rooted attitudes and behavior, such as prejudice, the most effective strategy is to:
    a. place people in a situation in which they must change their behavior, then changes in attitudes will follow.
    b. give people lots of vivid and personal information that contradicts their attitudes, then changes in behavior will follow.
    c. offer people rewards and praise for changing their behavior, then changes in attitudes will follow.
    d. have a highly attractive and credible speaker present arguments that contradict the person's attitudes, then changes in behavior will follow.

Answer: a
Page: 276

43. According to the "psychology of inevitability," if an individual anticipates close contact with a group against which he or she is prejudiced:
    a. that individual will change his or her prejudiced attitude so that it becomes more favorable toward the group.
    b. it will tend to increase that individual's prejudice toward the group.
    c. there will be no change in the individual's attitude because he or she is being forced into the situation.
    d. that individual will pretend to be less prejudiced toward the group, but the real prejudice will not change.

Answer: c   44. In their investigations of the early years of school
Page: 277–278   desegregation, Pettigrew and other researchers
                       found that violence tended to result when:
                       a.   people were not given a choice about whether
                            desegregation would occur.
                       b.   desegregation took place in the South, rather
                            than the North.
                       c.   desegregation policies were implemented in a
                            hesitant, gradual, or inconsistent manner.
                       d.   no efforts were made to reduce prejudice prior
                            to desegregation.

Answer: b   45. In general, early efforts to desegregate the schools
Page: 279   resulted in:
                       a.   an increase in the self-esteem of minority chil-
                            dren, but a surprising decrease in the self-
                            esteem of nonminority children.
                       b.   an unanticipated decrease in the self-esteem of
                            minority children.
                       c.   reduced prejudice among minority children,
                            but not among nonminority children.
                       d.   better academic performance among nonmi-
                            nority children.

Answer: c   46. Aronson argues that the most effective way to
Page: 277   reduce prejudice is to:
                       a.   allow people to choose whether or not they
                            will desegregate so that cognitive dissonance
                            causes them to change their attitudes.
                       b.   use information campaigns to change people's
                            attitudes.
                       c.   require people to desegregate with no options
                            of going back to segregation.
                       d.   try to keep prejudiced groups apart as much as
                            possible to reduce frustration and competition.

Answer: c
Page: 280

47. How did Muzafer Sherif reduce the tension at the camp between the Eagles and Rattlers?
    a. After all the competition between the boys had been created, the head counselor had to sit the boys down and tell them that it was an experiment. The little speech saved the day.
    b. They had a big campfire and all the boys had a good time.
    c. They deliberately broke the water supply system, so it took all the boys in both groups working together to fix it.
    d. The situation got out of hand. The parents had to come and get the boys sooner than was expected.

Answer: b
Page: 280–281

48. Mutual interdependence refers to a situation in which:
    a. you depend on someone else to help you accomplish your goals.
    b. individuals need, and are needed by, one another to accomplish their goals.
    c. individuals allow each other the freedom to accomplish their own independent goals.
    d. individuals compete in a friendly way to accomplish a goal that each person values highly.

Answer: b
Page: 282–283

49. The major feature of jigsaw groups that Aronson believes accounts for their success in reducing the negative effects of prejudice is:
    a. lack of competition among children.
    b. the necessity of depending on all group members for vital information.
    c. the forbidding of any teasing or abuse of minority children.
    d. the breaking down of a large, formal classroom into small, informal groups so the children get a chance to know each other.

Answer: d
Page: 284

50. According to Aronson, which of the following is a result of a jigsaw classroom?
    a. Anglo children experienced a reduction in self-esteem.
    b. Anglo children learned less than in a traditional classroom.
    c. minority children experienced a reduction in self-esteem.
    d. minority children performed better than in a traditional classroom.

Answer: b
Page: 283

51. According to *The Social Animal,* the jigsaw technique was successful because:
    a. it appealed to natural altruistic tendencies in children before they outgrew them.
    b. it capitalized on children's self-interest to do well in school.
    c. teachers played little or no role in the learning process.
    d. cooperation allows everyone to perform equally well in school.

Answer: d
Page: 283–285

52. Suppose you know a black person who feels that he is the victim of sexual discrimination and prejudice. According to experimental data, which of the following strategies will be effective in reducing this prejudice?
    a. competing more aggressively with whites for economic and political power
    b. creating counter-stereotypes aimed at the prejudiced group, such as "whitey"
    c. drawing together with other blacks into highly cohesive groups which do not include whites
    d. working interdependently with white people in situations which allow both an equal status

Answer: a
Page: 283–285

53. Suppose you were a woman who felt she was the victim of sexual discrimination and prejudice. According to experimental data, which of the following strategies will be effective in reducing this prejudice?
    a. working interdependently with men in situations which allow you both an equal status
    b. drawing together into highly cohesive groups which do not include men
    c. assigning women leadership roles to demonstrate they can perform as well as, or better than, men
    d. changing people's attitudes by pointing out the injustice of prejudice against women

Answer: d
Page: 286

54. Recent research has shown that children who cooperate with each other in interdependent classroom situations:
    a. like each other less.
    b. show decreases in their self-esteem.
    c. enjoy school less.
    d. develop more empathy.

Essay Questions

1. What is prejudice and how is it related to the phenomenon of stereotyping? How do stereotypes influence the kinds of attributions that are made regarding the behavior or personalities of members of a stereotyped group? In your answer, provide research examples that illustrate the role of attributions in stereotyping and prejudice.

2. The year is 1954, and the Supreme Court has just made its ruling in the case of *Brown* v. *the Board of Education of Topeka, Kansas.* Desegregation of the schools will proceed. You've been called upon to provide expert social-psychological testimony on how best to implement desegregation. What specific advice would you give policy-makers? What factors should they consider in planning desegregation efforts so that the expected positive outcomes are more likely to occur? Cite research to support your recommendations.

3. Daryl and Sandra Bem suggest that prejudice against women in our society is an example of a "nonconscious ideology." What is meant by this term? Describe at least one piece of research that supports this position.

4. How can economic or political forces foster prejudice between different groups in society? What role does competition and conflict over resources play in this process? Provide one historical example and one piece of research evidence to support your answer.

5. What is meant by the term "authoritarian personality" and how is it used to explain the phenomenon of prejudice? What are the characteristics and origins of this personality type? What research evidence supports or casts doubt on the notion that an "authoritarian personality" is a strong determinant of prejudice?

6. Briefly describe the features of the "jigsaw" classroom by comparing it to the way classrooms traditionally operate. What are the principles underlying the jigsaw technique that promote positive outcomes for students? How is the jigsaw technique related to the development of empathy?

8

Liking, Loving,
and Interpersonal Sensitivity

Terms & Concepts

reward theory of attraction
the foot-in-the-door technique
transsituational rewards
the pratfall effect
gain-loss theory of attraction
Rubin's liking and loving scales
passionate love
companionate love
triangle of love theory
intimacy
passion
commitment

romantic love
consummate love
evolutionary social psychology
exchange relationship
communal relationship
self-disclosure
authenticity
straight talk
feelings vs. judgments
feelings vs. intentions

Chapter Overview

Chapter 8 examines a broad range of social-psychological processes and factors that influence why people like each other. The merits of the reward theory of attraction—that we like those whose attributes or behavior are in some way rewarding to us—are explored, as well as its limitations in covering the full spectrum of phenomena associated with interpersonal attraction. In addition, the characteristics of various forms of attraction and attachment, such as liking and loving, are discussed. Finally, the chapter addresses some of the problems in communication that crop up in long-term, close relationships. Strategies for enhancing communication and intimacy in such relationships are explored in detail. Major points covered in the chapter are outlined below.

Research indicates that, contrary to the common-sense advice of Dale Carnegie, praise and favors are not universally rewarding and, thus, do not always lead to greater attraction. If the praise seems unwarranted, or if we think someone has an ulterior motive in praising us, our liking for the praiser will not increase and, in fact, may even decrease. Similarly, although we do like people who do us favors, getting someone to do us a favor is a more certain way of using favors to increase our attractiveness.

Reward theory suggests that we will like people more if they have pleasant or positive characteristics. While often true, under certain conditions this prediction does not hold. For example, research on the effects of a "pratfall" indicates that a highly competent person is liked more when he or she commits a small blunder than if he or she performed in a perfectly competent manner.

Physical beauty plays an important role in determining whether people will be initially attracted to each other. People also tend to perceive physically attractive people as having more desirable personality traits than less-attractive individuals. These perceptions can have profound effects on how people are treated and how they, in turn, behave toward others. Thus, in a study by Snyder, Tanke, and Berscheid, men who thought they were talking on the phone with an attractive woman rated her more positively, compared to men who thought they were talking with a less-attractive woman. More interestingly, however, independent judges who listened to the woman's half of the conversation—but who did not see her photo—also rated the attractive woman more positively, indicating that the expectations and behavior of the male subject had a strong impact on the behavior of the woman with whom he interacted.

Generally speaking, the single most powerful determinant of whether we like someone is whether that person likes us. Moreover, research indicates that mere perception of being liked can initiate a spiraling series of events that promote increasingly positive feelings and behavior between two people. That is, when we believe someone likes us, we tend to act on those beliefs—treating that person in a friendly, warm manner. Our behavior, in turn, leads the other person to feel liked, and to treat us in a friendly manner.

Although there is a strong relationship between similarity and attraction, other factors can weaken this relationship. For example, research indicates that we are more inclined to like someone whose attitudes are dissimilar to ours, as long as we are secure in the knowledge that this person already likes us—despite our different beliefs. Similarly, when we feel strongly about an issue we tend to find a person more attractive when they initially disagree with us, but are later "converted" to our way of thinking. Research also suggests that, under certain limited conditions, marital satisfaction is greater in relationships in which partners have dissimilar, but complementary, needs and characteristics.

Research on the "gain-loss" theory of attraction reveals that we tend to like someone more if they initially express disliking for us, but gradually come to feel positively toward us. Contrary to reward theory, our attraction is greater under such conditions than if the person had consistently expressed positive views about us all along. Gain-loss theory has important implications for long-term relationships. Over time, the positive regard of people who love us becomes less rewarding; yet, because we have grown accustomed to their affection, their power to hurt us is all the greater when, for whatever reason, they become critical or withhold their affection from us.

Social psychologists draw a distinction between liking and loving, generally viewing these two experiences as qualitatively different. Liking is marked by admiration and friendly affection; loving generally includes feeling of strong attachment, intimacy, and a deep concern for the beloved's welfare. In addition, researchers have developed different ways of classifying love. One theory suggests there are two forms of love: passionate and companionate. Another classification, the triangle of love theory, describes love as some combination of intimacy, passion, and commitment. Both theories make the distinction between love based on strong emotions, sexual desire, and intense preoccupation with the beloved and love that is a milder, more stable experience marked by feelings of trust, dependability, and warmth.

A distinction can be made between communal relationships, where people respond to others based on the others' needs, and exchange relationships, where the focus is on equity between participants. The closer a relationship is, the more communal it is, as demonstrated in research studies.

Honest and sensitive communication plays a vital role in establishing and maintaining intimate relationships over time. Yet, this is no easy matter. A general lesson of our society is to protect ourselves by concealing our feelings and to react defensively to others when engaged in an interpersonal conflict. One strategy for effective communication lies in learning how to use "straight talk" in our dealings with others. Straight talk involves a clear expression of our feelings, rather than blaming or attacking the other person with our negative judgments. This form of communication facilitates conflict resolution by allowing the other person to react to our concerns in a nondefensive manner, thereby preventing negative feelings from escalating.

Lecture Ideas & Teaching Suggestions

The Importance of Self-disclosure. As discussed in Chapter 8, a major obstacle to resolving interpersonal conflicts is the reluctance to reveal one's vulnerabilities. This reluctance inhibits effective communication, making it difficult for people to state their feelings and concerns without becoming defensive and judgmental toward the other person. Similarly, research indicates that self-disclosure is a key ingredient in developing and maintaining a close relationship. One way to augment your coverage of material on intimacy and communication is to provide students with a closer look at the role of self-disclosure in close relationships.

For example, research suggests that in order for intimacy to develop, self-disclosure generally must be reciprocal: as one partner begins to open up and reveal personal information, the other person responds in kind, disclosing information of a similar level of intimacy. Sharing intimate information about oneself implies to the other person that you trust him or her, and it is gratifying to have that trust returned when the other person also self-discloses. An experiment by Chaiken and Derlega (1974) illustrates the importance of reciprocity in self-disclosure. In their study, subjects observed a conversation between two women in which the first woman either disclosed intimate information about a sexual relationship or merely discussed a superficial problem about school. In response, the second woman either disclosed equally intimate or superficial information about herself. Subjects rated the second woman as more likable when she responded in a reciprocal fashion to the first woman's disclosures. When her responses were not reciprocal, she was evaluated negatively. Specifically, subjects perceived her as cold when her self-disclosures were less intimate than the other woman's. When she disclosed more intimate information than the other woman, subjects perceived her as psychologically maladjusted and indicated that they would be unlikely to want her as a friend.

Taking a different approach to the topic of self-disclosure, Derlega and Grzelak (1979) have identified four basic functions it serves for the individual: 1) self-expression—it allows us to "get things off our chests"; 2) self-clarification—it helps us to understand more clearly our own thoughts and feelings; 3) social validation—it provides feedback regarding the appropriateness of our feelings and perceptions; 4) social control—it allows us to influence the other person's impression of us, since we can control how much and what kinds of information we choose to reveal about ourselves.

Details of the above research may be found in: Chaiken, A.L., & Derlega, V.J. (1974). Liking for the norm-breaker in self-disclosure. *Journal of Personality, 42,* 112–129; Derlega, V.J., & Grzelak, A.L. (1979). Appropriate self-disclosure. In G.J. Chelune (Ed.), *Self-disclosure: Origins, patterns and implications of openness in interpersonal relationships.* San Francisco: Jossey-Bass. Finally, for a look at gender differences in self-disclosure, see

Derlega, V.J., & Chaiken, A.L. (1976). Norms affecting self-disclosure in men and women. *Journal of Consulting and Clinical Psychology, 44,* 376–380.

Loneliness. In recent years, researchers interested in love and friendship have increasingly turned their attention to the problem of loneliness, the flipside of intimacy. Research suggests that loneliness is quite common in our society and is frequently experienced by college students, especially those who are living away from home for the first time. As a result, this topic may be of special interest to your students.

How can we tell if someone is lonely? Perlman and Peplau (1982) have defined loneliness as "the unpleasant experience that occurs when a person's network of social relations is deficient in some important way, either quantitatively or qualitatively" (p. 31). Although researchers have offered a number of other definitions, common to all of them is the notion that loneliness is a highly subjective experience that cannot be identified by merely observing someone's behavior. You may wish to illustrate this point by asking students to consider and describe the difference between being "alone" versus being "lonely." For most people, being alone can often be a welcome and enjoyable experience, while loneliness is always associated with negative states of emotion. What are some of these emotions? Rubenstein and Shaver (1982) asked people to describe in detail how they felt when lonely. An analysis of these descriptions yielded four factors: desperation (e.g., feelings of panic and helplessness), depression, impatient boredom, and self-deprecation.

Two forms of loneliness—social and emotional—have been distinguished by Weiss (1973). Social loneliness results from insufficient ties to social networks such as groups of friends, co-workers, clubs, etc. Emotional loneliness arises when a person lacks a deep emotional connection with someone, such as a romantic partner, parents or children, or an intimate friend. A study by Russell, Cutrona, Rose, and Yurko (1984) supports Weiss's distinction. In their survey of 1,000 college students, they found that social loneliness stemmed from a lack of satisfying friendships, while emotional loneliness was associated with the absence of a romantic relationship.

Focusing on situational sources of loneliness, Perlman and Peplau (1982) have identified four kinds of events that tend to precipitate loneliness in most people: 1) when a close relationship ends (e.g., death, divorce); 2) physical separation from loved ones (e.g., moving to a new geographical area); 3) various changes in status (e.g., loss of job, when one's children "leave the nest"); and 4) when, for any number of reasons, the quality of an existing relationship is reduced (e.g., illness of one's partner). As is evident, societal conditions including high geographical and social mobility, rising divorce rates, and chronic unemployment can play an important role in the otherwise very private experience of loneliness.

For more information on this research and other aspects of loneliness, see: Peplau, L.A., & Perlman, D. (1982). *Loneliness: A sourcebook of current theory, research, and therapy.* New York: Wiley; Perlman, D., & Peplau, L.A. (1982). Toward a social psychology of loneliness. In Duck, S. and Gilmur, R. (Eds.), *Personal relationships* (Vol. 3): *Personal relationships in disorder.* New York: Academic Press; Rubenstein, C., & Shaver, P. (1982). *In search of intimacy.* New York: Delacorte; Russell, D., Cutrona, C.E., Rose, J., & Yurko, K. (1984). Social and emotional loneliness: An examination of Weiss's typology of loneliness. *Journal of Personality and Social Psychology, 46,* 1313–1321; Weiss, R.S. (1973). *Loneliness: The experience of emotional and social isolation.* Cambridge, MA: MIT Press.

Romantic Jealousy.   What can social psychology tell us about jealousy in relationships? White (1981) has observed that two factors are generally involved in any jealous reaction: feelings of personal inadequacy and the desire for an exclusive relationship. In addition, he proposes that a person who experiences romantic jealousy is threatened with two basic losses: the loss of the actual rewards provided by the relationship, and the loss of self-esteem that results from rejection by one's partner. An investigation by Mathes, Adams, and Davies (1985) supports White's theory. They asked subjects to imagine losing a romantic partner due to several factors, including: a) a rival (partner leaves you for someone else); b) rejection (no rival, partner simply ends relationship); c) destiny (e.g., partner takes a new job in a distant city); or d) fate (death by car accident). In all cases, losing the partner involved the loss of the rewards provided by the relationship. However, they predicted that the self-esteem component of jealousy would be engaged when the relationship ended due to simple rejection or being replaced by a rival. This is exactly what they found. Jealous reactions were greatest when subjects imagined their partners leaving them for someone else, and least when the relationship was lost due to fate. Thus, a threat to the individual's self-esteem appears to play a central role in the experience of romantic jealousy. Mathes et al. also found that each component of White's theory of jealousy was associated with a different emotion. Loss of esteem tended to provoke anger, while loss of relationship-rewards generally produced feelings of depression.

Details of this research may be found in: White, G.L. (1981). A model of romantic jealousy. *Motivation and Emotion, 5,* 295–310; Mathes, E.W., Adams, H.E., & Davis, R.M. (1985). Jealousy: Loss of relationship rewards, loss of self-esteem, depression, anxiety, and anger. *Journal of Personality and Social Psychology, 48,* 1552–1561.

Projects and Discussion Topics

1. PROJECT: Make a list of your attitudes and preferences in a variety of domains, including: music, movies, politics, religion, as well as a variety of social issues such as capital punishment, abortion, the environment, nuclear arms, affirmative action, etc. Ask a couple of close friends to indicate their attitudes and preferences on these issues. Next, ask a couple of people you have known for a while—but have not become friends with—to describe their views on these same issues. Compared to your acquaintances, are your friends' attitudes more similar to your own? What role do you think similarity plays in your relationship with your close friends? If they were to change their minds on some of the issues in which your views agreed, do you think it would affect your friendship and your feelings for them? If so, which issues would have the greatest impact on your relationship? If your friends' attitudes are somewhat or highly dissimilar to your own, what other characteristics of your friendship do you think compensate for this fact? Write a brief report describing your observations and reflections on this exercise.

2. PROJECT: How common is the gain-loss effect in relationships? Have you ever experienced it? For example, have you ever started off knowing or believing someone didn't like you, but later found out that he or she did? Did his or her attraction to you seem particularly rewarding as a result? Similarly, have you ever felt "taken for granted" by a good friend and, then, after withdrawing your interest or affection, found your friend was especially eager to re-establish good relations with you? Have you ever found yourself on the "other end" of this kind of relationship—where you initially disliked someone, but later grew to like him or her? Or where you took a friend for granted, and later felt hurt or insecure when he or she seemed to be ignoring you? Write a report of your experiences, using the "gain-loss" theory of attraction to analyze them. Ask a

few friends the same questions to see if their experiences are similar to your own, and include them in your report.

3. PROJECT: Research on physical attractiveness indicates that people tend to form long-term relationships with others whose level of physical attractiveness "matches" theirs. Search through copies of your local or regional newspaper for the wedding or engagement announcements, which are usually accompanied by pictures of the newlyweds or engaged couples. (These announcements are typically published once a week in the "features" section of the newspaper. If only a few photos are published, you may need to find several back copies of the newspaper at your campus or public library.) Look at the pictures of the couples carefully. Is there a tendency for both people to be equally attractive? Bring your newspaper clippings to class and report your findings.

4. PROJECT: Create a scenario in which you and someone you care about are involved in an interpersonal dispute. In writing the scenario, first describe why you and/or the other person are hurt and angry with each other. Then, go on to create a dialogue in which you and your friend communicate defensively about the problem—accusing, judging, making excuses, etc. Describe how the conflict ended, how you felt during and after the interaction, as well as how your friend felt. In the past, have you had real experiences similar to this one? Next, re-write the scenario, but in this version have you and your friend engage in "straight talk." How do you feel about the interaction this time around? How does your friend feel? What obstacles, if any, do you foresee in using "straight talk" with your friends and loved ones in your everyday life? In your report, present your scenarios and reflections on this exercise.

5. DISCUSSION: Based on the experiments you have read about, how important are "good looks" in determining whether one person is attracted to another? Do these findings correspond with your own personal experience? Apart from the research evidence, how important do you think physical attractiveness *should* be in friendship and love?

6. DISCUSSION: In our society, it is relatively uncommon for people to use "straight talk" in their relationships. Why do you think this is so? What are the personal and societal obstacles to using "straight talk," and how might they be overcome? For example, do

you think children should be taught in school how to engage in effective communication and conflict resolution? Would it be feasible for them to practice such techniques with teachers and other authority figures, as well as peers? Finally, are there circumstances in which you feel it would be unwise to engage in "straight talk"? If so, what are those circumstances?

7. DISCUSSION: In small groups, students can take turns role-playing a scenario in which two friends or romantic partners are involved in a conflict. (For example, one friend/partner might be angry because the other showed up two hours late to go to a party they had planned to attend.) To begin with, the role-players should attempt to resolve their dispute by using defensive and ineffective forms of communication—accusing, blaming, and judging each other. After finishing, the actors should take turns describing their experience during the interaction, explaining how the other person's comments made them feel and why they responded as they did. Next, the same partners should "re-play" their scenario, this time using "straight talk" to the best of their ability. Again, the actors should discuss how they felt during the interaction, and whether they found themselves slipping back into ineffective patterns of communication. Meanwhile, the audience should observe the interaction, reserving their comments until after each performance is completed and the actors have had a chance to speak. Using different scenarios, take turns with role-playing so everyone in the group who wants to participate can do so. (Note: If students have conducted Project 4, their scenarios can be used for this role-playing exercise.)

Experiential Exercises

1. ROOMMATES. The professor can develop a short questionnaire with 10 questions dealing with roommate issues. These can deal with smoking in the room, cleanliness, time to study, sharing food, having friends over and many more. The questionnaires are filled out by individuals. Then the class mingles for 5 minutes to locate others who agree on one major issue. Three or four of them form a roommate group and sit down. They go through each issue and see if they agree or disagree and try to compromise. Then they prioritize their list from most important to least important.

During the oral debriefing the discussion can revolve around what norms did they set for their group. If people feel comfortable, they might discuss the reasons a person would work or not work out in the group. The best place to handle the liking question is a written debriefing paper. It is not just personality characteristics, but it is also agreement on key issues that make up a good room-mate mix.

Petranek Consulting Services, Inc. has developed this value game, ROOMMATES. There are three others, PARTNERS (marriage), TASKS (employment), and SPIRITUALITY (where people find the spirit in their lives) that tackle the issue of liking someone. These experiential exercises lend themselves to good classroom discussion and analysis papers. These value exercises can be purchased from:

Petranek Consulting Services, Inc.
2712 Harmony Way
Evansville, IN 47720
Phone: 812-426-1617

Additional Readings

Adams, V. (1980, May). Getting at the heart of jealous love. *Psychology To-day*, pp. 38–47, 102–108. (Reviews research on types and causes of jeal-ousy, as well as gender differences in jealous behavior.)

Batson, C.D. (1990). How social an animal? The human capacity for caring. *American Psychology, 45,* 336–346.

Berscheid, E. (1985). Interpersonal attraction. In G. Lindzey & E. Aronson (Eds.), *Handbook of social psychology.* New York: Random House.

Brehm, S. (1985). *Intimate relationships.* New York: Random House.

Cash, T.F. & Janda, L.H. (1984, December). In the eye of the beholder. *Psychology Today*, pp. 46–52. (Examines the role of physical attractiveness in dating preferences, employment, and other areas.)

Chapdelaine, A., Kenny, D. & LaFontana, K. (1994). Matchmaker, match-maker, can you make me a match? Predicting liking between two unac-quainted persons. *Journal of Personality and Social Psychology, 67*(1), 83–91.

Davis, K.E. (1985, February). Near and dear: Friendship and love compared. *Psychology Today*, pp. 22–30. (Similarities and differences between love and friendship are explored.)

Hatfield, E. & Sprecher, S. (1986). *Mirror, mirror: the importance of looks in everyday life.* Albany, NY: State University of New York Press.

Hendrick, C. & Hendrick, S. (1983). *Liking, loving and relating.* Monterey, CA: Brooks/Cole.

Hogan, R., Curphy, A.J. & Hogan, J. (1994). What we know about leadership: Effectiveness and personality. *American Psychologist, 49*(6), 493–504.

McGue, M. & Lykken, D.T. (1992). Genetic influence on risk of divorce. *Psychological Science, 3*(6), 368–373.

Psychology Today. (1994, March/April). (Three feature articles are devoted to the study of love.)

Thompson, B. & Borrello, G.M. (1992). Different views of love: Deductive and inductive lines of inquiry. *Current Directions in Psychological Science, 1*(5), 154–156.

Trotter, R.J. (1986, September). The three phases of love. *Psychology Today.* September 1986, pp. 46–54. (A discussion of Sternberg's three-dimensional theory of love, which involves commitment, intimacy and passion.)

Walster, E. & Walster, W. (1978). *A new look at love.* Reading, MA: Addison-Wesley.

Multiple-Choice Questions

Answer: c
Page: 290–291

1. The general reward theory of attraction is based upon which of the following basic principles?
   a. The more often we see another person (repeated exposure), the more we will like him or her.
   b. The more control we can exert over another person, the more we will like him or her.
   c. We tend to like a person whose behavior provides us with maximum reward at minimum cost.
   d. We tend to like a person who grows to like us after initially disliking us.

Answer: d
Page: 292

2. The advice given by Dale Carnegie, if one wishes to "win friends," is most consistent with which of the following theories?
   a. cognitive dissonance theory
   b. self-perception theory
   c. the gain-loss theory of attraction
   d. reward theory

Answer: d
Page: 292

3. Suppose you turn in a paper that is graded by two professors. Professor Jones is very complimentary whereas Professor Smith is very critical of your work. Generalizing from the results of a similar experiment described in the text, you would believe that Professor _____ is more intelligent and you would like best Professor _____.
   a. Jones; Jones
   b. Smith; Smith
   c. Jones; Smith
   d. Smith; Jones

Answer: d
Page: 293

4. As Edward Jones says, "Flattery will get you some-where," except when:
   a. you are flattering a person with very high self-esteem.
   b. the person overhears you saying good things about him or her to somebody else.
   c. the person you are flattering is too often flat-tered by others.
   d. the person you are flattering thinks you are trying to manipulate him or her.

Answer: d
Page: 293–294

5. When people do favors for us, we:
   a. only like them better when our self-esteem is low.
   b. only like them better if the favor was unantici-pated.
   c. don't like them better, because they seem supe-rior and make us feel insecure.
   d. only like them if we don't feel indebted to re-turn the favor.

Answer: b
Page: 294–295

6. If you persuade someone to do you a favor, it is likely that:
   a. he or she will like you less.
   b. he or she will like you more.
   c. you will like him or her less because you feel indebted.
   d. his or her self-esteem will decrease.

Answer: b
Page: 294–295

7. In general, getting someone else to do you a favor is _____ effective in increasing his liking for you than your doing a favor for him, due to _____.
   a. less; his negative reinforcement
   b. more; his dissonance reduction
   c. less; your dissonance reduction
   d. more; your positive reinforcement

Answer: b
Page: 296

8. Aronson's text describes an experiment in which subjects watch a victim supposedly receive electric shocks. Subjects were given the opportunity to vote as to whether the victim should continue to receive the shocks, and the shocks were either terminated or not. Which group of subjects came to like the victim most?
    a. those who voted to terminate the shocks, but the shocks were not terminated
    b. those who voted to terminate the shocks, and the shocks were terminated
    c. those who voted to not terminate the shocks, but the shocks were terminated
    d. those who voted to not terminate the shocks, and the shocks were not terminated

Answer: b
Page: 298

9. Suppose you are observing a highly popular and well-respected politician and a college student eat lunch. Both proceed to spill gravy on their neckties. Generalizing from research cited in Aronson, your liking of the politician will most likely _____ and your liking of the college student will _____.
    a. increase; increase
    b. increase; decrease
    c. decrease; decrease
    d. decrease; increase

Answer: a
Page: 298

10. When a near-perfect person commits a blunder, his or her attractiveness generally _____. When a mediocre person commits the same blunder, his or her attractiveness generally _____.
    a. increases; decreases
    b. stays the same; decreases
    c. decreases; decreases
    d. decreases; increases

Answer: c
Page: 299

11. In studies of "the pratfall effect," Deux has shown that men prefer a _____, but women are more likely to prefer a _____.
    a. highly competent male blunderer; highly competent female blunderer
    b. highly competent female blunderer; highly competent male blunderer
    c. highly competent male blunderer; highly competent nonblunderer, regardless of sex
    d. highly competent blunderer, regardless of sex; highly competent nonblunderer, regardless of sex

Answer: b
Page: 299–300

12. In a study by Walster and her associates, in which students were randomly matched for a computer date after taking a battery of psychological tests, it was found that:
    a. intelligence and attitude similarity were significantly related to mutual liking.
    b. the physical attractiveness of the individuals involved was significantly related to mutual liking.
    c. complementary needs such as dominance/submissiveness were significantly related to mutual liking.
    d. comparable levels of self-esteem were significantly related to mutual liking.

Answer: c
Page: 299–300

13. Walster and her colleagues randomly matched incoming students to determine what they looked for in a potential blind date. Which of the following characteristics best determined whether or not subjects liked each other?
    a. a sense of humor
    b. intelligence
    c. physical attractiveness
    d. similarity of attitudes

Answer: a
Page: 299–300

14. From a study in which college students were subjects in a "computer dating" experiment, the primary determinant of how much subjects initially liked their dates was:
    a. the date's physical attractiveness.
    b. the date's personality.
    c. the date's sensitivity.
    d. the similarity of attitudes and backgrounds of the experiment's participants.

Answer: a
Page: 300

15. Generalizing from research presented in the text, on a first date, the partner people like most is the one whose physical attractiveness _____; in long-term relationships, they prefer a partner whose physical attractiveness _____.
    a. is greatest; matches their own level of attractiveness
    b. is greatest; is greatest
    c. matches their own level of attractiveness; matches their own level of attractiveness
    d. matches their own level of attractiveness; is greatest

Answer: d
Page: 300

16. According to research on dating, people:
    a. with low self-esteem are more selective about whom they will accept as dates, because they are less willing to take risks.
    b. with low self-esteem are more likely to initiate interactions with attractive people, since they have less to lose by being rejected.
    c. with high self-esteem are less likely to initiate interactions with attractive people, because they want to protect their self-esteem.
    d. tend to have relationships with someone who matches their level of physical attractiveness.

Answer: d
Page: 300

17. Dion and her colleagues showed subjects pictures of attractive, average, and unattractive people. The results of her study indicated that:
    a. men prefer attractive men and women, but women prefer average men and women.
    b. men and women prefer attractive people of the opposite sex but average people of the same sex.
    c. men prefer attractive women and average men whereas women prefer average men and attractive women.
    d. all subjects preferred attractive people regardless of sex.

Answer: a
Page: 301

18. In an experiment by Karen Dion and Ellen Berschied concerning physical attractiveness in children, it was found that:
    a. physically attractive boys were liked better than unattractive boys.
    b. unattractive boys were perceived as less aggressive than attractive boys.
    c. physically attractive children got better grades than unattractive children.
    d. teachers tended to feel more compassion for the unattractive children.

Answer: c
Page: 301–302

19. Dion asked women to examine reports of behavior disturbances caused by attractive and unattractive boys and girls. Which group of children were most likely to be blamed for the disturbance and thought to be chronic trouble makers?
    a. unattractive boys
    b. unattractive girls
    c. unattractive boys and girls
    d. unattractive boys and attractive girls

Answer: d
Page: 302

20. According to Frieze and her associates, how are attractiveness and salary related for men and women?
   a. For both attractive men and women their starting salary was higher than people who were not as attractive.
   b. Attractive men had their starting salaries higher but it was not higher over the years. Attractive women got paid the same when they started and over the years because it was a patriarchal system.
   c. For attractive women their starting salary was not affected and neither was their salary over several years.
   d. Attractive men had higher starting salaries and earned more money over many years. Attractive women had only higher salaries over the years and for their starting salary.

Answer: c
Page: 303–304

21. What did Downs and Lyons discover with judges making decisions with male and female defendants charged with a misdemeanor or a felony and their physical attractiveness?
   a. Both attractive males and females got lower bail and lower fines when charged with a misdemeanor or a felony.
   b. Attractive females got lower bail and lower fines when charged with a misdemeanor or a felony, but it was not true for attractive males.
   c. Attractive males and females got lower bail and lower fines when charged with a misdemeanor, but when a felony was involved, there was no difference between attractive males and females and unattractive males and females.
   d. Attractive males received lower bail and lower fines for both a misdemeanor and a felony, but this did not apply to attractive females.

Answer: d
Page: 302–303

22. Harold Sigall and Elliot Aronson conducted an experiment in which a female confederate was made up to appear either physically attractive or unattractive. Posing as a graduate student in clinical psychology, she interviewed college men and evaluated half favorably and half unfavorably. The results showed that:
    a. she was disliked more when she was homely than when she was attractive, regardless of the evaluation she gave.
    b. she was disliked more when her evaluation was negative than when it was positive, regardless of her physical attractiveness.
    c. she was well-liked in every condition except the one in which she was unattractive and also gave a negative evaluation.
    d. when she was attractive, the kind of evaluation she gave had a strong effect on men's liking for her, but when she was unattractive, it had virtually none.

Answer: b
Page: 303–304

23. In their study of the influence of physical attractiveness on court decisions, Downs and Lyons found that:
    a. judges assessed lower fines and bail only for attractive women.
    b. judges assessed lower fines and bail for attractive defendants only when misdemeanors were involved.
    c. judges assessed higher fines and bail for unattractive males only when felonies were involved.
    d. judges assessed similar fines and bail for both attractive and unattractive defendants.

Answer: a
Page: 304

24. Suppose you see two men. One is sitting with a highly attractive woman. The other is with an unattractive woman. Generalizing from research presented in Aronson:
   a. the man with the attractive woman will be seen as friendlier and more self-confident.
   b. the man with the unattractive woman will be seen as friendlier and more self-confident.
   c. there will be an interaction; only attractive men benefit from sitting with unattractive women.
   d. the attractiveness of the woman does not generalize to the man.

Answer: a
Page: 305–306

25. The main reason we tend to like people whose opinions are similar to our own is probably that they:
   a. provide consensual validation for our beliefs.
   b. have backgrounds similar to ours.
   c. are better able to empathize with us.
   d. keep us from having to consider alternative opinions.

Answer: a
Page: 306

26. What does Aronson say is one of the most powerful determinants of whether you will like another person?
   a. if that person likes you
   b. if that person and you are about equally attractive
   c. if that person and you have similar attitudes
   d. if you have high self-esteem

Answer: b
Page: 307

27. In Walster's experiment in which women were asked for a date by a young man prior to receiving favorable or unfavorable personality evaluations from a psychologist, the results showed that subjects:
   a. liked the young man more when the evaluation was positive, since he was associated with a reward.
   b. liked the young man more when the evaluation was negative, because he gave their lowered self-esteem a greater boost.
   c. liked the young man more when the evaluation was positive, because they felt they deserved to be asked for a date.
   d. expected the date to be less enjoyable when the evaluation was negative.

Answer: c
Page: 307–308

28. Suppose you are a young man who asks a young woman for a date, and she accepts. Assuming that the following situations occurred prior to your date, which of them would probably cause your liking for her to increase?
   a. You just saw a psychologist, who gave you a positive evaluation of your personality.
   b. Because you felt indebted to her, you went to a lot of trouble to get tickets for the play you will see.
   c. She turned you down on two previous occasions before accepting this date.
   d. Some of her attitudes were similar to yours and some were not.

Answer: a
Page: 308

29. Suppose two young men had taken a test of intelligence. Ralph believed he did very well and Fred believed he did poorly. Both have the occasion to meet a young woman. Which of the following best describes how they would most likely react, based on her physical attractiveness?
   a. Ralph would like her more if she is attractive, Fred if she is unattractive.
   b. Fred would like her more if she is attractive, Ralph if she is unattractive.
   c. Ralph and Fred would both like her more if she is attractive.
   d. In this instance, attractiveness would not be related to how much the men like the woman.

Answer: a
Page: 308–309

30. According to research conducted by Grube and his colleague, compared to men with low self-esteem, men who have a favorable view of themselves tend to:
   a. be attracted to women who are assertive and independent.
   b. be attracted to women who are willing to do them favors.
   c. be attracted to women who are submissive and dependent.
   d. be attracted to women who play "hard to get."

Answer: b
Page: 309

31. Generalizing from research conducted by Rubin, if you were an unattractive man and wanted your physical unattractiveness to not influence whether women would date you or not, you would be best advised to go into which of the following occupations?
   a. iron worker
   b. physician
   c. bartender
   d. plumber

Answer: b
Page: 309–310

32. The gain-loss theory of attraction predicts that:
    a. you like people more when they say all positive things about you than if they say some negative things.
    b. you like people more when they begin by disliking you and gradually increase their liking for you.
    c. you like people more when they initially like you and then gradually decrease their liking for you.
    d. the more people like you, the less you like them.

Answer: c
Page: 309–310

33. When someone is initially critical of you and later becomes complimentary:
    a. you tend to distrust him or her.
    b. you like him or her less because you suspect flattery.
    c. you like him or her more than someone who has always been complimentary.
    d. you like him or her less than someone who has always been complimentary.

Answer: d
Page: 311–313

34. In Aronson and Linder's "gain-loss" experiment, subjects overheard a confederate give a series of evaluations of them which were (1) consistently positive, (2) consistently negative, (3) negative and then increasingly positive (gain), and (4) positive and then increasingly negative (loss). The results showed that, in terms of mean liking for the confederate, subjects rated (from positive to negative) the confederates as follows:
    a. 1 4 3 2
    b. 1 3 4 2
    c. 3 1 4 2
    d. 3 1 2 4

Answer: a
Page: 311–313

35. You are at a party and are engaged in a discussion with someone you just met. The topic is capital punishment, an issue you feel very strongly about. Based on your discussion, your chances of liking this person will be greatest if he or she:
a. initially disagrees with you, but ultimately comes to accept your position.
b. shows integrity by refusing to be persuaded to adopt your position.
c. consistently agrees with your position.
d. forces you to think up good arguments to defend your beliefs.

Answer: b
Page: 311–313

36. Suppose you take a class from each of the following four professors: 1, 2, 3, and 4. You write five papers and get the following grades: 1: A A A A A, 2: D D C B A, 3: A A B C F, 4: D D C D D. Generalizing from Aronson, which professor will you like the most?
a. 1
b. 2
c. 3
d. 4

Answer: c
Page: 316–317

37. Your friend Ellen is talking to you about Jim, a guy she's been dating now for six months. In describing their relationship, Ellen says, "If Jim and I stopped seeing each other, I would be miserable. I feel I can confide in him about virtually anything!" Based on Rubin's research, which of the following conclusions would you be likely to draw?
a. Ellen is too dependent on Jim and may get hurt.
b. Ellen is living in a fantasy world.
c. Ellen loves Jim.
d. Ellen and Jim's love will not endure because there has to be more passion.

Answer: c
Page: 316–317

38. Compared to passionate love, companionate love tends to:
    a. assume less importance in a long-term relationship.
    b. decline over the course of a relationship.
    c. deepen over the course of a relationship.
    d. be rapid in onset.

Answer: c
Page: 317

39. According to Sternberg, romantic love is the combination of:
    a. commitment and intimacy.
    b. commitment and passion.
    c. intimacy and passion.
    d. commitment, intimacy, and passion.

Answer: c
Page: 317–318

40. "I think you are an extremely attractive person." From which of the following sources would this statement probably have the greatest positive effect on your self-concept?
    a. a close friend
    b. your spouse
    c. an attractive stranger
    d. someone who just did you a favor

Answer: c
Page: 319

41. In Joanne Floyd's experiment, young children were asked to share trinkets with another child, who was either a close friend or a stranger. They were led to believe that the other child was acting in either a generous or a stingy manner toward them. The results showed that:
    a. they were stingy to stingy strangers and to stingy friends.
    b. they were generous to generous strangers and to generous friends.
    c. they were generous to stingy friends and to generous strangers.
    d. they were generous to generous friends and to stingy strangers.

Answer: c
Page: 321

42. Higher levels of satisfaction in marriage tend to be associated with:
    a. long, uninterrupted periods of harmony, marked by few disagreements.
    b. a nontraditional attitude regarding the roles of men and women.
    c. a nonaggressive, but confrontational, style of resolving conflicts.
    d. the couple's willingness to frequently express their positive feelings toward each other.

Answer: d
Page: 324

43. "Straight talk" refers to a style of communication in which:
    a. you tell a person directly what you think of him or her, without beating around the bush.
    b. people discuss their conflicts face-to-face rather than complaining about each other to someone else.
    c. people can resolve all of their conflicts, without any discomfort.
    d. you offer a clear statement of your feelings and concerns, without accusing or judging the other person.

Answer: b
Page: 324

44. Which of the following statements provides the best illustration of "straight talk"?
    a. "You wouldn't act like that if you really cared about me."
    b. "I've been feeling competitive with you ever since you got that promotion."
    c. "If you want to act like a phony, the choice is yours."
    d. "Don't be upset—I didn't mean to hurt your feelings."

Answer: a
Page: 324

45. The general lesson of our society is to hide one's vulnerabilities from another person. This strategy:
    a. often results in defensiveness and poor communication.
    b. is seldom useful in some situations, especially when dealing with a true enemy.
    c. is essential for survival in our society.
    d. prevents us from understanding why we feel vulnerable.

Answer: a
Page: 324

46. According to Aronson, open and effective communication is especially difficult in many situations because:
    a. people are not fully aware of their own needs and feelings.
    b. people express their feelings without making sure the other person is ready to hear about them.
    c. people have no trouble expressing their negative feelings, but are less likely to express their positive feelings.
    d. one person almost always takes more blame and responsibility for the conflict than the other.

Answer: c
Page: 325

47. In communicating effectively with another person, giving that person immediate feedback regarding your own feelings is useful:
    a. because it keeps the person from having his or her feelings hurt.
    b. because it prevents disagreements from occurring.
    c. because it increases the person's insight into the impact of his or her actions.
    d. because it prompts disagreements to occur that can be resolved.

Answer: a
Page: 325–326

48. According to Aronson, expressing one's feelings, rather than one's judgments about another person, is important primarily because:
   a. expressing feelings is less hurtful than expressing judgments.
   b. people need to know whether their feelings are legitimate.
   c. it's not right to feel judgmental about another person.
   d. expressing our feelings makes the other person feel trusted.

Essay Questions

1. What does the reward theory of attraction predict regarding the probability that we will like people; a) who are similar to us? b) who do us favors? c) who evaluate us positively? d) who are highly competent? Given your knowledge of research on interpersonal attraction, to what extent are the above predictions supported or open to question? Illustrate your answer with specific examples of research.

2. Mary has just made a new acquaintance. She wants to be liked by this person and would like to see a friendship develop. What characteristics of interpersonal attraction might she want to consider to achieve her goals? Discuss three studies from your readings on interpersonal attraction and their implications for Mary's situation.

3. Describe both the reward theory of attraction and the gain-loss theory of attraction. How do these two theories differ in their predictions regarding the conditions under which people come to like each other? Discuss a research finding that supports one theory over the other.

4. To what extent are physically attractive people perceived and treated differently than less-attractive people? What effect, if any, does this treatment have on their behavior? In more general terms, what is the role of "good looks" in determining whether people are attracted to each other? Support your answer with examples of relevant research.

5. What kinds of distinctions have social psychologists made between liking and loving, as well as different forms of love? What are the characteristics of these various forms of attachment and attraction? Are they mutually exclusive within a given relationship, or do they have the capacity to co-exist?

6. The gain-loss theory of attraction suggests that individuals are likely to face certain obstacles in maintaining a long-term, loving relationship. What is the nature of these problems? How, and to what extent, might these problems be reduced?

7. Define the term "straight talk" and discuss its relevance to interpersonal sensitivity and communication. What are the important characteristics of this form of "feedback" that make it effective? Why is it so often so difficult to engage in straight talk when communicating with other people? Give an example of how a person might deal with an interpersonal conflict by using "straight talk" and contrast it with how someone might approach the same problem using a less-effective approach to communication.

9

Social Psychology as a Science

Terms & Concepts

experimental condition	third factors
extraneous variables	correlated variables
independent variable	experimental realism
dependent variable	mundane realism
cause and effect	cover story
random assignment	debriefing

Chapter Overview

Chapter 9 provides a discussion of the major features and advantages of the experimental method in social psychology. The difficulties posed by laboratory experimentation—both methodological and ethical—are also addressed. To illustrate these important issues, experiments introduced in earlier chapters are examined in detail. Highlights of the chapter are summarized below.

The use of random assignment constitutes the crucial difference between experimental and nonexperimental approaches. Under conditions of random assignment, each subject has an equal chance to be in any condition in the study. Thus, if we find a difference between conditions in an experiment, it is unlikely that this would be due to individual differences in any single characteristic—since all of these characteristics were distributed randomly across all conditions. As a result, any differences between conditions could be attributed to the effects of the independent variables.

Unlike research involving correlational methods, experiments can determine the causal relationship between two variables. With correlational research, we cannot tell whether variable A is the cause of variable B, or vice versa. In fact, there may be no causal relationship at all between A and B; a third variable—often unknown to the researcher—may be the cause of both A and B.

Control over the experimental setting is important because it allows the researcher to draw valid conclusions about the experimental results. An experiment, however, must also have impact on subjects if its findings are to have any real meaning and not simply be the trivial results of an artificial situation. Impact, or experimental realism, occurs when a subject finds the events of an experiment interesting and absorbing and, thus, reacts in a natural manner. Mundane realism, the degree to which the experimental setting approximates real life, also can impact, although it is not always possible to attain. The difficulty for experimenters is that these two crucial factors—impact and control—often work in opposite directions. The challenge, then, is to maximize impact on subjects without sacrificing control over the experimental situation.

To achieve valid and meaningful results, it is frequently necessary to disguise the true purpose of the study through the use of a "cover story." If subjects are aware of the hypothesis before participating in the study, they are unlikely to act in a spontaneous manner. Rather, they will tend to perform in a way that makes them look good or "normal," or they may try to "help out" the experimenter by behaving in a way that confirms the hypothesis.

The use of deception in experiments, as well as the tendency for some experiments to cause discomfort for subjects, raises serious ethical problems for the researcher. First, it is simply unethical to tell lies to people. In addition, deception prevents subjects from giving their informed consent to participate in a study and, thus, can lead to an invasion of privacy. These issues are especially problematic when the experimental procedure involves unpleasant experiences.

Aronson proposes five ethical guidelines in deciding whether to conduct a given experiment: 1) Procedures that cause intense pain or discomfort should be avoided. 2) Experimenters should be alert to alternative procedures to deception, using them whenever viable. 3) Experimenters should give subjects the real option of quitting the experiment if their discomfort becomes too intense. 4) Experimenters should spend considerable time with each subject during the debriefing session, gradually and carefully explaining the experiment, its true purpose, and the reasons for any deception. They should make every effort to protect the dignity of subjects and to make sure they leave feeling good about themselves and their role in the experiment. 5) Before entering the lab, researchers should be certain their experiment is sound and important. They should not conduct an experiment involving deception or discomfort in order to address a trivial research question.

Social psychologists also face a moral dilemma regarding what they discover in the pursuit of a scientific understanding of behavior. For example, research findings can be used to develop sophisticated and efficient techniques for controlling people's behavior. There is always the possibility that some individuals will use such techniques to exploit others for their own gain. While there is no perfect solution, Aronson's personal approach to this moral dilemma is "to educate the public about how these techniques might be used and to remain vigilant against their abuse as I continue to do research aimed at furthering our understanding of us social animals—how we think and how we behave."

Lecture Ideas & Teaching Suggestions

Finding Flaws in Experiments. One approach to exploring the important features of experimental methodology is to present students with examples of flawed experiments, interspersed with some properly conducted studies. After describing each study, you can challenge students to try to determine what, if anything, is wrong with each one. For example, you might describe a two-condition study in which the experimenter ran all subjects in one condition during the first three weeks of the semester and then—due to an equipment or staffing problem—ran all subjects in the second condition during the last two weeks of the semester. If students understand the concept of random assignment, they should quickly spot the potential for systematic differences in subjects' behavior that would invalidate the experimental findings. (For example, subjects may be more distracted by exam pressures at the end of the semester, or there may be personality differences in the kinds of people who sign up for an experiment early in the semester, compared to those who sign up late in the semester—e.g., the tendency to procrastinate, attitudes toward science, etc.)

To take another example, you could describe a study that examined whether being insulted by someone leads to feelings of hostility and aggression. In this study, male and female subjects interact with a confederate who either does or does not insult them. The researcher then asks each subject if he or she felt like hitting the confederate at any point during the interaction. The results of the study reveal that, among subjects who were insulted, only male subjects indicated that they wanted to hit the confederate. Men who were not insulted, and females in both conditions, did not express a desire to hit the confederate. The researcher concludes that there is a strong gender difference in the effects of insults on aggressive feelings. Students who understand the problem of demand characteristics will be able to spot the flaw in this study: Admitting to aggressive feelings—especially those involving physical harm—is less acceptable for women than for men in our society. More generally, simply asking subjects how they feel is usually an ineffective procedure, especially when undesirable behaviors are being investigated. You might then ask students how the use of a good cover story and a different measure of aggressive feelings would help to improve this study.

Finally, you might describe a study on similarity and attraction, in which the researcher first determined each subject's attitudes on a variety of topics and then gave them a description of a person who held nearly identical attitudes. The researcher then asked subjects how much they thought they would like this person and, lo and behold, nearly all subjects said they would like this person very much and would like to have a chance to meet him or her. The researcher concludes that similarity does lead to attraction—"birds of a feather do flock together." Here, the simple point is there was no manipulation of the independent variable and, hence, no subjects who saw descriptions of dissimilar others to serve as a comparison group. As a result, the researcher has no basis upon which to draw any conclusions from his or her "experiment."

(NOTE: One way to generate more examples is to take existing experiments and create flaws in them. Another possibility is to ask students in small groups to come up with their own flawed studies to see if they can stump their classmates.)

Values and Science. In their commitment to the goals of science, researchers typically strive to conduct their investigations in an objective, value-free manner. It is possible, however, for values to influence research in a variety of ways. In your discussion of scientific methods in social psychology, you might also wish to introduce your students to the more "subjective" side of the research enterprise.

For example, the impact of prejudiced beliefs on the conclusions drawn from research is reflected in the discussion of early studies on gender differences in persuasion, presented in Chapter 7. To briefly summarize, research conducted by Janis and Field in the 1950s indicated that women were more easily persuaded than men. Subsequent research, however, revealed that this apparent difference was due to the specific topics used as stimuli in the Janis and Field experiment. Because these topics were more reflective of masculine interests, female subjects evidently had little knowledge about them and, as a result, tended to conform to the opinions of others. In contrast, later research by Sistrunk and McDavid found that when topics involved traditionally feminine domains of interest, men were more easily persuaded than women. This example illustrates the unintended impact of values on how research is conducted, as well as how research findings are interpreted. Not only were the stimulus materials used in the Janis and Field study biased in favor of masculine performance, but the results of this study went unquestioned for several years—undoubtedly because they were consistent with stereotypes regarding women's greater gullibility and lack of firm convictions. To borrow Bem and Bem's terminology, such is the power of a "nonconscious ideology."

Values that are at odds with those of the scientific community can also have implications for social-psychological research. For example, several years ago, Senator William Proxmire of Wisconsin publicly criticized research on love conducted by Ellen Berscheid and Elaine Hatfield, claiming that the American public would prefer to remain ignorant of the dynamics underlying the "mystery" of love and romance. Thus, in his view, certain domains of life are sacred and should be protected from the cold scrutiny of scientific inquiry. One way to stimulate discussion on this topic is to ask students if they agree with Proxmire's position. Should certain topics—such as love, religious faith, or the sublime effect of a beautiful poem—be off-limits to scientists? Will scientific knowledge of certain aspects of life destroy our capacity to participate fully and unself-consciously in such experiences? Is it, as Proxmire has argued, a waste of public funds to support research on such topics?

Values are also implicit in the kinds of topics researchers choose to investigate. Often such decisions are influenced by the pressing social problems of the day, rather than some abstract set of scientific criteria. Thus, Latane and Darley's research on bystander intervention was stimulated by growing alarm regarding the potentially dehumanizing effects of urban life. Milgram's research on obedience to authority was a response to the horrors of Nazism. Similarly, waves of research interest in racial and gender prejudice, pornography, violence and aggression, and a host of other phenomena have been strongly influenced by current social values and concerns.

Finally, it is worth noting that certain values are implicit in the special emphasis that social psychologists place on "situational" causes of behavior. This focus has clear implications for the kinds of solutions to social problems that researchers are likely to propose. Policy recommendations based on social-psychological research are more likely to involve modifications of institutional arrangements or changes in the structural conditions of society, while individual-level interventions are apt to receive less attention.

Field Experimentation. In your coverage of methods in social psychology, you may wish to supplement the chapter's treatment of laboratory experimentation with a discussion of other methods used by researchers. In particular, the topic of field experimentation may merit special attention since, in recent years, researchers have increasingly sought to test their hypotheses within natural settings. In part, this turn to the field reflects the desire of many experimenters to increase the generalizability of their findings beyond the lab and into the real world.

Field experiments resemble laboratory experiments in allowing the researcher to manipulate independent variables and to assign subjects to experimental conditions on a random basis. In addition, they offer the advantage of observing people in their natural environment. And, because subjects typically do not know they are in an experiment, they are likely to respond to the experimental manipulations in a spontaneous manner. (It should also be noted, however, that laboratory experiments that are high in experimental realism also achieve this effect.) Unfortunately, field experiments have their share of drawbacks as well. First, the control over extraneous variables that is easily achieved in the lab is usually more difficult to establish in a field setting. In a laboratory experiment, the researcher can ensure that the setting is virtually identical for all subjects. This is impossible in the field because any number of conditions can—and are likely to—change over the course of running the experiment. For example, other people (who are not in the study) may be present in the setting in some cases, but not others. Their presence may interfere with, or otherwise influence, the experimental procedure or subjects' behavior. In general, the best the researcher can do is to minimize the impact of such extraneous variables, taking steps to ensure that these factors do not have a systematic impact on the results of the study. Another disadvantage of field experimentation is that it is often difficult to conduct a study involving complex variables or several variables that must be manipulated simultaneously. As a result, some hypotheses cannot be easily or adequately tested in field settings. Additional background on field experimentation and other research methods used in social psychological research may be found in: Aronson, E., Ellsworth, P.C., Carlsmith, J.M., & Gonzales, M.H. (1990). *Methods of research in social psychology*. Reading, MA: Addison-Wesley; and Judd, C.M., Smith, E.R., & Kidder, L.H. (1991). *Research methods in social relations*. New York: Holt, Rinehart & Winston.

Projects and Discussion Topics

1.   PROJECT: Examine several research reports describing experiments in the field of social psychology. Good sources of such articles are *The Journal of Personality and Social Psychology, Personality and Social Psychology Bulletin, The Journal of Experimental Social Psychology,* and *The Journal of Applied Social Psychology*. (These journals should be available at your campus library or the library of a nearby university.) Select two articles that you find interesting, one describing an experiment with high experimental realism, and another with low experimental realism. For each article, describe or identify: a) the title, authors, journal, and date of the article; b) the

purpose of the study; c) the independent and dependent variables; d) the various experimental conditions or treatments; e) the "cover story," if any; f) the study's degree of experimental realism; g) the presence of "suspicious" subjects or other complications, if any, and how these problems were handled; h) how the experimenter controlled extraneous variables; i) ethical concerns raised by the study; j) the study's results. Finally, briefly summarize the conclusions drawn by the researchers, as well as any possible alternative explanations for the experimental findings.

2. PROJECT: Come up with a social-psychological question that interests you, develop a hypothesis, and design an experiment to test it. (If you have trouble coming up with a question, choose an experiment you are familiar with and design a new experiment to test the same hypothesis.) Write a report of your experimental design and procedure, and include the following information: a) the hypothesis or research question addressed in your study; b) the independent and dependent variables; c) the various experimental conditions; d) how you would assign subjects to conditions; e) how you would control for extraneous variables; f) your "cover story"; g) any ethical issues raised by your study; h) how you would protect the rights of your subjects; i) how you would conduct the post-experimental session. Finally, describe any difficulties you had in designing your experiment and any problems you think you might encounter if you were to conduct it. (Note: this project also works well in class as a discussion item.)

3. DISCUSSION: Select an experiment you have read about that you feel raises serious ethical concerns. Do you think this study should have been performed? That is, does the knowledge gained from this study justify the deception or discomfort experienced by subjects? If the experiment's negative impact on subjects was only temporary, does this fact diminish the ethical problems to an acceptable level in your opinion? In general, what standards of ethics would you follow if you were a researcher?

4. DISCUSSION: Would you question the ethics of the Milgram study if none of the subjects had administered shocks beyond the "moderate shock" level? One study found that when people were told that a high proportion of Milgram's subjects was obedient, they rated the procedure as more harmful than if they were told

that only a low proportion obeyed the experimenter's orders. What do you make of these findings? Should researchers restrict themselves to conducting experiments that reveal flattering information about human nature and behavior? Would this even be possible? Why or why not?

5. DISCUSSION: Consider the issue of the researcher's moral responsibility for how her or his discoveries are put to use. For example, research on persuasion and self-justification has yielded a number of potent strategies for influencing people's behavior. These techniques can be used for good or ill, depending on the purposes of those who possess the knowledge and resources to use them. Do you feel it is immoral or dangerous for researchers to develop this knowledge, without being able to control how it is used? Do you think some form of control over the use of research findings could or should be implemented? If so, how? Finally, do you think it is right for potent techniques of persuasion to be employed to change people's behavior, without their knowledge? Would you feel the same way if it were used "for their own good"—such as influencing people to stop smoking or to use condoms to prevent AIDS? If you were a researcher, how would you deal with this moral dilemma?

Experiential Exercises

1. The professor can conduct an experiment in class and discuss the various procedures. On page 301–302 Karen Dion showed a picture of a "cute" boy and read a story about this boy throwing a rock at a dog. The subjects rated how well they liked the boy on a 1–7 scale. It could also be done for a "cute" girl with the same story. Another group of subjects were shown a picture of an "ugly" boy with the same story. They also rated how well they liked the boy. This could be done with an "ugly" girl too.

   In the classroom the students could be randomly assigned to group A or group B. Then group B steps into the hall while the first group sees and hears the story. After that group B comes into the classroom and sees the second picture. The ratings are tallied on the board for Group A boy and girl and Group B boy and girl. A discussion would follow about how close this exercise is to the ideal experimental model in the text. Students will experience the research even though all the controls are not in place.

2. Attractiveness Rating Exercise. This exercise and others appeared in Chapter 4 on Social Contagion. These could be applied here as well.

Additional Readings

Aronson, E., Ellsworth, P.C., Carlsmith, J.M. & Gonzales, M.H. (1990). *Methods of research in social psychology*. Reading, MA: Addison-Wesley.

Aronson, E., Brewer, M. & Carlsmith, J.M. (1985). Experimentation in social psychology. In G. Lindzey & E. Aronson (Eds.), *Handbook of Social Psychology*. New York: Random House.

Baumrind, D. (1964). Some thoughts on ethics of research: After reading Milgram's behavioral study of obedience. *American Psychologist, 19,* 421–423. See also: Milgram, S. (1964). Issues in the study of obedience: A reply to Baumrind. *American Psychologist, 19,* 848–852.

Berkowitz, L. & Donnerstein, E. (1982). External validity is more than skin deep: Some answers to criticisms of laboratory experiments. *American Psychologist, 37,* 245–257.

Estes, W.K. (Ed.). (1994). *Psychological Science, 5*(3). (Special section including general article by Robert Rosenthal (pp. 127–134) and four commentaries regarding the current state of ethics in scientific research.)

Fisher, C.B. & Fyrberg, D. (1994). Participant partners: College students weigh the costs and benefits of deceptive research. *American Psychologist, 49*(5), 417–427.

Gibson, E.J. (1994). Has psychology a future? *Psychological Science, 5*(2), 69–76.

Pope, K.S. & Vetter, V.A. (1992). Ethical dilemmas encountered by members of the American Psychological Association: A national survey. *American Psychologist, 47*(3), 397–411.

West, S.G. & Gunn, S.P. (1978). Some issues of ethics in social psychology. *American Psychologist, 33,* 30–38.

Multiple-Choice Questions

Answer: d
Page: 330

1. According to the text, the first step in the scientific method is:
   a. assigning subjects randomly to groups.
   b. specifying the independent and dependent variables.
   c. answering the ethical questions implied by the research question.
   d. observation.

Answer: a
Page: 331

2. Aronson believes that the study of social psychology is:
   a. an art and a science.
   b. an art but not a full-blown science.
   c. science but not an art.
   d. an incomplete science.

Answer: b
Page: 332–334

3. In the Aronson and Mills experiment, the _____ was (were) the independent variable(s) and the _____ was (were) the dependent variable(s):
   a. severity of initiation; young women who participated
   b. severity of initiation; women's liking for the discussion group
   c. severity of initiation; boring discussion group
   d. liking for discussion group; severity of initiation

Answer: a
Page: 333–334

4. Suppose you constructed an experiment to better understand the effect of the content of a speech on how persuaded people were by it. In this experiment, the independent variable would be:
   a. the content of the speech.
   c. how persuaded the subjects were.
   c. the characteristics of the subject.
   d. how the speech was delivered.

Answer: c
Page: 333–334

5. The factor systematically varied by the experimenter is usually termed:
   a. the dependent variable.
   b. the extraneous variable.
   c. the independent variable.
   d. the control variable.

Answer: c
Page: 333–334

6. In conducting an experiment, the researcher's goal is to:
   a. determine whether experimental findings also operate under real-world conditions.
   b. determine whether the theory of random assignment actually works when put into practice.
   c. determine whether manipulations of the independent variable cause systematic differences in subjects' behavior.
   d. predict whether subjects will believe the "cover story" used in the experiment.

Answer: b
Page: 334

7. Suppose you conducted an experiment to study the effect of violence in television shows on aggressiveness in children. The dependent variable would be:
   a. the factors that distinguished between one group of children and another.
   b. how aggressive the children were.
   c. whether or not the children should be exposed to the violence.
   d. how violent the programs were.

Answer: b
Page: 333–334

8. The dependent variable in an experiment is used to measure:
   a. the effects of extraneous variables in the experimental setting.
   b. the effects of the independent variable.
   c. the degree of experimental realism achieved in the experiment.
   d. the degree of mundane realism achieved in the experiment.

Answer: b
Page: 334

9. Which of the following word pairs corresponds most closely to "cause-effect"?
   a. experiment-correlation
   b. independent variable-dependent variable
   c. experimental realism-mundane realism
   d. control-impact

Answer: c
Page: 335

10. In an experiment, extraneous (nonmanipulated) variables are controlled by:
   a. having more than one experimenter interact with all subjects in the study.
   b. using subjects who are similar to each other in nearly all respects.
   c. making all aspects of the procedure identical for all conditions, except for the independent variable manipulation.
   d. the assignment of subjects to experimental conditions based on the characteristics of the subjects.

Answer: b
Page: 335

11. Experimentation is used in social psychology primarily because:
   a. it allows for more precise quantification of the dependent variable than other research techniques.
   b. it allows for greater control of the relevant variables than other research techniques.
   c. it is less time-consuming than other research techniques.
   d. it presents fewer ethical problems than other research techniques.

Answer: d
Page: 336–337

12. In the context of an experiment, "random assignment" means that:
   a. subjects are assigned at random to different "cover stories."
   b. subjects are selected at random from a large population of potential subjects.
   c. subjects are assigned to only one experimental condition.
   d. each subject has an equal chance to be in any condition in the study.

Answer: a
Page: 336–337

13. According to Aronson, the most important condition which must be met before any experiment can lead to definite cause-and-effect conclusions is:
   a. random assignment of subjects to groups.
   b. the presence of a correlation between variables.
   c. the presence of broad demand characteristics.
   d. the manipulation of all dependent variables.

Answer: d
Page: 338

14. The crucial difference between experimental and nonexperimental methods of investigation is that experimental methods involve:
   a. the quantification of empirical findings.
   b. establishing a relationship between two or more variables.
   c. the use of deception.
   d. the use of random assignment.

Answer: c
Page: 339

15. In social psychological experiments, the experimenter tries to:
   a. create an exact duplicate of conditions found in the real world.
   b. control conditions in natural, real-world situations.
   c. create a functional equivalent to conditions found in the real world.
   d. let the subject know what behavior is expected of him or her.

Answer: c
Page: 336–338

16. Simply knowing that achievement is positively correlated with happiness tells us:
    a. that there is a causal relationship between achievement and happiness.
    b. that a third variable is the cause of both achievement and happiness.
    c. that as achievement increases, happiness also increases.
    d. that achievement causes happiness, *or* that happiness causes achievement.

Answer: d
Page: 336–338

17. If researchers find a positive correlation between cowardice and nosebleeds, it most likely means that:
    a. cowardice is a cause of nosebleeds.
    b. nosebleeds are a cause of cowardice.
    c. that a third variable—a genetic, hormonal factor—causes both cowardice and nosebleeds.
    d. any, all, or none of the above.

Answer: b
Page: 339

18. Generally, the relationship between control and impact is such that:
    a. as impact increases, control increases.
    b. as impact increases, control decreases.
    c. as impact increases, control shifts from the independent to the dependent variable.
    d. as impact increases, control shifts from the dependent to the independent variable.

Answer: c
Page: 339–340

19. The main reason social psychologists want their experiments to have impact on subjects is that, without impact:
    a. an exact duplicate or real-world situation cannot be achieved.
    b. subjects will be bored and, thus, will refuse to participate in the experiment.
    c. subjects' reactions will not be spontaneous and, thus, the results of the experiment will have little meaning.
    d. subjects will probably guess the hypothesis of the experiment.

Answer: d
Page: 339–340

20. _____ realism refers to the impact an experiment has upon a subject; _____ realism refers to the degree to which laboratory procedures are similar to commonly occurring events in the outside world.
    a. Experimental; dependent
    b. Mundane; procedural
    c. Independent; dependent
    d. Experimental; mundane

Answer: c
Page: 339–340

21. An experiment that gets the subject involved and interested but that does not represent events that occur in the real world is:
    a. high in experimental control, low in correlational control.
    b. high in mundane realism, low in experimental realism.
    c. high in experimental realism and low in mundane realism.
    d. high in correlational control and low in experimental control.

Answer: c
Page: 339–340

22. Suppose you volunteered to be a subject in a psychology experiment in which you were locked into a sound-proof booth and were told that your brain waves were being measured. Furthermore, you truly believed that your brain wave pattern was being used to predict your basic personality traits. According to Aronson, this experiment would have _____ mundane realism and _____ experimental realism.
   a. low; low
   b. high; high
   c. low; high
   d. high; low

Answer: a
Page: 441

23. Jane is a subject in Milgram's study of obedience. As she delivers increasingly severe shocks to the "learner," she feels a great deal of anxiety, engages in nervous laughter, and breaks out into a sweat. Caught in the grip of conflicting emotions, she would like to stop but feels she must continue to obey the orders of the experimenter. She has never encountered a situation like this before. Based on this description, what can we conclude about the Milgram experiment?
   a. It was high in experimental realism.
   b. It was high in experimental and mundane realism.
   c. It was low in experimental and mundane realism.
   d. It was high in mundane realism.

Answer: a
Page: 340–341

24. Cover stories are used to:
   a. mislead subjects about the true purpose of the experiment.
   b. direct the subject's attention toward the specific behavior being studied.
   c. decrease experimental realism.
   d. decrease mundane realism.

Answer: c
Page: 341

25. If subjects know the true purpose of an experiment while participating in it, the most serious risk is if they:
   a. refuse to continue their participation in the experiment.
   b. tell the experimenter ways that the experiment could be improved.
   c. act in ways that they believe will make them look good or "normal."
   d. ruin the "cover story" by telling other subjects about the hypothesis of the experiment.

Answer: c
Page: 341

26. In Asch's study of conformity, which involved a comparison of the lengths of different lines, subjects were told that the experiment was about perceptual judgment. Telling subjects this:
   a. involved the unnecessary use of deception, which Asch later regretted.
   b. aroused a great deal of suspicion because the line-judging task was too easy.
   c. was part of the experimenter's cover story.
   d. created a high level of mundane realism in the experiment.

Answer: d
Page: 343

27. Many subjects in a study by Robyn Dawes, Jeanne McTavish, and Harriet Shaklee experienced considerable discomfort after their participation in a study of how people respond to "social dilemmas." This study was included in *The Social Animal* to illustrate:
   a. the pitfalls inherent in doing research involving deception.
   b. the hazards of failure to carefully debrief subjects after their participation in an experiment.
   c. the need to screen subjects before conducting an experiment, to make sure they are in good psychological health.
   d. that no code of ethics can anticipate all problems, even when an experiment is carefully planned and conducted.

Answer: d
Page: 343–344

28. According to the text, ethical dilemmas faced by experimental social psychologists stem from two conflicting values to which most researchers subscribe. These values are reflected in the belief _____, versus the belief _____.
    a. that they must advance their scientific careers; that research should address important social problems
    b. that informed consent is desirable; that deception cannot be avoided in research
    c. that most people benefit from participating in research; that some people may be harmed by experimental deception
    d. that free scientific inquiry is important; that the dignity of humans and their right to privacy should be respected

Answer: c
Page: 345

29. Which of the following is not an ethical guideline proposed by Aronson in conducting an experiment?
    a. Procedures that cause intense pain or discomfort should be avoided.
    b. Experimenters should be ever alert to alternative procedures to deception. If some other viable procedure can be found, it should be used.
    c. Deception, in general, can be justified in all experiments, provided that the subjects are adequately debriefed at the end.
    d. Experimenters should provide their subjects with the real option of quitting the experiment if their discomfort becomes too intense.

Answer: b
Page: 346

30. Psychiatric interviews of subjects in Milgram's obedience study (in which subjects believed they were delivering intense electric shocks to another person) conducted one year following the study, revealed:
a. that many subjects still had negative feelings toward the experimenter who deceived them.
b. that many subjects believed their participation in the study had been both instructive and enriching.
c. only a few subjects experienced long-term negative effects as a result of the study.
d. that some subjects still believed they had actually shocked the confederate.

Answer: a
Page: 345

31. The postexperimental session (debriefing):
a. allows the experimenter to explain the details to the participants to protect the dignity of the participants.
b. should fool the subject in order to be effective and gain more information.
c. increases the mundane realism of the experiment.
d. is a chance to conduct even more research.

Answer: b
Page: 345

32. Debriefing a subject at the end of an experiment:
a. is unethical if the subject already seems upset by the experimental procedure.
b. is a valuable way of undoing some of the discomfort and deception that may have occurred during the experiment.
c. has been shown to be relatively ineffective in undoing possible harmful effects to the subject.
d. helps to keep the subject unaware of the true nature of the experiment.

Answer: b
Page: 449

33. If deception is used, its negative effects best can be overcome by:
    a. never telling the subject anything.
    b. debriefing the subject.
    c. using role playing techniques.
    d. paying the subjects more money.

Essay Questions

1. Why do social psychologists conduct experiments? Choose an experiment (such as the "initiation" study by Aronson & Mills) and use it to illustrate the advantages of the experimental method. What problems would a researcher encounter if he or she tried to study the same phenomenon as it occurs in the real world?

2. Fran Flanders, an advice columnist for a regional newspaper, was curious about why people are attracted to each other. She had a feeling that similarity leads to attraction, but she decided to conduct a scientific investigation to test her hunch. She found several couples who had been dating for a year or more and gave them a questionnaire that measured their attitudes and opinions on a variety of topics. Next, Fran gave the same questionnaire to several pairs of individuals who knew each other only as casual acquaintances. When she examined the questionnaire responses, lo and behold, she found that the attitudes of the couples who had been in long-term relationships were far more similar than the attitudes of casual acquaintances. "Great," Fran concluded, "I knew it all along! Now I can tell my readers that the key to good relationships is having similar attitudes!"

   Do you agree with Fran's conclusion? Why or why not? If you were an experimental social psychologist, what approach would you take to testing Fran's hunch about why people like each other?

3. Why is the random assignment of subjects to groups such an important component of experimental research? What is gained by randomly assigning subjects? What would be lost if subjects were not assigned randomly?

4. Explain the meaning of the terms "control" and "impact" as they pertain to social-psychological experiments. Why is each of these

factors important in conducting effective research? What difficulty does the need for both pose for the careful researcher?

5. According to Aronson, what are the three basic ethical problems that social psychologists face in conducting experiments? Would a carefully devised code of ethics, if stringently followed, be able to completely eliminate such problems? If researchers refrained from doing research involving deception, would these ethical issues be settled once and for all? Why or why not?

Readings About the Social Animal

Multiple-Choice Questions

Chapter 1   Research in Social Psychology as a Leap of Faith

Elliot Aronson

Answer: a   1.   What does Aronson mean when he says that science is a "self-corrective enterprise"?

      a.   even if a certain study is not perfect, other researchers will improve on it.

      b.   researchers conduct experiments as a way of improving—"correcting"—the human condition.

      c.   the inherent tendency of all human action is to gradually improve over time, and science, as a human endeavor, exhibits this same quality.

      d.   a panel of experts reviews each and every research article before it is accepted for publication, and this ensures that no errors in scientific research go undetected before the results are made public.

Answer: b   2. Aronson invokes James' notion of a "leap of faith" to argue that:

a. religious faith is an important topic of social-psychological research because our beliefs affect our attitudes, which, in turn, affect our behavior.

b. researchers should do the best work they can, with the understanding that when other researchers analyze their studies, they will probably improve on it, thus benefiting science as a whole.

c. if you have faith that you can do a particular study, then you will succeed.

d. science alone cannot solve our social problems; we must trust in higher powers that are not open to scientific investigation.

Answer: a   3. Aronson uses the example of Seymour's advice to his younger brother, Buddy, from a short story by Salinger, to suggest that:

a. a researcher should attempt to answer questions that have always interested him.

b. a researcher should always try to study the questions that others have identified as the most important.

c. researchers should always strive to be "provocative rather than right".

d. writing novels is more valuable than conducting scientific research because literature is easier for more people to understand than science, so literature can have a much larger social impact.

e. it is not wise for there to be two scientists in one family, because they will rarely, if ever, agree on anything.

Answer: c   4. Aronson maintains that "one of the by-products of
                    excessive caution is excessive self-consciousness."
                    In the context of conducting research, this state-
                    ment means that:
                    a. scientists should not always be concerned with
                        following proper methodological procedures.
                    b. engaging in scientific inquiry, which is by na-
                        ture a slow, careful enterprise, leads one to de-
                        velop a cautious and conservative personality.
                    c. being too careful and cautious can stifle scien-
                        tific inquiry by making researchers reluctant to
                        pursue interesting and unusual questions.
                    d. if a researcher is not careful, science can de-
                        generate into an undisciplined, "circus-like"
                        enterprise.
                    e. many researchers are by nature shy and with-
                        drawn, which means that their findings often
                        go unnoticed because they fail to publicize
                        them.

Chapter 2   On Baseball and Failure

Elliot Aronson

Answer: c

1. According to Aronson, why are experiments in social psychology more difficult than in other scientific disciplines?
   a. human subjects have highly complex and variable responses.
   b. it is difficult to get funding for research with human subjects.
   c. human subjects have their own theories about the phenomena being studied.
   d. as a younger science, social psychology does not have a base of established theories.

Answer: a

2. Aronson loves social psychology because:
   a. it reminds him of baseball where errors are part of the game.
   b. he can learn about human nature and apply that knowledge to improve the world.
   c. he likes interacting with people.
   d. doing research is like a private investigator solving a case.

Answer: d

3. What is Aronson's second law?
   a. Science looks for lawful generalizations, but people are unique individuals.
   b. The amount of a person's self-justification is indirectly related to their self-esteem.
   c. People behave, but social forces influence and direct that behavior.
   d. People who are unafraid to make mistakes are unlikely to make anything of great value.

Chapter 3   Opinions and Social Pressure

Solomon E. Asch

Answer: a

1. The Asch experiment forces subjects to choose be-
    tween two powerful conflicting forces. They are:
    a. their own sense perceptions and the influence
        of group opinion.
    b. obedience and rebellion.
    c. the desire to be "contrary" and the need to "fit
        in".
    d. the contrived reality of the research laboratory
        and the "real world" contextual influences that
        operate outside of the experimental setting.

Answer: c

2. In Asch's experiment, what percentage of subjects
    exercised complete independence—that is, what
    percentage never agreed with the opinions of the
    majority?
    a. 75%
    b. 50%
    c. 25%
    d. 0%

Answer: d

3. Asch's experiment sought to determine the influence of majority opinion on individual opinion along two dimensions—the size of the majority and its degree of unanimity. Which of the following statements correctly describes what Asch found out about these two key variables?
   a. Individual opinion was not influenced by the size of the majority, but it was influenced by having a partner who also went against the majority.
   b. Individual opinion was influenced by the size of the majority, but it was not influenced by having a partner who also went against the majority.
   c. Individual opinion was not influenced either by the size of the majority or by the presence of a partner who also dissented.
   d. Individual opinion was influenced by both the size of the majority and the presence of a partner who also went against the majority.

Answer: d

4. Which of the following was *not* studied by Asch in his experiments on opinion and group pressure?
   a. the effect of the size of the majority
   b. the degree of unanimity of majority opinion
   c. the effect of the "desertion" of a partner to the majority
   d. the effect of the similarity of partners' social backgrounds on their willingness to form dissenting alliances against majority opinion

Chapter 4   Behavioral Study of Obedience

Stanley Milgram

Answer: b

1. The major reason why Milgram conducted his experiments on obedience was:
   a. he received a large research grant from the federal government to investigate how citizens might be made more loyal and obedient.
   b. to understand how the Nazi regime could have carried out its genocidal plans during WWII.
   c. to discover whether anti-social persons were more cruel than pro-social persons.
   d. to analyze the psychological and physiological responses to stress of persons who possess "authoritarian" personality traits.

Answer: b

2. In Milgram's study, the primary dependent variable was
   a. how profusely the subject sweated, stuttered, and trembled when he continued to administer shocks to the "learner".
   b. the maximum shock a subject administered before refusing to continue in the experiment.
   c. the number of times the experimenter had to prod the subject to continue to administer the shocks.
   d. how painful the subject considered the shocks to be to the learner, as measured on a 14-point scale.

Answer: b

3. Which of the following was an unexpected manifestation of tension that Milgram and his associates observed in some subjects?
   a. drop in their blood pressure
   b. nervous laughter
   c. sadistic comments
   d. Some subjects tore up the money they received for participating in the experiment, which Milgram interpreted as an act of defiance toward the authority of the experimenter.

Answer: d   4.   According to this article, several features of the
                       Milgram experiment help to account for the high
                       levels of obedience displayed by the subjects.
                       Which of the following is *not* one of those fea-
                       tures?

                       a.   Subjects believed the experiment would in-
                            crease scientific knowledge on an important
                            subject.
                       b.   The subjects felt a sense of obligation and
                            commitment to continue the experiment, even
                            after they began to feel uncomfortable admin-
                            istering high-voltage shocks.
                       c.   lack of guidelines about the limits of experi-
                            mental research
                       d.   The experiment allowed subjects to discuss
                            their actions among themselves, so that they
                            could come to a consensus that it was right to
                            continue to follow the experimenter's orders.

Chapter 5   "From Jerusalem to Jericho": A Study of Situational and Dispositional Variables in Helping Behavior
John M. Darley and C. Daniel Batson

Answer: d

1. The "Good Samaritan" experiment was designed to assess the influence of which of the following types of variables?
   a. exogenous and endogenous
   b. egoistic and altruistic
   c. latent and manifest
   d. situational and personality

Answer: b

2. Only one of the two independent variables in the "Good Samaritan" experiment was found to be significantly related to *whether and how much* help was given. This variable was:
   a. the content of the talk the subjects were to give.
   b. how hurried the subjects were.
   c. the type of religiosity exhibited by the subject.
   d. the degree to which the victim seemed to be in need of help.

Answer: c

3. Darley and Batson found that type of religiosity affected the *kind* of aid a subject offered to the victim. Specifically, they observed that:
   a. "rigid" helping styles were prevalent among subjects who viewed religion as a "quest" for meaning in their personal and social worlds.
   b. subjects who held orthodox religious beliefs tended to listen carefully to the victim's claims that he was really all right.
   c. subjects who scored high on the "religion as quest" scale were more mindful of the victim's definitions of his own needs.
   d. religiously orthodox subjects were cold and callous toward the victim.

Answer: d

4. From the results of the "Good Samaritan" experiment, Darley and Batson conclude that:
   a. seminary students, as a group, are more hypocritical than the general population.
   b. being in a hurry is inversely related to being religious, probably because hurried persons are very involved in worldly, material concerns and do not consider other-worldly, religious issues.
   c. personality variables are strong predictors of whether or not a person offers assistance to someone in need.
   d. situational variables affect whether or not a person offers assistance to someone in need.

Answer: b

5. In discussing their findings, Darley and Batson suggest that the best explanation for why some subjects failed to stop and render assistance is because:
   a. they were too preoccupied memorizing their speeches to even notice the victim.
   b. they experienced a conflict between helping two different persons—the experimenter and the victim.
   c. they were afraid that the victim was really a very dangerous street person who would harm them.
   d. being shy, quiet individuals, as most seminarians are, they did not want to create a scene on the sidewalk, especially if the victim turned out to be drunk or disorderly.

Chapter 6 A Focus Theory of Normative Conduct: Recycling the
Concept of Norms to Reduce Littering in Public Places
Robert B. Cialdini, Raymond R. Reno, and Carl A. Kallgren

Answer: a
1. Cialdini, Reno, and Kallgren found in their first study about littering that when people exited a parking garage, they were least likely to litter
   a. when the confederate littered one piece of litter into a clean environment.
   b. when the confederate did not litter in a clean environment.
   c. when the confederate littered into a dirty environment.
   d. when the confederate did not litter into a dirty environment.

Answer: b
2. In the study about littering, Cialdini, Reno, and Kallgren found that gender
   a. played a major role with males littering more in all five studies.
   b. played a minor role with males littering more only once.
   c. played a major role with young females littering the most.
   d. played no role because the rates were the same for males and females in all five studies.

Answer: d
3. One major conclusion from the littering studies by Cialdini, Reno, and Kallgren was
   a. observing a person littering is the most important variable in explaining littering.
   b. seeing litter at an amusement park influenced people more than seeing it on hospital grounds.
   c. reading a sign that warned people not to litter influenced them the most.
   d. realizing the norm in the environment is not to litter was the most important variable.

Answer: c

4. In the fifth study on littering Cialdini, Reno, and Kallgren found that when an area filled with litter was swept into piles or not swept at all, subjects
   a. mostly littered all the time because it did not matter if the litter was organized or not.
   b. rarely littered because they could see there was already too much litter.
   c. littered least if a confederate littered when there were swept piles of litter.
   d. littered the least when the confederate did not litter when the litter was scattered all over.

Chapter 7 Making Sense of the Nonsensical: An Analysis of Jonestown

Neal Osherow

Answer: b

1. Osherow points out that Jim Jones carefully controlled the information that was available to his followers in order to prevent them from developing a questioning attitude regarding the Temple. In addition to controlling the flow of information, Jones also employed which of the following techniques to keep followers from adopting a critical view of life in the Temple?
   a. killing the messenger of bad news
   b. attacking the credibility of the sources of critical information
   c. developing an elaborate coded language, which was known only to the Temple faithful
   d. conducting rigorous and systematic brainwashing sessions where Temple followers who were beginning to question Jones' teachings would be reprogrammed

Answer: c

2. Despite his obviously inhumane practices and the internal inconsistencies in his preachings, Jones was able to maintain his followers' loyalty. Osherow explains this with all but which of the following:
   a. People seek to justify their choices by altering their attitudes.
   b. If people experience pain and humiliation as part of belonging to a group, then they tend to value membership in that group more highly.
   c. Using power to make people comply is more effective in the long run than setting up a situation where people internalize social controls.
   d. Slowly but continually increasing the level of demands on a person's time and energy lead them to make greater commitments.

Answer: a   3.   Osherow notes that after the Jonestown mass suicide, cults and unusual religious practices came under close media scrutiny. One result of this was that
many "untraditional" religious practices were seen
as dangerous. According to the article, which of
the following questions can serve as a basis for dis-
tinguishing between beneficial alternative lifestyles
and dangerous cult practices?
    a.   Does membership in a group close off other
         life choices?
    b.   Is the group committed to "revolutionary ac-
         tions"?
    c.   Is individual responsibility preached as part of
         the religious doctrine?
    d.   Is there a single leader who controls the group?

Answer: d   4.   According to Osherow, the author of the article on
Jonestown, the mass suicide of nearly a thousand
people can best be understood as an act of:
    a.   prejudice.
    b.   reactance.
    c.   aggression.
    d.   conformity.

Answer: c   5.   The "upper echelon" of Jones' followers were typically attracted to membership in the Temple by:
    a.   their need for clothing, food and shelter.
    b.   their need for a "family" environment.
    c.   their interest in a utopian socialist society free
         from racism.
    d.   their belief that Jones was the Messiah.

Chapter 8   Effects of Varying the Recommendations in a
Fear-Arousing Communication
James M. Dabbs, Jr. and Howard Leventhal

Answer: d

1. Which of the following variables was *not* investigated in the Dabbs and Leventhal experiment on tetanus inoculation?
   a. effectiveness of inoculation
   b. painfulness of inoculation
   c. level of fear
   d. allergic reaction to inoculation

Answer: d

2. The dependent variables used in the Dabbs and Leventhal experiment to assess the effect of fear arousal on persuasion were:
   a. subjects' intentions to take shots and their level of fear as measured on a 7-point anxiety scale.
   b. subjects' intentions to take shots and their evaluations of the importance of shots in preventing disease.
   c. subjects' actual shot-taking behavior and their perceptions of how painful the shots were.
   d. subjects' intentions to take shots and their actual shot-taking behavior.

Answer: c

3. Dabbs and Leventhal's main experimental finding was that:
   a. the dependent variables were affected by manipulations of belief in the effectiveness of tetanus shots.
   b. the dependent variables were affected by manipulations of pain.
   c. the dependent variables were affected by manipulations of fear.
   d. the dependent variables were unaffected by any of the experimental manipulations.

Answer: d   4. Dabbs and Leventhal point to several factors that they did not systematically control, which could have affected their results. Among these factors are:

    a. the order of presentation of the manipulations of fear, effectiveness, and pain.

    b. the subjects' direct experience with medical practices and techniques.

    c. the subjects' academic field of study—science and pre-med students may have been more knowledgeable about inoculation procedures than students majoring in the humanities or social sciences.

    d. the effects of not giving all subjects in the experiment specific instructions on how to get a tetanus shot.

Chapter 9   Attribution Versus Persuasion as a Means for
Modifying Behavior
                    Richard L. Miller, Philip Brickman, and Diana Bolen

Answer: c   1.   The hypothesis of Miller et al.'s first experiment,
                    which attempted to modify children's littering be-
                    havior, was that:
                    a. both attribution and persuasion manipulations
                        would lead to initial behavioral change and to
                        stable, persistent behavior modification.
                    b. attribution manipulation would lead to behav-
                        ioral change; persuasion manipulation would
                        not.
                    c. both attribution and persuasion manipulations
                        would lead to initial behavioral change, but only
                        attribution would have a more long-lasting
                        effect on behavior modification.
                    d. only those children who were lectured on the
                        ecological problems of littering and pollution
                        would exhibit any significant change in their
                        littering behavior.

Answer: c   2.   Miller et al. gave subjects a pretest before conduct-
                    ing Study 1 in their research on the relative effects
                    of attribution versus persuasion in producing be-
                    havioral change. The importance of conducting
                    this pretest was:
                    a. to get the children prepared for the increased
                        number of tests, drills, and assignments that
                        the experiment would involve.
                    b. to introduce the students to the experimenters.
                    c. to discover existing differences among the
                        classrooms in how much they littered.
                    d. to discover how knowledgeable the children in
                        each classroom were regarding issues of ecol-
                        ogy and pollution.

Answer: d

3. In discussing their results on the relative effectiveness of persuasion and attribution techniques in producing behavioral change, Miller et al. advance which of the following explanations for their findings?

   a. Persuasive techniques are superior to attribution techniques because they involve more forceful appeals.

   b. Persuasive techniques do not threaten the self-concept, and that is why they are more effective.

   c. Attribution techniques are relatively less successful because they are less likely to arouse resistance, counterarguing, or reactance.

   d. Attribution techniques are relatively more successful because they suggest something positive about the subjects and bolster their self-concepts.

Answer: d

4. Miller et al. warn against seeing their findings either as the basis for specific educational reforms or as an effective step toward ending social inequalities. They cite several reasons why they hold this less-than-optimistic view. Which of the following is *not* one of those reasons?

   a. Long-standing individual differences are unlikely to be rectified by short-term interventions.

   b. Attribution techniques are incompatible with the traditional educational curriculum and procedures.

   c. Using false attributions, even for good ends, involves a risk to the teacher's sense of credibility.

   d. All children should be given a chance to succeed, but designing programs to aid a particular group gives them an unfair competitive advantage.

Chapter 10   The Impact of Mass Media Violence on U.S. Homicides

David P. Phillips

Answer: a

1. Phillips chose to study the effects of publicized prizefights on homicide rates because:
   a. violence in prizefights is presented by the media as rewarded, exciting, real, and justified.
   b. prizefights have never been studied before, except in the laboratory.
   c. prizefights are especially popular among people who are highly aggressive, compared to less-aggressive people.
   d. Phillips wanted to see if boxing, as a particularly violent sport, elicited more violent behavior than other sports such as hockey, football, or soccer.

Answer: a

2. Drawing on laboratory research conducted by Berkowitz, Phillips tested the "modeling of aggression" hypothesis. Phillips' data indicated that:
   a. highly publicized fights are followed by larger increases in homicides than less-publicized fights.
   b. "aggressor" modeling exists after a prizefight.
   c. "victim" modeling doesn't exist after a prizefight.
   d. viewers of prizefights engage in "non-modeling" in which they model neither aggressors nor victims.

Answer: a   3. Phillips' study of the effects of media violence has added to laboratory research on media violence in which of the following ways?

   a. It supported the link between media violence and aggression found in the laboratory.
   b. It has shown that the link between media violence and aggression is nonexistent.
   c. It has demonstrated that the presentation of media violence—especially prizefights—must be carefully controlled or everyone who witnesses such events is likely to become a perpetrator of violence.
   d. It has demonstrated that although prizefights lead to imitative aggressive behavior, other factors such as "precipitation" and "gambling" cannot be ruled out as rival explanations for the findings.

Answer: a   4. Phillips' study of the correlation between the occurrence of a prizefight and homicides found that after a prizefight:

   a. homicides increased significantly, with the greatest number of homicides occurring three days after the prizefight.
   b. homicides decreased significantly, demonstrating the catharsis effect.
   c. homicides increased significantly, with the greatest number of homicides occurring with the first three hours after the prizefight.
   d. homicides increased only if the "underdog" won the fight.

Chapter 11 Contrast Effects and Judgments of Physical
Attractiveness: When Beauty Becomes
a Social Problem

Douglas T. Kenrick and Sara E. Gutierres

Answer: c

1. In their series of three studies on the "contrast effect" and ratings of physical attractiveness, Kenrick
and Gutierres hypothesized that:

a. exposing judges to extremely unattractive
stimuli before they rated a photo of a woman
of "average" attractiveness would have no effect
on how the judges rated the photo.

b. exposing judges to extremely attractive stimuli
before they rated a photo of a woman of "average" attractiveness would result in the judges
rating the photo as more attractive.

c. exposing judges to extremely attractive stimuli
before they rated a photo of a woman of "average" attractiveness would result in the judges
rating the photo as less attractive.

d. exposing judges to extremely unattractive
stimuli before they rated a photo of a woman
of "average" attractiveness would result in the
judges rating the photo as less attractive.

Answer: d

2. The results of the first experiment conducted by Kenrick and Gutierres supported their hypothesis. However, one alternative explanation could not be completely ruled out: The subjects who were watching *Charlie's Angels* may have been more generally negative in their judgments toward women than control subjects, due to differences in personality, background, or some other unknown characteristic. To control for this in Study 2, Kenrick and Gutierres:
   a. had all subjects complete a full battery of psychological tests designed to detect differences in personality.
   b. assigned subjects to experimental conditions on a "matched sample" basis; that is, they made sure that the subjects in the experimental and the control groups were as much alike as possible.
   c. used subjects who were watching a television show other than *Charlie's Angels*.
   d. manipulated exposure to media beauty by using a different attractiveness stimuli *and* randomly assigned subjects to experimental conditions.

Answer: c

3. In Study 3 of their series of experiments on the "contrast effect," Kenrick and Gutierres modified their procedures in order to examine the effect of two additional variables on judgments of attractiveness. These two variables were:
   a. providing subjects with occupational information on the woman in the photo and the inclusion of female judges.
   b. the inclusion of female judges and the inclusion of photos of male targets.
   c. exposure to peer evaluations (by having confederates comment on the photo) and the inclusion of female judges.
   d. exposure to peer evaluations (by having confederates comment on the photo) and the inclusion of photos of male targets.

Answer: b

4. Taken as a whole, the results of the studies conducted by Kenrick and Gutierres on the "contrast effect" support which of the following statements?

   a. Initial judgments of a potential romantic partner's attractiveness may set into motion a "self-fulfilling prophecy".

   b. Initial impressions of potential romantic partners will be adversely affected by recent exposure to media images of highly attractive individuals.

   c. Male and female judges rated the photos very differently, indicating that only men are influenced by media images and cultural standards of physical beauty.

   d. Individuals who encounter a "representative" sample of opposite-sex persons in their everyday life will not develop a bias against average-looking potential partners.

Chapter 12 The Effect of Attitude on the Recall of Personal Histories
Michael Ross, Cathy McFarland, and Garth J.O. Fletcher

Answer: b

1. Ross et al.'s research on how attitudes affect recall attempted to answer which of the following questions?
   a. Would recall of repressed childhood memories be aided by psychological therapy or counseling that was designed to change a person's current attitudes?
   b. Would subjects' recall of their past behaviors be influenced by manipulations of their current attitudes?
   c. Are subjects' current attitudes the result of their need to justify their past behaviors?
   d. Contrary to "common sense," is it easier to recall when long-standing habits were first formed than when more recent habits were formed?

Answer: b

2. The results of the Ross et al. study on the relation between attitudes and recall demonstrated that:
   a. positive messages influenced attitudes more strongly than negative messages did.
   b. negative messages influenced attitudes more strongly than positive messages did.
   c. both positive and negative messages were equally effective in influencing attitudes.
   d. no attitude shifts toward personal hygiene habits were obtained as the result of exposure to persuasive communications.

Answer: b

3. Ross et al., in their discussion of possible interpretations of their findings on the relationship between attitudes and recall, rule out the "self-presentation" interpretation because:
   a. the subjects' responses were anonymous.
   b. the results of the "self-monitoring" variable showed that the effect of attitude on behavior was stronger among low self-monitors, which works against the self-presentation hypothesis.
   c. the results of the "self-monitoring" variable showed that the effect of attitude on behavior was weaker among self-monitors, which works against the self-preservation hypothesis.
   d. there is no difference in recall between familiar supporting arguments and novel opposing arguments.

Answer: a

4. Stated in the most general, but direct, terms, the research results from the Ross et al. study on the link between attitudes and behavior reveal that:
   a. attitudes can influence the recall of past behaviors.
   b. behavior can affect attitudes.
   c. attitudes can direct behavior.
   d. past behavior can affect future behavior.

Chapter 13   Attitude Accessibility as a Moderator of the Attitude-Perception and Attitude-Behavior Relations: An Investigation of the 1984 Presidential Election
Russell H. Fazio and Carol J. Williams

Answer: b

1. In their review of research on consistency between attitudes and behavior, Fazio and Williams note that there are two major approaches to studying the attitude-behavior link—the "when" approach and the "how" approach. The major difference between these two approaches is:
   a. in the "when" approach, the focus is on the process by which attitudes guide behavior, whereas in the "how" approach the focus is exclusively on identifying variables that mediate the attitude-behavior relation.
   b. the "when" approach focuses on the question of when attitudes predict subsequent behavior, whereas the "how" approach focuses on the process by which attitudes guide behavior.
   c. the accessibility of attitudes from memory is more important to the "when" approach than to the "how" approach.
   d. the "when" approach has a more cognitive focus, whereas the "how" approach looks at how persons' unconscious motivations govern their behavior.

Answer: d

2. In Fazio and Williams' study of attitude accessibility, they hypothesized that individuals who responded relatively quickly to statements about the 1984 Presidential election candidates would:

   a. be more likely to vote in the election than individuals who responded more slowly.

   b. be more likely to report that they intended to vote for one candidate but would actually vote for the other candidate.

   c. report perceptions of the performance of the two candidates in a later Presidential debate that conflicted with their initial attitudes toward the two candidates—that is, they responded too hastily and later changed their opinion regarding the best candidate.

   d. report perceptions of the performance of the two candidates in a later Presidential debate that were in agreement with their initial attitudes toward the two candidates, and would also actually vote for the candidate whom they had initially favored.

Answer: d

3. Results of the Fazio and Williams' study of the moderating effect of "attitude accessibility" demonstrated that:
   a. there is no relation between attitude extremity and latency of response to attitudinal inquiries—that is, there is no relation between how strongly a person feels about someone or something and how quickly they respond to statements about that person or thing.
   b. the relation between attitude and behavior is stronger among subjects with low attitude accessibility.
   c. individuals with high attitude accessibility tend to be right-wing extremists, as evidenced by the landslide victory of Reagan over Mondale in the 1984 election.
   d. attitude accessibility affects the link between attitudes and perceptions and the link between attitudes and behaviors—that is, individuals with relatively accessible attitudes show greater selective perception and greater attitude-behavior consistency.

Answer: c

4. Fazio and Williams discuss the implications of their findings on the functioning of "attitude accessibility" for which of the following real-world contexts?
   a. curbing the effects of media violence on heavy viewers of television crime dramas
   b. revising Presidential debate formats to make them less favorable to the incumbent
   c. designing political or marketing campaigns that target certain population segments as recipients of persuasive communications
   d. reforming political campaign practices that use highly impactful—but misleading—messages to sway voters' opinions

Chapter 14   Videotape and the Attribution Process: Reversing
Actors' and Observers' Points of View

Michael D. Storms

Answer: b

1. Storms' research on experimental manipulation of visual orientation has its theoretical foundation in the work of Jones and Nisbett (1971) on attribution. In that work, Jones and Nisbett argue that:
   a. actors tend to explain their own behavior as resulting from internal, personal causes, whereas observers explain actors' behavior as resulting from external, environmental causes.
   b. actors tend to explain their own behavior as resulting from external, environmental causes, whereas observers explain actors' behavior as resulting from internal, personal causes.
   c. altering actors' attributions is the key to successful psychological therapy.
   d. attributions are unaffected by point of view or perspective.

Answer: c

2. The main hypothesis in Storms' research on the effect of videotape reorientation of actors' and observers' causal attributions involved which of the following specific predictions?
   a. Observers who saw themselves on videotape would become relatively more situational in attributions of the actors' behavior.
   b. Actors who saw themselves on videotape would become relatively less dispositional in attributions of their own behavior.
   c. Actors who saw themselves on videotape would become relatively less situational in attributions of their own behavior.
   d. Visual orientation would have no influence on attributions.

Answer: a

3. Storms argues that the relatively greater amount of change from initially dispositional attributions toward situational attributions, compared to the lesser amount of change from initially situational attributions toward dispositional attributions, is probably the result of:
   a. a high base rate of importance for personal, dispositional attributions among most persons, that is, a "ceiling effect" for dispositional attributions was found.
   b. experimenter "demand characteristics".
   c. the tendency of observers who saw a videotape from the actors' point of view to develop a "self-discovery" perspective.
   d. the tendency of most people to not "blame the victim".

Answer: d

4. Storms discusses the implications of the effects of videotape reorientation on attributional processes for psychological therapy and human relations training. While he points out the possible beneficial effects of having a patient develop a "self-viewing" perspective, Storms also notes that this could sometimes be "distherapeutic" mainly because:
   a. it could make patients think that they didn't need to continue to seek professional help.
   b. self-viewing, by increasing persons' situational attributions, could lead patients to blame all of their problems on society rather than on themselves.
   c. the costs of therapy are already high, and introducing the use of costly videotape technology would push patient fees even higher, making therapy even more inaccessible to the average citizen.
   d. patients may discount the effects of situational forces on their behavior and end up blaming themselves too much, which can actually lead them to get worse, not better.

Chapter 15   Strangers to Ourselves: Discovering
the Adaptive Unconscious

Timothy D. Watson

Answer: b

1. Wilson in his work on introspection related a story about his friends buying a home and found that
   a. the people, who made a list of all the pros and cons for their new home, were the most satisfied.
   b. the real estate agent had the "Buyers Lie" as a guideline and did not believe in buyers making lists with pros and cons.
   c. when the buyer had a list of pros and cons and had a real estate agent follow these, the buyer was the happiest.
   d. the buyer was the happiest when the price of the home was a lot cheaper than the people had ever imagined in their introspection.

Answer: a

2. Wilson found that with introspection and self-narrative when subjects analyze five art posters and then took one home,
   a. the people, who made no lists and picked the poster on gut feelings, were the happiest with their poster.
   b. the people, who approached the task like Benjamin Franklin would have with a list of pluses and minuses, were the happiest with their poster.
   c. the people, who randomly picked a poster, were the happiest with their poster.
   d. the people, who had no choice in the selection of their poster, were the happiest with their poster.

Answer: c

3. With introspection and self-narrative Wilson found in studies when a student thought about being depressed (rumination) or thought about other things (distraction),

    a. the rumination students had a clear idea of their depression and move on towards healing themselves.

    b. the distracted students were no better or worse than the others because they had not worked on their problem.

    c. the distracted students were less depressed than the ruminating students.

    d. the ruminating students, who could come up with a list of reasons for their depression, ended up being the better adjusted.

Answer: d

4. In regards to introspection and self-narratives Wilson would recommend which of the following the most?

    a. Thinking extensively about events and one's depression is most helpful.

    b. Making a list of the pros and cons about a decision is most helpful.

    c. Ruminating in therapy is most helpful.

    d. Writing incoherently at first about an issue and then writing coherently about the issue is most helpful.

Chapter 16 Dissonance, Hypocrisy, and The Self-Concept

Elliot Aronson

Answer: d

1. Festinger introduced his theory of cognitive dissonance in the mid 1950s. At the time, it challenged which dominant theory in psychology?
   a. adaptation
   b. classical conditioning
   c. repression
   d. reinforcement

Answer: b

2. According to Aronson, the primary appeal of the theory of cognitive dissonance was that:
   a. it established social psychology as a valid discipline.
   b. it generated a broad range of testable hypotheses.
   c. it could be studied fairly inexpensively.
   d. research could be conducted without the use of deception.

Answer: a

3. Aronson was strongly influenced by Festinger's theory of cognitive dissonance. However, he revised Festinger's theory because he felt dissonance was better explained as the result of:
   a. a threat to the self-concept.
   b. a violation of social norms.
   c. a conflict between opposing thoughts.
   d. external justification.

Answer: c

4. Aronson got college students to use condoms by having them do two things: videotaping a speech advocating the use of condoms and:
   a. having them empathize with an AIDS victim.
   b. informing them of the dangers of unsafe sex.
   c. having them think about times they themselves did not use condoms.
   d. having them watch the film with a student audience.

Answer: a

5. According to Aronson, people with constructive self-compassion have a _____ and _____ self-esteem.
   a. high; well-grounded
   b. high; fragile
   c. low; well-grounded
   d. low; fragile

Chapter 17   Compliance Without Pressure:
The Foot-in-the-Door Technique

Jonathan L. Freedman and Scott C. Fraser

Answer: d

1. The main prediction in Freedman and Fraser's first field experiment on compliance, in which they were ostensibly concerned with the inventory of household products in subjects' homes, was that the subjects:
   a. in the One-Contact condition would be most likely to comply with a large request.
   b. in the Agree-Only condition would refuse to carry out the first, smaller request.
   c. in the Familiarization condition would refuse to comply with the first, smaller request.
   d. in the Performance condition would be more likely to agree to the larger request than subjects in any other experimental condition.

Answer: a

2. The major reason why Freedman and Fraser found it necessary to conduct a second experimental test of their compliance hypothesis was:
   a. the first experiment didn't adequately answer the questions of why and how agreeing to an initial request increases compliance with a second request.
   b. the first experiment didn't adequately answer the questions of why and how complying with the first, smaller request failed to increase compliance with the second, larger request.
   c. the first experiment involved unethical experimental practices that invalidated the findings.
   d. the second experiment was conducted to take advantage of a new interviewing technique that allowed the same experimenter to contact the subjects on both the first and second requests.

Answer: b

3. In their second experiment, where subjects were asked to install a large sign on their front lawns, Freedman and Fraser found all of the following results *except:*

a. there were no significant differences among the experimental conditions in the proportion of subjects who complied with the initial request.

b. in the conditions where the first and second requests were similar in nature, there was significantly more compliance than in the conditions where the first and second requests were different in nature.

c. merely having been given a first request tended to increase compliance with a second request, regardless of whether subjects agreed to perform the first request.

d. having different interviewers for the first and second requests had no significant effect on the degree of compliance with the second request.

Chapter 18   Reducing Weight by Reducing Dissonance: The Role
of Effort Justification in Inducing Weight Loss
Danny Axsom and Joel Cooper

Answer: a

1. Axsom and Cooper, in their experiment on the effectiveness of different weight-loss therapies,
maintain that the therapeutic process is influenced
by which of the following concepts?
a. effort justification
b. the psychodynamic schema of id, ego, and
superego
c. systematic desensitization
d. the idea, borrowed from architecture, that "less
is more"

Answer: b

2. According to the article on weight reduction by
Axsom and Cooper, the factor that underlies the
effectiveness of virtually all forms of psychotherapy
is:
a. changing a negative self-concept to a positive
self-concept.
b. expending effort to participate in the therapy.
c. learning logical, rational decision-making procedures.
d. learning to accept oneself for the person one is.

Answer: d

3. The results of Axsom and Cooper's weight-reduc-
tion experiment showed that by the end of the fifth
(and last) session, subjects in the high-effort condition had lost _____ weight than those in the
low-effort condition. A year later, subjects in the
high-effort condition had lost _____ weight
than those in the low-effort condition.
a. significantly more; significantly more
b. significantly more; about the same amount of
c. slightly less; significantly more
d. slightly more; significantly more

Answer: d

4. In Axsom and Cooper's experiment, which of the following pairs of variables were manipulated?
    a. choice/weight loss
    b. effort/weight loss
    c. length of session/level of effort
    d. effort/choice

Answer: b

5. Axsom and Cooper argue that the continued weight loss experienced by some of their subjects during the six months following the experiment occurred primarily because:
    a. the eating plan used in the experiment was highly effective and nutritionally sound.
    b. subjects continued to pursue the goal of weight loss, which had been made more attractive by the experimental manipulation of effort justification.
    c. the experiment led to the formation of an "antecedent" that helped subjects follow the successful weight-loss techniques they had learned.
    d. the initial loss of weight reduced subjects' anxiety about being overweight in a society that overemphasizes being thin and fit.

Chapter 19 Dishonest Behavior as a Function of Differential Levels of Induced Self-Esteem

Elliot Aronson and David R. Mettee

Answer: a

1. Aronson and Mettee's main hypothesis is that persons who experience lowered self-esteem will be more likely to cheat than persons who experience heightened self-esteem. The major assumption underlying this prediction is that:

   a. dishonest behavior is inconsistent with high self-esteem, and people strive for cognitive consistency.
   b. persons who are most susceptible to having their self-esteem lowered are already predisposed to engage in cheating behavior.
   c. persons with high self-esteem never cheat because they have "more to lose" and little to gain by cheating.
   d. low self-esteem creates an attitude of "I have nothing to lose," so that persons with low self-esteem are more likely to risk being caught cheating.

Answer: d

2. The *main* reason that Aronson and Mettee administered the California Personality Inventory (CPI) to their subjects in the card-cheating experiment was:

   a. to measure the subjects' chronic self-esteem.
   b. to determine whether some subjects might be too sensitive to participate in an experiment involving deception.
   c. to determine which subjects displayed personality characteristics that would lead them to engage in cheating or other dishonest behavior.
   d. to provide the experimenters with a "cover" for manipulating subjects' self-esteem by providing bogus test results.

Answer: c

3. By analyzing both the cheating behavior of subjects and their chronic levels of self-esteem as measured by the CPI, Aronson and Mettee found evidence for which of the following?
   a. People with high chronic self-esteem were disproportionately clustered in the "High Self Esteem" (HSE) experimental condition.
   b. In the "No Feedback" condition (NSE), more "low chronics" cheated than "medium chronics."
   c. The greatest proportion of cheaters were "low chronics" in the "Low Self Esteem" (LSE) experimental condition.
   d. The greatest proportion of cheaters were "low chronics" whose self-esteem was not manipulated by the experimenters.

Answer: c

4. In discussing the results of their study on self-esteem and cheating, Aronson and Mettee acknowledge that alternative explanations of their findings are possible. In their view, the *major* rival explanation is:
   a. anger and aggressiveness directed toward the experimenter by subjects in the low self-esteem condition.
   b. cognitive consistency theory.
   c. compensation—that is, low self-esteem subjects cheated to make sure they won some money, thus "compensating" for not having done well on the bogus personality test.
   d. reward-reinforcement theory—"It pays to cheat."

Chapter 20 Using Cognitive Dissonance to Encourage Water Conservation

Chris Dickerson, Ruth Thibodeau, Elliot Aronson &
Dayna Miller

Answer: a

1. Of the four conditions tested in Dickerson et al.'s study of water conservation among women taking showers, which was the one designed to arouse the most dissonance (the "hypocrisy" manipulation)?
   a. mindful plus commitment
   b. mindful only
   c. commitment only
   d. unmindful and no commitment

Answer: c

2. The results of Dickerson et al.'s water conservation experiment revealed a statistically significant difference between:
   a. the mindful and unmindful groups.
   b. the committed and uncommitted groups.
   c. the hypocrisy group and the control group.
   d. the hypocrisy group and all other groups.

Answer: d

3. The major dependent measurement recorded of subjects' behavior that was used as the basis for analyzing the results of Dickerson et al.'s water conservation experiment was:
   a. the attitudes the subjects held about the value of water conservation.
   b. the degree to which subjects agreed with statements such as "I always turn off the water when soaping up."
   c. whether or not subjects were willing to sign a petition that advocated water conservation.
   d. how long subjects ran the water during their showers.

Answer: b

4. One argument that is an alternative to the dissonance reduction explanation given by Dickerson et al. is that subjects in the "hypocrisy" condition:

a. were more likely to hold liberal political beliefs and thus be more friendly to ideas such as recycling and water conservation.

b. were "primed" to think more about water conservation, thus enhancing those attitudes.

c. actually felt less dissonance in the "hypocrisy" condition and therefore were less likely to conserve water.

d. felt a temporary decline in their self-esteem and were therefore more compliant to the experimenter's requests.

Chapter 21   Self-theories of Intelligence

Carol S. Dweck

Answer: b

1. Carol Dweck in her article, Self-theories of Intelligence, valued which of the following persons the most?
   a. Charles Darwin for his theory of evolution and his superior intellectual ability.
   b. Michael Jordan who was cut by his high school coach in basketball and then through his relentless practice became a super basketball player.
   c. Thomas Edison for his raw intelligence and his many inventions like the light bulb and phonograph.
   d. Tiger Woods for his natural ability as an athlete and his instinctual skill as a businessman to make millions of dollars.

Answer: a

2. Which of the following statements are true according to Carol Dweck in her article, Self-theories of Intelligence?
   a. Students with a malleable belief in intelligence are more likely to take risks in learning, put more effort into learning and learn a greater variety of ideas.
   b. "Gifted" students should be treated special and be reminded that they were given a great deal of intelligence, and they have a responsibility to the community to utilize their native intelligence.
   c. Poorer students, who have a fixed view of their intelligence, often work harder, ask for more help when learning and realize that they will have to adjust to their lower intelligence.
   d. Students, who have a malleable view of intelligence, are the smartest students and come from high social class families.

Answer: d

3. Carol Dweck and her colleagues discovered from their work on self-theories of intelligence that with gender
   a. males benefit more from a malleable view of intelligence than do females.
   b. females who have a fixed view of intelligence are generally superior to males with the same view.
   c. males who have a fixed view of intelligence score the same on English tests as females with a malleable view of intelligence.
   d. females with a malleable view of intelligence close the gender gap in mathematics with males.

Answer: c

4. When Carol Dweck and her colleagues were working with self-theories and intelligence, they conducted an experiment, in which students completed an easier task and afterwards were given one of three different praises. Then all the students were engaged in a difficult task and they all did poorly. Finally the students were allowed to choose a task that made them look good or pick a task involving risk but could learn more. What did they discover?
   a. When children were told "you must be smart at these problems" after the ease task, they generally chose the task where they would learn more because they wanted to prove themselves.
   b. When children were told "you did well" after the ease task, they generally picked the task in which they would learn more.
   c. When children were told "you must have worked hard at these problems" after the ease task, they generally chose the task where they would learn more because they felt like they could take a risk.
   d. It did not matter what the children were told because they all believed their intelligence was fixed and they picked the task to make themselves look good.

Chapter 22   The Effects of Observing Violence

Leonard Berkowitz

Answer: b

1. Berkowitz's study of the effects of filmed aggression on behavior was designed to test which of the following theories?
   a. the serial killer syndrome
   b. catharsis
   c. cognitive dissonance
   d. compliance

Answer: b

2. Berkowitz's experimental findings suggest that one of the key factors affecting whether viewing filmed violence will lead to aggressive behavior is:
   a. if the violence is especially graphic.
   b. if the violence is portrayed as justified.
   c. if the type of violence in the film is consistent with the viewer's past behavior.
   d. if the violence is seen in a large group.

Answer: c

3. Which of the following is *not* a conclusion about aggressive behavior drawn by Berkowitz as a result of his research?
   a. People who have been angered and then see filmed violence will act more aggressively than people who have not been angered before seeing filmed violence.
   b. Aggressive behavior is most often directed toward specific targets.
   c. Films with violent themes and scenes make anyone who sees them act more aggressively and at approximately the same level of aggression.
   d. A frustrated person can enjoy fantasy aggression.

Answer: a

4. From his own research and from his analysis of related work by others, Berkowitz maintains that the most important danger in viewing film violence is that:

a. for a short period right after viewing violence, a person is predisposed to act violently.

b. it has long-term effects on memory, which can lead the viewer to act aggressively for a long period after viewing the film.

c. violent films are so impactful that the emotional trauma of viewing them is never eliminated.

d. a "systematic desensitization" to violence occurs, such that the more viewers watch violent films, the more violence those films must contain in order to have the same arousing effects.

Chapter 23   The Facilitation of Aggression by Aggression: Evidence
Against the Catharsis Hypothesis
Russell G. Geen, David Stonner, and Gary L. Shope

Answer: b   1.   Geen et al. argue that the mixed and inconclusive
data on aggression catharsis is probably the result
of:
a.   poor operationalization of the concept.
b.   differences in experimental conditions that affected inhibitions against aggression.
c.   differences in types of subjects used in different experiments.
d.   differences in experimenter demand characteristics.

Answer: a   2.   In their "attack manipulation," which was designed
to create different levels of instigation to aggres-
sion, Geen et al.:
a.   had the confederate shock the subjects when
he disagreed with their attitudes on 12 controversial issues.
b.   had the confederate shock the subjects when
they made mistakes on a code-learning task.
c.   insulted the subjects during an interview conducted prior to the experiment.
d.   intentionally recruited two separate groups of
subjects—one that scored high on chronic levels of aggression and one that scored low on
the same measure.

Answer: d   3.   In the Geen et al. experiment on aggression, subjects administered the most intense shocks in
which of the following treatment conditions?
a.   "attack—experimenter shocks" condition
b.   "attack—no shocks" condition
c.   "attack—confederate shocks" condition
d.   "attack—subject shocks" condition

Answer: b

4. Geen et al. acknowledge that there are two plausible explanations for their findings that aggressing leads to committing further acts of aggression. These two explanations involve:
   a. a weakening of restraints against violence/desire to punish.
   b. weakening of restraints against violence/consistency-seeking behavior.
   c. weakening of restraints against violence/desire for justice or revenge ("an eye for an eye").
   d. physiological catharsis/increased instigation to aggress.

Chapter 24 Peacetime Casualties: The Effects of War on the Violent Behavior of Noncombatants

Dane Archer and Rosemary Gartner

Answer: b

1. Archer and Gartner maintain that State violence is not included in investigations of murder and aggression mainly because:
   a. the State is a complex bureaucracy that can easily conceal its actions from public scrutiny.
   b. State violence enjoys legitimacy.
   c. the media is in collusion with government to suppress all news of State violence.
   d. the effects of State violence are relatively minor compared to the vast number of crimes committed by individuals.

Answer: c

2. Archer and Gartner maintain that war, as the most dramatic form of State violence, may result in increases in post-war homicide rates mainly because of which of the following processes?
   a. catharsis
   b. arrested moral development
   c. social learning
   d. frustration-aggression

Answer: b

3. Archer and Gartner's analysis of post-war homicide rates reveals that warring nations:
   a. were less likely to experience homicide rate increases than non-combatant nations.
   b. were more likely to experience homicide rate increases than non-combatant nations.
   c. with the highest numbers of wartime casualties were less likely to have homicide rate increases, because the citizens of those countries had already experienced too much death and destruction.
   d. were more likely to experience homicide rate increases than non-combatant nations, but only among minority populations.

Answer: c

4. Even though it is a commonly accepted hypothesis, the "violent veteran" explanation for post-war homicide rate increases is not supported by Archer and Gartner's analysis of the evidence. They based their dismissal of this "myth" on:

   a. their extensive interviews with veterans of three different wars.

   b. the fact that homicide rate increases *during* the wars were as high as *after* wars, so that veterans could not have been responsible for the wartime homicides.

   c. the fact that post-war increases in violence and homicide occurred among demographic groups who did not serve in combat.

   d. the fact that research has shown that military training "wears off" very quickly after combat duty ceases.

Chapter 25   Deindividuation and Anger-Mediated Interracial
Aggression: Unmasking Regressive Racism
Ronald W. Rogers and Steven Prentice-Dunn

Answer: c

1. In their study of interracial aggression, Rogers and
    Prentice-Dunn predicted that if the white subjects
    in their experiment were not angered, they would:
    a. experience deindividuation.
    b. attack black victims more severely than white
        victims.
    c. attack white victims more severely than black
        victims.
    d. quickly make friends with all of the victims,
        regardless of race.

Answer: b

2. Which of the following variables was *not* investi-
    gated by Rogers and Prentice-Dunn in their study
    of interracial aggression?
    a. deindividuating vs. individuating cues
    b. low shock intensity vs. high shock intensity
    c. race of victim
    d. insult to the subjects vs. no insult to the sub-
        jects

Answer: c

3. In the Rogers and Prentice-Dunn experiment on
    interracial aggression, they found evidence of a sig-
    nificant interaction effect between which of the
    following variables?
    a. deindividuation and race
    b. deindividuation and insult
    c. race and insult
    d. shock intensity and race

Answer: d   4. Rogers and Prentice-Dunn's findings on interracial aggression suggest the operation of what they term "regressive racism". This process:

a. can be fully explained using the "ambivalence-amplification" hypothesis of Katz.

b. can account for whites' aggressive behavior toward blacks, but cannot explain blacks' aggressive behavior toward whites.

c. involves the expression of unprejudiced values that are fully internalized.

d. refers to the tendency for persons of any race to adopt chronologically earlier styles of interracial behavior when they are aroused.

Chapter 26 Predictors of Naturalistic Sexual Aggression

Neil M. Malamuth

Answer: d

1. Malamuth notes that in his research program on sexual aggression, he has employed two types of aggression measures—a laboratory measure and a naturalistic measure—which have opposite advantages and disadvantages. The advantage of the laboratory measure of aggression is that:
    a. it is a self-report measure and, therefore, is immune to errors occurring from social desirability pressures.
    b. it assesses behavior in a setting that is high in ecological validity.
    c. almost all previous research has used it, so it allows for comparisons among studies.
    d. it is an objective measure that does not rely on subjects' self-reports.

Answer: b

2. Which of the following was *not* one of the six predictor variables that Malamuth used in his study of self-reported naturalistic sexual aggression?
    a. sexual responsiveness to rape
    b. exposure to media violence
    c. hostility toward women
    d. antisocial personality characteristics

Answer: d   3. Malamuth's findings on the predictors of naturalistic sexual aggression demonstrate that:
a. all of the predictor variables he identified were significantly related to naturalistic sexual aggression.
b. the primary causal factor in naturalistic sexual aggression is psychoticism—that is, having an antisocial personality.
c. the Additive model of combining predictors was superior to the Interactive model in accounting for the occurrence of naturalistic sexual aggression.
d. the presence of any one of the predictor variables—by itself—is unlikely to lead to high levels of sexual aggression.

Answer: a   4. In discussing the implications of his findings on the occurrence of naturalistic sexual aggression, Malamuth argues that his results lend support to other research on:
a. how media depictions of violence may change persons' attitudes in such a way that actual aggressive behavior occurs.
b. how increasing prison sentences for rapists may actually lead them to commit more acts of violence, both while they are in prison and once they are released.
c. how research on sexual aggression should continue to search for single, primary factors that predict when sexual aggression will occur.
d. how rapists develop rationales and justifications for their acts.

Chapter 27   The Nonverbal Mediation of Self-Fulfilling Prophecies in Interracial Interaction

Carl O. Word, Mark P. Zanna, and Joel Cooper

Answer: b

1. The general hypothesis of the Word et al. study on interaction between whites and blacks is that:
   a. black job applicants will respond to what they perceive as whites' negative attitudes toward them with increased friendliness, in an attempt to change the whites' negative evaluations of them.
   b. whites and blacks will engage in a sequence of nonverbal, reciprocal interactions that result in a self-fulfilling prophecy.
   c. black job applicants will receive the same amount of "immediate" nonverbal communications from a white interviewer as will white job applicants.
   d. all recipients of more "immediate" non-verbal communications—regardless of race—will be judged more harshly than recipients of less "immediate" non-verbal communications.

Answer: b

2. In the Word et al. study on interracial interaction, all of the following were significant results *except:*
   a. white interviewers sat closer to white applicants than to black applicants.
   b. white interviewers made fewer speech errors talking with black applicants than with white applicants.
   c. white interviewers spent less time with black applicants than with white applicants.
   d. job applicants in the "nonimmediate" condition were judged to be less adequate for the job than job applicants in the "immediate" condition.

Answer: a

3. According to Word et al., the practical, "real world" implications of their findings on self-fulfilling prophecies in interracial interactions are most applicable to the problem of:
   a. black unemployment.
   b. race riots.
   c. affirmative action.
   d. desegregation.

Answer: d

4. Word et al. draw on the findings from a number of related studies to develop a rationale for their experiment on interracial interactions. Which of the following researchers do they mention as being associated with the idea that "blackness" is a stigmatizing trait in American society?
   a. Merton
   b. Rosenthal
   c. Mehrabian
   d. Goffman

Chapter 28   The Effect of Stereotype Threat on the Standardized
Test Performance of College Students
Joshua Aronson, Claude Steele, Moises Salinas, and
Michael Lustina

Answer: c   1.   Aronson, Steele, Salinas, and Lustina conducted
their experiment on stereotype threat to study the
effect of
a.   testing situations on performance.
b.   biased test items on performance.
c.   apprehension on test performance.
d.   socioeconomic studies on test performance.

Answer: d   2.   The results of Aronson, Steele, Salinas, and
Lustina's first two studies revealed:
a.   African American students who felt they were
not discriminated against did as well as Caucasian students.
b.   African American students did more poorly
than Caucasian students on math tests, but did
as well as Caucasian students on verbal tests.
c.   African American students did more poorly
than Caucasian students only on culturally-
biased items.
d.   African American students did as well as Caucasian students when all subjects were told
their abilities were not being tested.

Answer: a   3.   Based on Aronson, Steele, Salinas, and Lustina's
experiments, a person's performance on a standardized test may be hindered by:
a.   caring too much about the significance of the
outcome.
b.   the perception of discrimination.
c.   lack of experience with cultural norms.
d.   low self-esteem.

Chapter 29 Experiments in Group Conflict

Muzafer Sherif

Answer: b

1. The main reason Sherif and his colleagues studied a carefully selected group of boys in a summer camp was:
   a. to compare boys who went to camp with a matched sample of boys who did not go to camp to see if participating in group activities influenced cooperative social skills.
   b. to study the formation and development of group cohesion and group conflict.
   c. to discover the personality traits that were correlated with social interaction skills and demonstrated leadership abilities.
   d. to discover whether and how leaders differ from followers, by comparing their family backgrounds.

Answer: b

2. The subjects in Sherif's Robber's Cave experiments were:
   a. boys labeled as juvenile delinquents.
   b. normal, healthy, intelligent boys from stable, white, middle-class homes.
   c. normal boys from a variety of racial backgrounds chosen from a program for underprivileged children.
   d. boys from two sixth-grade classes in one of the Norman, Oklahoma, school districts.

Answer: d

3. Sherif found in his experiment at Robber's Cave that which of the following conditions needed to exist before status hierarchies developed among the boys in a particular peer group?
   a. They needed to engage in competitive games with each other.
   b. They needed to engage in cooperative activities with each other.
   c. They needed to be given unequal rewards.
   d. None of the above; status hierarchies emerged naturally.

Answer: d

4. Sherif describes that the boys at Robber's Cave were immediately divided into two groups. Quickly, a leadership hierarchy developed within each group. Sherif explains that this hierarchy developed:
   a. as a result of competition between the two groups.
   b. as a result of cooperation between the two groups.
   c. as a result of giving the groups unequal opportunities and rewards.
   d. naturally as part of the group formation process.

Answer: d

5. Sherif and his associates eventually restored harmonious relations between the Rattlers and the Eagles by:
   a. having the two groups engage in competitive games.
   b. bringing the two groups together for common social events such as movie-watching and eating.
   c. forcing the two groups to cooperate through threats of expulsion from the camp.
   d. creating a common, "superordinate" goal.

Chapter 30   Jigsaw Groups and the Desegregated Classroom:
              In Pursuit of Common Goals

Elliot Aronson and Diane Bridgeman

Answer: c   1.   Aronson and Bridgeman review studies that demonstrate the disappointing results of desegregation in improving group relations, self-esteem and academic performance. They argue that these negative results are mainly due to:
                  a.   the failure of authorities to support integration efforts.
                  b.   inadequate funding for schools.
                  c.   the interaction of lack of "equal-status contact" with the competitive structure of the classroom.
                  d.   lack of discipline in classrooms, so that children are not compelled to cooperate.

Answer: d   2.   Aronson and his colleagues developed the technique known as the "jigsaw" classroom primarily to:
                  a.   provide data for a theoretical analysis comparing the effects of cooperation versus competition.
                  b.   take advantage of the altruistic motivations of students, which are stifled by a competitive classroom environment.
                  c.   replicate the findings of the famous "Robber's Cave" experiment in another "naturalistic" setting—the classroom.
                  d.   develop a cooperative structure for integrated classrooms that could be readily implemented and evaluated—that is, to develop an "action research" program.

Answer: b   3.   Aronson and Bridgeman discuss research on the effect of jigsaw techniques on academic performance. This research, conducted by Lucker et al. (1977), found that:

a. both minority and Anglo students significantly improved their academic performance as a result of the jigsaw technique.

b. minority students performed significantly better in jigsaw classes than in traditional classes.

c. unlike most other students, high-ability students suffered from the jigsaw technique, as evidenced by the decline in their reading scores after the jigsaw technique was implemented.

d. all students—Anglo and minority alike—in jigsaw classrooms showed increases in self-esteem and increases in "liking" school.

Answer: a

4. In comparing the jigsaw technique to other techniques designed to develop interdependent classroom learning, Aronson and Bridgeman note that the major difference between the jigsaw technique and other approaches such as "TGT" and "STAD" is:

a. jigsaw attempts to minimize competition; TGT and STAD promote and use competition *across* groups, while encouraging *within-group* cooperation.

b. jigsaw can be effective only where the entire traditional classroom structure of competition is eliminated, whereas TGT and STAD promote and utilize competition.

c. jigsaw is based on established social-psychological principles, whereas other interdependent learning programs do not have a solid, scientific foundation.

d. jigsaw improves both academic performance and racial/ethnic relations, whereas other interdependent learning programs only improve academic performance.

Chapter 31   Jackie Robinson, Branch Rickey, and the Social Psychology of Affirmative Action

Anthony Pratkanis and Marlene Turner

Answer: a

1.   In Pratkanis and Turner's article on Branch Rickey and Jackie Robinson, a key factor in increasing the success of integration is:
a.   conveying the inevitability of change.
b.   having different behavioral options.
c.   using minority people of superior ability.
d.   maintaining reasonable quotas.

Answer: d

2.   According to Pratkanis and Turner, the Pee Wee Reese Principle describes the phenomenon that:
a.   social expectations guide behavior.
b.   minorities will only be assimilated into society if they are challenged.
c.   discrimination has a reciprocal effect: people discriminated against become prejudiced against their discriminators.
d.   violating norms can change accepted biases.

Answer: d

3.   Which of the following, according to Pratkanis and Turner, is NOT one of the reasons why some people see affirmative action as being preferential towards black Americans.
a.   Some people think minorities are intellectually inferior.
b.   Some people feel affirmative action violates norms of procedural justice.
c.   Some people who have suffered financial setbacks may blame black Americans for their woes.
d.   Some people feel affirmative action gives black Americans a false sense of hope.

Answer: c

4. At the time that Branch Rickey attempted to racially integrate baseball, many people felt that blacks and whites would not be able to get along. However, social psychologists cite four factors that enhance positive intergroup relations. Which of the following is NOT one of those factors?

a. The interaction should have the support of authorities.

b. Members of both groups need to be dependent on each other.

c. Members of the two groups should take turns being in leadership positions.

d. Members of the two groups should seek a common goal.

Chapter 32   "Playing Hard to Get": Understanding an Elusive
Phenomenon
Elaine Walster (Hatfield), G. William Walster, Jane Piliavin, and
Lynn Schmidt

Answer: a   1.   In their review of research on the "hard to get"
                     phenomenon, Walster et al. cite several theories
                     that could explain why playing "hard to get" in-
                     creases one's desirability. Which of the following
                     theories was included in their review?
                     a.   dissonance theory
                     b.   modeling theory
                     c.   reactance theory
                     d.   balance theory

Answer: b   2.   As Walster et al. describe in considerable detail,
                     they attempted five experimental tests of their hy-
                     pothesis before designing an experiment that con-
                     firmed their prediction. The major reason why
                     Experiment VI succeeded when the previous five
                     had failed was:
                     a.   the experimenters stopped using students as
                          subjects, because students did not have much
                          experience with the "hard to get" phenome-
                          non.
                     b.   after reinterviewing their subjects and listen-
                          ing carefully to their comments, the experi-
                          menters discovered that there were both
                          advantages and disadvantages in attempting to
                          date "hard to get" and "easy to get" women, so
                          they refined their procedures.
                     c.   they realized that it was only necessary to ma-
                          nipulate one variable—how "hard to get" a
                          woman was for the subject; whereas earlier
                          they had also tried to manipulate how "hard to
                          get" the woman was for other men.
                     d.   they had been pursuing the wrong research
                          strategy by insisting on measuring the "selec-
                          tivity" of "hard to get" women.

Answer: b   3. The main finding of the Walster et al. experiments on the "hard to get" phenomenon is:

    a. selectively "hard to get" women will be the least liked.

    b. selectively "hard to get" women will be liked more than uniformly "hard to get" women.

    c. selectively "hard to get" women will be liked less than uniformly "easy to get" women.

    d. selectively "hard to get" women will only be asked out for one date.

Chapter 33 The Search for a Romantic Partner: The Effects of Self-Esteem and Physical Attractiveness on Romantic Behavior

Sara B. Kiesler and Roberta L. Baral

Answer: c

1. The main hypothesis in the Kiesler and Baral experiment on the relationship between self-esteem and attractiveness was:
   a. the less attractive a subject was, the lower his self-esteem would be.
   b. subjects would always prefer attractive partners over less-attractive partners.
   c. moderately attractive subjects with low self-esteem would tend to select moderately attractive partners over highly attractive partners.
   d. there is no relation between subjects' self-esteem and choosing an attractive partner; what matters is whether the subjects are highly attractive.

Answer: d

2. Checks on the self-esteem manipulation, which asked subjects to rate their "present emotional feelings" and their performance on an intelligence test, revealed that:
   a. subjects in the low self-esteem condition tended to feel better than subjects in the high self-esteem condition.
   b. subjects in the low self-esteem condition tended to rate their test performance higher than subjects in the high self-esteem condition.
   c. overall, the self-esteem manipulation was not effective.
   d. overall, the self-esteem manipulation was effective.

Answer: c

3. Kiesler and Baral interpret their findings on the relationship between self-esteem and choice of romantic partner in which of the following ways?

a. High self-esteem persons are less "practical" and "realistic" in their choice of romantic partner, which is consistent with their scores on the California Personality Inventory (CPI).

b. People with high self-esteem feel threatened if someone doesn't like them and, thus, have a greater need for affection and reassurance than people with low self-esteem.

c. Changes in perception of the self affect perceptions of the chances of success in choosing romantic partners.

d. Their results are valid regardless of subjects' assessments of the likelihood of rejection by highly-attractive romantic partners.

Chapter 34   Social Perception and Interpersonal Behavior: On the Self-Fulfilling Nature of Social Stereotypes
Mark Snyder, Elizabeth Decker Tanke, and Ellen Berscheid

Answer: a

1. The central hypothesis of Snyder et al.'s experiment on social stereotypes can be most accurately stated as:
   a. stereotypes help to create a self-fulfilling prophecy.
   b. the stereotype that physically attractive people are really more likable, friendly, and confident than unattractive people is erroneous.
   c. we tend to "fill in the gaps" in our knowledge about someone by selecting information that tends to disconfirm our stereotypes.
   d. even if we treat people in a hostile fashion, they will tend to try to counteract our negative behavior by acting in a very friendly way, thus disconfirming our stereotypes about them.

Answer: d

2. Snyder et al. not only had male "perceivers" rate their partners' personality characteristics, they also had "observers" judge the women's conversational interaction with the male subjects. This was done to:
   a. provide a check on the manipulation of the target women's attractiveness.
   b. make sure that the male "perceivers" did not make mistakes in their ratings.
   c. see whether male "perceivers" made their initial assessments of the female partners' personality based on stereotyped beliefs about physically attractive women.
   d. see whether the "perceivers" initial impressions of their partners initiated a sequence of behaviors in which the female partners acted in ways that confirmed the "perceivers" stereotypes.

Answer: b

3. Which of the following is an accurate summation of the central finding in the Snyder et al. study of the relationship between stereotypes and social interaction?

    a. Male "perceivers" did not assess their female partners on the basis of stereotypes linking physical attractiveness and positive personality traits.

    b. Male "perceivers" impressions of their female partners created a self-fulfilling prophecy, whereby the female partners came to believe in ways that were consistent with the "perceivers" impressions of them.

    c. Male "perceivers" assessed their female partners on the basis of gender stereotypes linking physical attractiveness to femininity.

    d. "Observers" did not detect any differences in social interactions between women assigned to the attractive-target condition and women assigned to the unattractive-target condition.

Answer: a

4. In their discussion of the implications of their study of social perception, Snyder et al. maintain that most research and theory in social perception has focused on how people process information and has neglected:

    a. how people help to *create* the information they process.

    b. the *predictive* power of personality traits.

    c. the link between *physical* attractiveness and personality traits.

    d. the importance of beliefs about the *self* in determining people's behavior.

Chapter 35　Some Evidence for Heightened Sexual Attraction Under Conditions of High Anxiety
Donald G. Dutton and Arthur P. Aron

Answer: d

1. Dutton and Aron's series of three experiments on sexual attraction and emotional arousal was designed to test which of the following hypotheses?
   a. An attractive woman will be seen as more attractive by men who encounter her as they are experiencing a calm, relaxed physiological and emotional state.
   b. An attractive woman will be seen as more attractive when she is perceived to be in distress and needs help.
   c. An attractive man will show a preference for a less-attractive partner when he is in a state of physiological and emotional arousal.
   d. An attractive woman will be seen as more attractive by men who encounter her when they are experiencing strong physiological and emotional arousal.

Answer: b

2. Dutton and Aron discuss two major problems with their first experiment that led them to refine their procedure in Experiment 2. Which of the following was *one* of those two problems?
   a. Experimental subjects may have been less likely to contact the female interviewer for a date because they were more likely to be local residents who knew about the experiments.
   b. A difference in subject populations—that is, people who crossed the suspension bridge may have been different from those who crossed the control bridge.
   c. The suspension bridge tended to attract tourists, many of whom were foreign visitors who were unable to communicate properly with the female interviewer.
   d. The fact that the male and female interviewers in Experiment 1 obtained an identical pattern of results suggested to Dutton and Aron that something was wrong with their procedures in the first experiment.

Answer: b

3. Dutton and Aron found it necessary to conduct a third experiment, this time in a laboratory setting, mainly because of their inability to control for:
   a. poor weather conditions, which caused the field experiment to be delayed several times.
   b. the possibility that the female interviewer may have acted differently toward the two groups of subjects by exhibiting different forms of nonverbal behavior.
   c. the amount of time that the interviewer spent with subjects in each condition.
   d. the attractiveness of experimental subjects, who could not be screened for "good looks" in the field setting, as they could in a laboratory setting.

Answer: a

4. In discussing the theoretical implications of their findings on the emotion-sexual attraction link, Dutton and Aron argue that their results best support which of the following theories?
   a. cognitive labeling of emotion theory
   b. actor-observer theory
   c. the self-fulfilling prophecy
   d. deindividuation theory

Chapter 36   Keeping Track of Needs and Inputs of Friends
and Strangers

Margaret Clark, Judson Mills, and David Corcoran

Answer: d

1. According to Clark, Mills and Corcoran, if Barbara and Susan are very good friends who respond to each other based on the other's needs, their relationship would best be described as:
   a. implicit friends.
   b. explicit friends.
   c. an exchange relationship.
   d. a communal relationship.

Answer: c

2. In Clark et al.'s experiment, pairs of friends were believed to represent _____ relationships and strangers were believed to represent _____ relationships.
   a. need; communal
   b. exchange; input
   c. communal; exchange
   d. exchange; communal

Answer: a

3. Which of the following best summarizes the predictions made by Clark et al. regarding communal and exchange relationships?
   a. Friends are more likely to pay attention to each others' needs, whereas strangers are more likely to pay attention to each others' contributions.
   b. Both friends and strangers are more likely to pay attention to their own needs than to their partners' needs.
   c. Both friends and strangers are more likely to pay attention to their own contributions than to their partners' contributions.
   d. Friends are more likely to pay attention to each others' contributions whereas strangers are more likely to pay attention to each others' needs.

Answer: b

4. The results of Clark et al.'s experiment on exchange and communal relationships found that friends looked at the lights more often than strangers did in the _____ condition, and strangers looked at the lights more often than friends did in the _____ condition.
   a. inputs; needs
   b. needs; inputs
   c. communal; exchange
   d. exchange; communal

Suggested Videos and Films

Chapter 1: What is Social Psychology?

Invitation to Social Psychology (1975, 25 min., color). Methods and topics in social psychology are discussed, including aggression, helping behavior, attraction, attitudes, and obedience. Narrated by Stanley Milgram. MTI Teleprograms Inc., 3710 Commercial Avenue, Northbrook, IL 60062 (800-323-6301).

Methodology: The Psychologist and the Experiment (1975, 31 min., color). Introduces research methods and experimental design, through the example of Schachter's studies on fear and affiliation. (Also relevant to Chapter 9.) CRM-McGraw-Hill, P.O. Box 641, Del Mar, CA 92014-9990 (619-453-5000).

Social Psychology (1990, 30 min.). This film examines several research studies on stereotyping and prejudice, attributions, and the influence of social roles. Zimbardo's prison experiment and in-group/out-group experiments are analyzed. Insight Media, 121 W. 85th St., New York, N.Y., 10024.

Chapter 2: Conformity

Conformity and Independence (1975, 26 min., color). Classic studies of conformity by Asch, Sherif, and Milgram are analyzed, along with Moscovici's research on minority influence. MTI Teleprograms Inc., 3710 Commercial Avenue, Northbrook, IL 60062 (800-323-6301).

Four More Days (1971, 32 min., color). This film depicts the classic "Stanford prison study" conducted by Phillip Zimbardo and his colleagues. Film Library, New York University, 26 Washington Place, New York, NY 10002.

Group Dynamics: Groupthink (1973, updated 1989, 22 min., color). A presentation of Irving Janis's work on "groupthink," within the context of a board meeting at a pharmaceutical company. The major symptoms of groupthink are discussed, along with important historical events (e.g., the Bay of Pigs) that illustrate this phenomenon. CRM-McGraw-Hill, P.O. Box 641, Del Mar, CA 92014-9990 (619-453-5000).

Obedience (1963, 45 min., b&w). A presentation of Milgram's study of obedience. A classic. Film Library, New York University, 26 Washington Place, New York, NY 10002.

Moral Development (1973, 28 min.). This film recreates the procedure of Milgram's classic obedience study and examines the reaction of various subjects. Responses are analyzed within the context of Kohlberg's theory of moral development as characteristic of preconventional, conventional, or principled reasoning. CRM-McGraw-Hill Films, 674 Via de la Valle, P.O. Box 641, Del Mar, CA 92014.

When Will People Help? The Social Psychology of Bystander Intervention (1976, 25 min., color). Daryl Bem narrates this film which reenacts Latane and Darley's pioneering research on the bystander intervention. Harcourt Brace Jovanovich, 757 Third Avenue, New York, NY 10017.

Mob Psychology and Crowd Control: Disaster at Hillsborough (1994, 52 min., color). On April 15, 1989, the worst disaster in the history of English soccer took place when fans swarmed into bleachers, pushing others up against a wire fence, crushing 95 people to death. This program looks at the police investigation to determine what happened. Films for the Humanities and Sciences, P.O. Box 2053, Princeton, NJ 08543-2053 (800-257-5126).

Conformity, Obedience and Dissent (1990, 30 min.). This film examines why people conform, obey, and dissent in social situations by using examples based on Milgram's obedience study, studies of leadership styles, and the groupthink phenomenon. Insight Media, 121 W. 85th St., New York, NY 10024.

Chapter 3: Mass Communication, Propaganda and Persuasion

Effective Persuasion (1968, 11 min., b&w). Persuasion techniques are illustrated in excerpts of speeches by Martin Luther King, Adlai Stevenson, John F. Kennedy, and Winston Churchill. McGraw-Hill Book Company, 1221 Avenue of the Americas, New York, NY 10020 (800-421-0833).

Killing Us Softly: Advertising's Image of Women (1980, 45 min., color). A powerful demonstration of how advertising fosters gender stereotypes. (Also relevant to Chapter 7.) Cambridge Documentary Films, P.O. Box 385, Cambridge, MA 02139 (617-354-3677).

Still Killing Us Softly: Advertising's Images of Women (19??, 30 min.). A second film, based on lectures of Dr. Jean Kilbourne, that describes, through the use of ads from magazines, newspapers, album covers, and billboards, how the advertising industry portrays women and men, focusing on consumers' fears and desires. Cambridge Documentary Films, Inc., P.O. Box 385, Cambridge, MA 02139 (617-354-3677).

The Psychology of Mass Persuasion (19??, ? min.). Discusses the psychology of mass persuasions with a focus on (1) the psychological phenomenon of attitudes, (2) advertising's role in politics, and (3) how advertising and propaganda compare and contrast. HRM Video, 175 Tomkins Ave. No. V212, Pleasantville, NY 10570-0839 (800-431-2050).

Think Twice: The Persuasion Game (1978, 19 min., color). A look at how emotional appeals are used as a means of increasing the persuasive impact of a message. Iowa Films, Media Library, University of Iowa, Iowa City, IA 52242 (319-353-5885).

Chapter 4: Social Cognition

Attribution of Motives (1975, 22 min., color). The nature of our causal attributions is explored. University Films of Canada, 7 Hayden Street, Suite 305, Toronto, Ontario, Canada M4Y 2P2.

Impression Formation and Interpersonal Attraction (1975, 27 min., color). A presentation of attraction research, including work on first impressions, need complementarity, and implicit personality theories. (Also relevant to Chapter 8.) University Films of Canada, 7 Hayden Street, Suite 305, Toronto, Ontario, Canada M4Y 2P2.

Predicting Our World (1975, 28 min., color). Topics such as the need for control, risk taking, learned helplessness, and the "just world" phenomenon are explained and illustrated. University Films of Canada, 7 Hayden Street, Suite 305, Toronto, Ontario, Canada M4Y 2P2.

Productivity and the Self-Fulfilling Prophecy: The Pygmalion Effect (1975, 28 min., color). Presents several scenarios that illustrate the confirmation bias—how one's expectations can affect another person's behavior. (Also relevant to chapters 5 and 7.) CRM-McGraw-Hill, P.O. Box 641, Del Mar, CA 92014-9990 (619-453-5000).

Sports Psychology: The Winning Edge in Sports (1987, 60 min.). Sports psychologist Andrew Jacobs and nationally-known athletes discuss issues that affect team performance such as concentration, motivation, stress, and burnout. RMI Media Productions, Inc., 2807 W. 47th Street, Shawnee Mission, KS 66205; Distinctive Home Video Productions, 391 El Portal Rd., San Mateo, CA 94402 (415-344-7756).

Chapter 5: Self-justification

Attitudes about Attitudes (1975, 27 min., color). Topics include cognitive dissonance theory, predicting behavior from attitudes, and the 3-component model of attitudes. University Films of Canada, 7 Hayden Street, Suite 305, Toronto, Ontario, Canada M4Y 2P2.

Productivity and the Self-Fulfilling Prophecy: The Pygmalion Effect (1975, 28 min., color). Presents several scenarios that illustrate how one's expectations can affect another person's behavior. (Also relevant to chapters 4 and 7.) CRM-McGraw-Hill, P.O. Box 641, Del Mar, CA 92014-9990 (619-453-5000).

Social Animal (1963, 29 min.). This film introduces the general subject matter of social psychology, but focuses on attitude change and cognitive dissonance theory. The classic Festinger and Carlsmith (1959) experiment concerning subject's attempts to justify their behavior is discussed. Western Illinois University, Macomb, IL 61455.

The Holy Ghost People (1968, 53 min.). A TV documentary that chronicles the behavior of members of a fundamentalist religious congregation in Appalachia. During a revival meeting, people donate large sums of money, speak in tongues, and handle poisonous snakes. Although social psychological theories are not discussed, the film can be used as a good discussion starter, especially in concert with a discussion of the Jonestown or Waco disasters. CRM-McGraw-Hill Films, 674 Via de la Valle, P.O. Box 641, Del Mar, CA 92014.

Chapter 6: Aggression

Human Aggression (1976, 22 min., color). Discusses the frustration-aggression hypothesis, social learning theory, and group factors that influence aggressive behavior. Examines aggression in the context of youth gangs and police training. MTI Teleprograms Inc., 3710 Commercial Avenue, Northbrook, IL 60062 (800-323-6301).

Konrad Lorenz's Discussion with Richard Evans: Aggression (1975, 31 min., color). Ethologist Lorenz discusses and addresses criticisms of his theory of aggression. Aims Instructional Media Services, 626 Justin Avenue, Glendale, CA 91101 (800-367-2467).

Emotional Development: Aggression (1975, 19 min., color). A look at how aggression is learned and how it can be changed, from the perspective of social learning theory. CRM-McGraw-Hill, P.O. Box 641, Del Mar, CA 92014-9990 (619-453-5000).

Pornography: The Double Message (1985, 28 min.). This film examines research studies that suggest images of rape, domination, and bondage lead to insensitivity and unsympathetic attitudes toward victims of rape. Contains explicit material. Filmaker's Library, Inc., 124 E. 40th, New York, NY 10016 (212-808-4980).

Violence and Sex on TV (1994, 28 min., color). Specially adapted Phil Donahue program that explores the effect of on-screen violence on young people. Discusses whether viewing violence alters their view of reality, and whether the government should restrict content. Films for the Humanities & Sciences, P.O. Box 2053, Princeton, NJ 08543-2053 (800-257-5126).

Chapter 7: Prejudice

Guilty by Reason of Race (1972, 53 min., color). This powerful documentary chronicles the events surrounding the internment of Japanese-Americans in the U.S. during World War II. Footage includes interviews with those interned as well as those who made the decision to create the camps. Iowa Films, Media Library, University of Iowa, Iowa City, IA 52242 (319-353-5885).

Killing Us Softly: Advertising's Image of Women (1980, 45 min., color). A powerful demonstration of how advertising fosters gender stereotypes. Cambridge Documentary Films, P.O. Box 385, Cambridge, MA 02139 (617-354-3677).

Prejudice: Causes, Consequences, and Cures (1972, 23 min., color). A look at the nature of prejudice based on race, gender, and economic factors. CRM-McGraw-Hill, Box 641, Del Mar, CA 92014-9990 (619-453-5000).

Prejudice: Perceiving and Believing (1977, 28 min., color). This film examines stereotypes regarding gender, race, religion, and ethnicity. Narrated by Edward Asner. MTI Teleprograms Inc., 3710 Commercial Avenue, Northbrook, IL 60062 (800-323-6301).

Prejudice: The Eye of the Storm (19??, 25 min.). A documentary about the division of a third-grade classroom into blue-eyed and brown-eyed students assigned to inferior and superior roles. Explores how behavior changes dramatically depending on treatment and how frustrations and anger are the result of unequal rewards. Winner of the Peabody Award. Insight Media, 121 W. 85th St., New York, NY 10024; Iowa Films, University of Iowa, Iowa City, IA 52242 (319-353-5885).

Beyond Black and White (1974, 29 min.). A black child psychiatrist discusses black needs and white needs as human needs. Produced at the University of Michigan, the film features Dr. James Comer. Film Video Library, University of Michigan, 919 S. University Ave. Rm 207, Ann Arbor, MI 48109-1185 (313-764-5360).

Bill Cosby on Prejudice (1971, 24 min., color). Presents Bill Cosby, the comedian, as a super-bigot who presents himself as a man who sees others as inferior based on their minority status: Blacks, Italians, Scots, Midwesterners, women, and others. Cosby categorizes individuals by group based on common stereotypes, e.g., lazy, aggressive, irreligious, etc., and emphasizes the inherent contradictions and paradoxes when making stereotyped attributions and judgments. Indiana University, Bloomington, IN 47405-5901.

Chapter 8: Liking, Loving, and Interpersonal Sensitivity

Impression Formation and Interpersonal Attraction (1975, 27 min., color). A presentation of attraction research, including work on first impressions, need complementarity, and implicit personality theories. (Also relevant to Chapter 4.) University Films of Canada, 7 Hayden Street, Suite 305, Toronto, Ontario, Canada M4Y 2P2.

Introduction to Group Process: Member Behaviors in a Group (1982, 21 min.). This three-part tape examines the behavior that takes place in groups. The first segment identifies processes that occur in groups and looks at typical behavior in a newly formed group. The second part of the tape identifies these behaviors, and the final segment shows a constructive group. Health Sciences Consortium, Distribution Department, 201 Silver Cedar Ct., Chapel Hill, NC 27514-1517 (919-942-8731).

Your Erroneous Zones (1980, 97 min.). Based on Dr. Dyer's best-selling book, Dr. Dyer helps identify and expose your erroneous zones—the unhealthy behavior patterns that block you from all kinds of freedoms and experiences. Video Publishing House, 4 Woodfield Lake Ste 505, 930 N. National Pkwy., Shaumburg, IL 60175 (800-824-8889); Films, Inc., 5547 N. Ravenswood Ave., Chicago, IL 60640-1199 (312-878-2600).

Chapter 9: Social Psychology as a Science

Social Psychology: What, Why and How? (1975, 27 min., color). Covers experiments in the laboratory and in field settings, archival studies, and the relationship between theory and data. University Films of Canada, 7 Hayden Street, Suite 305, Toronto, Ontario, Canada M4Y 2P2.

Inferential Statistics: Hypothesis Testing—Rats, Robots, and Roller Skates (1976, 28 min., color). A humorous look at the basic elements of research methods, including hypothesis-testing, control groups, and the importance of random assignment. John Wiley & Sons Inc., 605 Third Avenue, New York, NY 10016 (212-867-9800).

Methodology: The Psychologist and the Experiment (1975, 31 min., color). Introduces research methods and experimental design, through the example of Schachter's studies on fear and affiliation. (Also relevant to Chapter 1.) CRM-McGraw-Hill, P.O. Box 641, Del Mar, CA 92014-9990 (619-453-5000).